D0179656

STORMS OF SILENCE

Joe Simpson is the author of several best-selling books, of which the first, *Touching the Void*, won both the NCR Award and the Boardman Tasker Award. His other books are *This Game of Ghosts*, *Dark Shadows Falling*, *The Beckoning Silence* and a novel *The Water People*.

BY JOE SIMPSON

The Water People (A Novel)
Touching the Void
This Game of Ghosts
Dark Shadows Falling
The Beckoning Silence

JOE SIMPSON

Storms of Silence

VINTAGE BOOKS
London

Published by Vintage 2007

10

Copyright © Joe Simpson, 1996

Joe Simpson has asserted his right under the Copyright, Designs
and Patents Act 1988 to be identified as the author of this work

Michael Dynes' article reproduced in the plate section is
© Times Newspapers Ltd 1995

First published in Great Britain in 1996 by
Jonathan Cape

Vintage Books
Random House, 20 Vauxhall Bridge Road,
London SW1V 2SA

www.vintage-books.co.uk

Addresses for companies within The Random House Group Limited
can be found at: www.randomhouse.co.uk/offices.htm

The Random House Group Limited Reg. No. 954009

A CIP catalogue record for this book
is available from the British Library

ISBN 9780099578116

The Random House Group Limited supports The Forest
Stewardship Council (FSC), the leading international forest
certification organisation. All our titles that are printed on
Greenpeace approved FSC certified paper carry the FSC logo.
Our paper procurement policy can be found at:
www.rbooks.co.uk/environment

Printed in the UK by CPI Bookmarque, Croydon, CR0 4TD

CONTENTS

To my friend and mentor
Tony Colwell

'He alone is an observer who
can observe minutely without
being observed.'
Johann Kaspar Lavater

INTRODUCTION
INNER VOICES

THE SNOW FELL like soft voices whispering through the walls of my tent. I lay back in my sleeping bag and listened to the dry scratching sounds, watching as grey-blue shadows briefly formed on the Gore-Tex and then slithered down in a murmur of indistinct husky rumours. I closed my eyes and the sounds swirled around inside the dome of the tent, filtering into my mind like words silently articulated in my head. I could not quite make sense of them. I seemed to be on the edge of a hundred conversations, confused by a quiet vortex of sounds, all talking to me. It made me think about avalanches.

I had developed a lively paranoia about these and other menaces. Even if my imagination was working over-time, I had heard these voices before and learned to heed them. Years ago, standing on a trembling snow slope, I had listened with rising panic to the silent murmuring threats from the quivering white surroundings. It was as if everything was holding its breath, waiting to see whether I would pay attention. Out of tiredness and stupidity I had closed my mind to the whispers.

Seconds later I was falling thousands of feet in the boiling maelstrom of an avalanche on the north-east face of the Courtes in the French Alps. I learned then that it was dangerous not to listen to voices.

In the Cordillera Huayhuash in 1985 a clear inner voice had kept me sane, forced me to live when everything told me that I was dead. Three and a half days I had spent alone with

1

a shattered leg, abandoned by a partner who had left me for dead, crawling through a wasteland of crevasses and jumbled rock debris, listening to a quiet insistent voice that cut cleanly through the hysteria of dying a lonely and pathetic death. Those days of utter loneliness were a form of sensory deprivation. I had never spent so long alone, hearing nothing, seeing no life at all, no insects or birds, no one. It was unnerving.

I replaced the emptiness with voices, filled my days with lunatic reveries, saw visions in ice cliffs, sang songs I didn't know I knew, and all the time I listened to that cold hard voice of reason which told me what to do. Since then I have always listened.

Even in the startling violence of a six hundred-foot fall down the west face of Pachermo in Nepal there was a voice speaking with quiet rational assurance to my frantic and confused mind. I had listened then to its hard unemotional commands as I struggled to climb back up an ice face with a shattered ankle and a lacerated bloody face. Something told me to keep trying and despite a sleepy and confused mind, concussed by the ferocious impact of my ice axe, the message seemed to get through.

I am not a religious man. I do not believe that some other being, an omnipotent godhead, was interceding on my behalf, lending me the strength to carry on. Yet I do believe in the power of voices, the silent witnesses of our past urging us on in the present. The whisperings of all my past experiences help me to sense when things are right or wrong, good or bad. Often it is a matter of common sense, sometimes it is like *déjà vu*, and at other times the prompting is quite irrational and inexplicable, as if I am in the company of ghosts. I listen to them all.

Occasionally there is a disturbing premonition that something terrible is about to happen, a rock fall or an avalanche, when there is nothing physical to suggest such a threat. For no apparent reason, you go left instead of straight up as you intended, and minutes later a fusillade of rocks crashes down the line of where you would have been standing. *Just coincidence*, you tell yourself, although secretly you are sure you knew that was going to happen!

Or you experience a calm recognition that you have done this thing before and know, without doubt, that all will be well. It is intuition combined with lessons well learned, or it may be quite inexplicable, but I listen anyway.

I have noticed how the threat of danger and violence seems to sharpen this sixth sense. Perhaps it is primordial and we experience a regression to a time when, like other animals, our senses were so much more acute, our protective antennae tuned to perfection.

There is an ever-present potential for savagery in nature. The animals walk a constant tightrope between eating and being eaten. They have developed what appears to be an uncanny sense of danger. It is such a constant in their existence that it dictates their every conscious move. Perhaps there are still faint traces in us of that ability which, at certain moments, we use without being aware of what it is we are relying upon.

At the same time as we have relinquished most of those acute animal instincts, we have gained immeasurably in our own capacity for violence. Could it be that without the mechanisms by which we are warned of attack we have also lost the ability to control violence? As a species we are certainly barbaric. Not far beneath the thin skin of our civilised manners lies a heart of darkness which emerges from time to time to mock our conceited assumption that we are above the realm of the animal's bestial behaviour.

It is a question that holds a certain fascination for me. Our capacity for aggressive inhumanity both repulses and attracts me. It is ironic that we label such behaviour as bestial, brutish, that of an animal, when in truth no animals would ever behave as irrationally, as savagely as humans. Animals still retain their acute sense of danger. They know when to flee and when to attack and do so only when required.

There are voices whispering warnings to us all the time but we have lost the ability to hear them. We have lost our senses, and in so doing, we have exiled ourselves from the animal world. The things that we have done, the genocide, the pollution, the parlous state to which we have reduced the planet, are all testament to our deafness.

Yet there are times when we catch faint echoes of lost senses, when soft voices whispering through tent walls can be faintly heard, when intuition demands to be heeded. I wanted to roll over and ignore the scratching sounds on the nylon but I had learned to listen the hard way, and the confused babble of a hundred conversations filtering into my mind made me sit up and listen. There were rumours of avalanches in the air.

PART ONE

I

THROWING THE RICE

We had pitched our tents at the head of a valley by a stream which carved its way steeply down into the Langtang valley two thousand feet below. An old yak shelter, a roofless rectangle of dry-stone walling, had been converted into a kitchen-cum-gambling den with stout branches and a blue plastic tarpaulin for the roof. Against the inner walls gunny-sacks of flour, rice, potatoes, and onions had been stacked up four feet high to provide extra draught-proofing for the gaps in the walling. Wicker baskets of tinned food, boxes of biscuits and climbing ropes formed an uncomfortable bench seat around the walls and a stone slab table had been built in the centre to clamp the central roof pole in place. A bower of thin whippy branches arched across the roof, holding up the heavy blue plastic tarp which was kept in place by a criss-cross of ropes and string anchored to heavy stones. The kerosene lamp hung from the strongest branch. A tattered and sun-bleached old tent inner hung in the doorway.

Before the storm we had been able to look out from the den and up towards the North Face of Gangchempo and a Matterhorn-shaped rocky summit looming above our base camp. We had climbed up a steep-sided valley with its boulder-strewn stream until it opened out about a thousand metres above the broad Langtang valley below. We had pitched camp at the point where it spread into a wide bowl encompassed by steep rocky hillsides. Above the camp, the summit rocks of Gangchempo dominated the view as it peeped over a foreground spur of rock. An ice-fall of blue seracs guarded the approaches to the mountain where a small glacier spilled out from beneath the north face.

It had seemed a logical place for a camp. There was water nearby and tough, stunted rhododendron bushes and boulders covered the hills, offering what appeared to be sufficient grip for any snow that might fall.

Ray Delaney and I had arrived first and, with all our years of mountaineering experience, had unerringly selected the worst possible site for our tents. A small spur rose above the yak shelter, narrow, rocky and uninviting. After hours of exhausting digging we had managed to pitch our small tents atop this spur on even smaller platforms. Kidney-bruising lumps protruded through the ground sheets, and unless I lay firmly wedged between rucksacks and ropes I awoke each morning in a cramped foetal position at the bottom of the tent. Any item left outside promptly began rolling down the spur towards the wide smooth valley floor where the rest of the team – Ian Tattersall (Tat), Richard Haszko, John Stevenson, Brendan Murphy and Kate Phillips – had quickly erected their tents. They had spent the rest of that first afternoon building elaborate patios and flower gardens at the entrances to their comfortable homes, laughing gleefully at our stupidity.

Our Liaison Officer was installed in a small dome tent in the lee of a large circular boulder near the yak shelter. Despite all the money which the regulations said we had to pay him so that he could equip himself properly, he seemed to have brought with him just one set of clothing, which looked suspiciously like pyjamas, and a large piece of leather. He had a pair of baseball boots and some strange puttee-like bandages for his lower legs. He intended using the leather as an insulating sleeping mat. Unfortunately it quickly became soaked, then froze, and stuck to the ground-sheet and his thin sleeping bag. After his first night at base camp he was not seen again for the rest of the expedition, electing to remain in his sleeping bag for the entire time while complaining bitterly of the cold. He did little in the way of liaising.

After building a small altar and erecting hundreds of feet of colourful prayer flags our Sirdar, Chwong Rinsi, had held a puja, with much burning of juniper and throwing of rice, while we made small offerings of chocolate and alcohol and tried to stop Richard from drinking it all. The sun had burned down from a clear blue sky as the smoke and prayers drifted up to our mountain with our fervent hopes for a safe climb and good weather. It had then snowed heavily.

During the first night of the storm, when the wind had come howling up the valley, the lid of Ray's plastic barrel had blown off and rolled down from our lofty spur. In the morning it was nowhere to be seen. Ray started digging. He began well, with a studious quartering search of the area around his tent, gradually extending his quest until it covered virtually the entire hanging valley. Every morning after that he awoke to find his diggings completely filled in and smoothed over. Unable to remember where he had already searched, he would start all over again. He must have shifted the volume of several Olympic swimming pools of snow each day only to find the following morning it was all back where it had started.

By the fourth day he began to flag. He stopped being methodical and decided to rely on intuition. After long contemplation of the wind direction, angle of slope, and experiments rolling my barrel lid down from his tent site, he would declare with absolute conviction that he knew exactly the only possible place in which it could be. The consequent evacuation of a shoulder-deep hole covering the area of a small terraced house only proved to him that he was wrong – and, yes, there had been a lot of rhododendron bushes around the base camp before the storm.

He would then retire to the cook tent in a grim mood to be laughed at by the team. After five days the cook boys and Chwong were laughing at him, and even the Liaison Officer was heard to emit some slightly manic guffaws from beneath the shadow of his boulder. It was pointed out to Ray that, as leader of the Gangchempo North Face expedition, he had a duty to boost the team's morale.

The whispering snowfall outside the tent seemed to have

stopped on the sixth morning, and I heard Ray struggling out of his tent.

'How is it?' I shouted hopefully.

'Snowing.'

'Yeah, but what's it like?'

'Well, snow is this cold white fluffy stuff that falls from the sky and has been doing it for the last week.'

'Thank you, Ray . . .'

'Good God!'

'What?'

'The flipping cook tent has almost disappeared. It must be waist-deep round here by now.'

'You're kidding?' I said, struggling out of my bag. I heard Ray laughing. 'What is it?'

'Haszko's tent is no more,' he said gleefully. 'Well, there's a little bit sticking out.'

'So, what's new?'

I emerged blinking in the white glare as I dug the drifts clear from the tent doorway. It was still snowing but there were hopeful signs of brightness in the south. Down in the bowl, the snow had drifted heavily against the tents. Richard's looked as if it had collapsed, and Brendan and Kate's small blue Gemini had been half-buried. What had once been a substantial twenty-foot-high boulder near John's tent was now all but submerged. There was no sign either of the Liaison Officer's tent and the yak shelter had drifts high up on the walls and partially covering the roof. Beyond the buried tents I could just make out the snowslopes on the other side of the bowl. They rose into the cloud at an angle of forty-five degrees and were deeply laden. Our position on top of the spur, perhaps a hundred feet above the hanging valley bowl, was not only uncomfortable, it also now looked a lot less safe to me.

'I don't like the look of those slopes at all,' I said to Ray, who had waded off to one side and was poking the snow with a ski-stick.

'You what?' he muttered distractedly as he scanned the area in the hope of spotting a small circular black plastic barrel lid.

'I said I was worried about avalanches.'

'What avalanches? I didn't hear any last night.'

'No, nor did I, but we might do pretty damn soon if it carries on like this.' He stopped digging and examined the slope above our spur.

'It should be all right. I mean there are a lot of rocks and bushes to hold it together.'

'Yes, there were a few days ago, but look at it now. They're much deeper in the snow than they were. And look at that,' I said, pointing to the altar and the prayer flags, or rather the complete absence of them. I watched as Brendan dug his way out of his tent and began wading towards the yak shelter. The snow was thigh deep, and occasionally drifted to waist level.

'It must have put down nearly two metres in the last week.'

'Come off it, that's over six feet, for God's sake.'

'Yeah, well, look at what Brendan's wading through. Anyway, whatever the depth, I'm beginning to wonder whether this camp is as safe as we thought.'

'Safe as houses. Anyway, it's finally clearing up. A bit of sun should soon consolidate this lot,' Ray said as he headed towards breakfast in the cook tent.

'Consolidate it on top of our heads, I shouldn't wonder,' I muttered as I waded after him.

'Never happen,' he shouted confidently.

Far above the tents the snowslopes settled uneasily. With a slight popping noise, a crack appeared on the surface of the slope, a thin dark shadow line rapidly filled by wind-harried spindrift. The wind scurried across the hillsides hustling veils of spindrift in tight eddies across the heavy drift. Dawn broke slowly as a weak sun filtered through the clouds.

The slope settled again and the crack reappeared. For a moment the forces bonding the thick layers of wind slab held firm and then with a hissing sound the crack raced across the upper edge of the snowfield and the whole lower slope slid down into the cloud-filled valley below. Three feet of clean-cut snow wall formed the shear point across hundreds of metres of the snowfield. From below came the rising heavy murmur of the avalanche. The clouds twisted aside as it pushed a mass of air ahead of it, gathering speed as it fell towards the white bowl of the hanging valley, the deep-cut stream, and the small cluster of half-buried tents sheltering on the far side of the bowl.

A light gleamed through the blue plastic roof covering the dry-stone walls of the yak shelter. Steam escaped past the nylon doorway. The shrill hiss of a released pressure cooker joined the roar of the double-burner primus stove and almost drowned a sudden outburst of laughter from within the shelter. It had snowed for five days and nights.

'Do you think we're safe here?' I asked again as Brendan dealt the cards.

'How do you mean?' Tat said.

'Well, there's been an awful lot of snow recently and I was thinking this morning that maybe this camp isn't safe any more. I mean we're surrounded on three sides by perfectly-angled avalanche slopes.'

'Naw. Never happen. Those slopes are well covered with rocks and bushes and stuff. That'll hold it all together.'

'Maybe that was true a few days ago, but I'm not so sure now.'

'And what could we do about it anyway?' Richard asked.

'We could move . . .' I suggested doubtfully, beginning to wish I hadn't brought up the subject.

'Move where, for God's sake?' Ray said, putting his cards down and standing up.

'But if we think it's a real threat, it would be stupid just to sit here and do nothing.'

'I must admit the tents are a bit exposed out there,' Tat said, looking around for support. 'We could all move in here, so we're all together in one spot. It would be safer here, wouldn't it?'

'No, you're just paranoid, Joe . . .' Ray grinned at me.

'Yes, and with good reason,' I muttered.

'It safe here,' Chwong Rinsi said. 'I have thrown the rice.'

I looked over at the smiling face of our Sirdar. 'He's thrown the rice. Ah well, that makes all the difference.' I smiled and

12

shrugged my shoulders. Faced with such irrefutable logic, I gave up.

Soon after that I was wondering what to do with a lousy Gin Rummy hand, and staring vacantly at the doorway, when it hit. There were ten of us in the cook shelter. Tat was sitting beside me on some flour sacks and leaning back against the rock wall of the shelter. Brendan and Kate faced us across the crude circular stone table with their backs to the door. Ray was stretching his legs, standing by the centre pole with one hand gripping the rough wood and the other holding the paper with the card scores on it. Richard sat sideways to the door, peering glumly at his cards. John, jammed in a corner full of boxes, was reading a Tom Clancy thriller. Chwong was gambling with the cook boy. Pemba had just released the pressure cooker. A mass of steam jetted towards the doorway. The tent inner shivered in the gust.

There was no warning sound at all. One moment I was staring at the tent inner door and the next second it was gone. I can't recall hearing any wind sound. A seemingly solid white tube instantly replaced the nylon door. I saw the blue roof lift and everything inside the shelter seemed momentarily to expand.

The powder snow exploded in my face. I still hadn't moved a muscle and was staring fixedly at the doorway and the solid white tube which seemed to be taking a long time to get inside. Part of my mind was screaming *'Avalanche!'* but I was quite incapable of translating the message into any form of physical reaction. It was like staring at a frozen tableau of figures; no one moved, their eyes staring from snow frosted faces in alarmed bemusement.

This is just the air blast, the rest is coming, the rest is coming!

At last a message came through that galvanised me into action. I knew what was coming. I had been there before. The notion of tons of snow bursting through the door at any moment made me throw myself sideways down among the flour sacks while trying to get an arm protectively across my nose and mouth. Unfortunately Tat had got the same message. We banged heads painfully and then had a brief undignified struggle to bury ourselves in the sacks. As we did so it stopped with the same shocking abruptness as it had started.

Everyone was absolutely still and silent – all but Tat and me in exactly the same positions and poses. The only difference was that everyone and everything was now totally white – hair, clothing, eyebrows, spectacles, rock walls, cards in the hand, and steaming white coffee mugs. The tent inner drifted down from wherever it had been blown and closed the open doorway.

'It was a bloody awful hand anyway,' Richard said and threw his cards on the table.

'Where did that come from?' someone asked.

'Outside,' Richard said helpfully.

Once the first shock of the avalanche had subsided and we stopped giggling nervously, we scrambled out of the shelter to survey the damage – not an easy task when you can see for no more than ten feet. The shelter had stood up remarkably well and none of the scattered tents seemed to have been hit. In fact there was no sign of avalanche debris anywhere. On our return to the shelter we found that the cook boys had lapsed into a fatalistic state of mind and, in spite of our cheery assurances, they remained grim and unsmiling.

'Well, now that the impossible has happened, what do you suggest we do?' I asked somewhat smugly.

'Was that actually an avalanche?' Brendan asked doubtfully. 'I mean, it wasn't . . .'

'No, in fact, it was the passing wind from a troupe of dancing girls. Quite common in these parts . . .'

'Shut up, Richard.'

'It does seem odd, especially as there's no debris outside,' Tat added.

'We missed the main event, or rather, it missed us. I reckon the big slopes on the other side of the stream avalanched but it didn't get this far,' Ray said, dusting powder snow from his seat and sitting down.

14

'More likely that it came down, hit the stream, which diverted it to the right, and off it went tearing down past us. Hence, no debris in the bowl or damage to the tents,' Tat surmised.

'So you reckon we were just hit by the air blast then?' John asked.

'Yeah, something like that. If it had crossed the stream I guess we might not be here now.'

'It's still snowing,' Kate said as she came in from inspecting her tent.

'Those slopes could go again,' John said. 'For all we know, that could have been just a small slide.'

'Yeah, and if the slopes above and behind us set off, we wouldn't have any stream to divert it,' I added, beginning to feel seriously paranoid again.

'Well, there isn't much we can do about it today,' Tat said. 'It'll be dark in a couple of hours. There's no safer place to camp up here, and it would be just as risky to try moving down in these conditions and in the dark. All the slopes bounding the stream could go and we would be stuck in the open.'

'Stay here then,' Ray suggested. 'I mean in the shelter. At least we would have some protection from the walls . . .'

'Yes, the tents are pretty exposed and scattered in the bowl,' Brendan said. 'If there was another slide in the night, it could take John's and Tat's tents out and the rest of us might not even know it.'

'Ray and I would be safe on our nice wee spur, anyway,' I said gleefully.

'Not if the slopes above us went,' Ray muttered.

'I thought you said this morning they wouldn't go?'

'Ah yes, well, as Leader I have the right to change my mind . . . rapidly.'

'Okay, so we all pack sacks with essentials and doss in here,' Tat reasoned. 'Let's hope we aren't hit, but we'll know where to look if anyone is buried.'

There was a general murmuring of assent from the team. The cook boys looked serious and scared. Chwong seemed unperturbed and was counting up his total winnings from the hapless cook boys. It looked as if we might just pay their wages directly to him at the end of the trip.

'What do you think, Chwong?' Ray asked. 'Is it dangerous here?'

'Not dangerous. Good place.' He smiled confidently. After all, he had thrown the rice.

By early evening things began to look up. Richard went out for a pee and was soon whooping and yelling and shouting for us to come outside.

'Look,' he said, clutching his old man in one hand and pointing to the west.

'I'd rather not, all the same,' Kate said.

'Full moon and clear sky,' he continued.

Sure enough most of the western sky was clear of clouds. The sun was sinking into the black, silhouetted horizon of distant summits casting a soft pink alpenglow over the clouds drifting out of our high valley.

'What does your altimeter-barometer thing say, Joe? What's the pressure doing?'

'Blowed if I know,' I muttered as I pressed an alarming array of buttons on a watch the size of a cricket ball on my wrist. 'Haven't quite got the hang of this yet.'

'It certainly looks like a major change,' Tat said, 'not just another front going over.'

'Ah, right,' I said hopefully. 'Yup, it looks as if it's gone up.'

'What's gone up?' Richard asked as he fought a losing battle with his salopettes. 'Pressure or height?'

'Good question. Let's see . . . height. Yes, we're higher than we were this morning.'

'That's no good. It means bad weather. If height goes up it means pressure has fallen, therefore bad weather. If it goes up, we go down. That's how you work it.'

'Oh! Hang on, I'm wrong, it's the pressure I'm looking at, not the height. Pressed the wrong button, I think. It's not easy, you know. You need a Ph.D. to understand the instruction booklet,' I said defensively. 'Anyway, it does mean good

16

weather if the pressure is rising, right?' I said to no one at all since they had given up and gone back into the shelter.

'You know what Ph.D. stands for, don't you?' someone said from inside.

'What?'

'Push here, Dummy.'

The next morning dawned bright and clear. I looked across at the faint scar that marked where the avalanche had broken off the previous afternoon. Tat had been right. It had swept down the stream, blasting past us in a flurry of powder. It didn't look a very big avalanche, and I began to wonder at how a bit of sunshine could completely change our mood from feeling caged in by a suddenly threatening and inescapable situation to a sense of optimism and swift disdain for our earlier fears. Perhaps Chwong had been right? Maybe there was something in the throwing of the rice? Or maybe, as I suspected, we were just lucky.

I ploughed my way down towards the shelter.

'Breakfast's on,' I yelled to Ray, who was energetically digging for his barrel lid down near the stream.

I sat next to Richard, who was tucking into pancakes and porridge. Pemba handed me a pancake and a hard boiled egg which I promptly cracked on Richard's shining pate to help break up the shell. It was a childish and mildly irritating habit that we had all fallen into, especially with Richard because it made such a satisfying noise.

'Top of the morning to you all,' I said happily, and Richard scowled.

'Do you think he'll ever find that lid?'

'Nope,' Tat said, a little too confidently.

'You haven't hidden it, have you?' Kate asked, and laughed.

'No, but if I do find it, I will.'

Ray came in and dusted snow off his shoulders over Richard's breakfast.

'Morning, Glorious One,' he said by way of appeasement. Richard scowled again and muttered something about children and little things and little minds.

'It's going to be rough getting up to the gear,' John said from the back of the shelter. On the day of the puja we had carried a load of crampons, ropes and stoves to a high point overlooking the glacier, a thousand metres above base camp. 'It'll all be buried by now,' I said, 'but I have a cunning plan. I can set this watch to start beeping once we are a thousand metres above here, which is . . . let's see . . .' There was a collective groan and a chorus of abuse. Richard cracked his egg on my head and everyone laughed except Richard who tried to get out of the way as I lunged for him. His egg hadn't been cooked.

An hour later we set off in single file, trudging wearily through the deep snow. I rested heavily on my ski-sticks, trying to protect my heavily strapped left knee. As I stepped down from a snow-covered boulder into a stream bed there was a lancing, ripping pain from the knee joint and I stumbled forward, losing my balance. I steadied myself and watched the others pull away from me as I flexed the injured joint. I knew at once that it wasn't strong enough for the climb. I thought of turning back. Then a wave of frustration ran through me and I put my head down and started the long climb up to the glacier. The fiery stabs of pain from the damaged cartilage increased. I thought of someone I didn't like and worked myself into a fury, stamping angrily up the track and ignoring the pain in my knee.

2

WALKING WOUNDED

I watched them move slowly away up a narrow snow ridge towards the upper slopes of the glacier. Once again I was left to contemplate yet another failure to climb a mountain. It was beginning to wear me down. I looked at the huddle of tents in the bowl of the valley below and the line of deeply cut footsteps rising up towards where I sat. It was going to be painful descending. I squeezed my left knee tentatively and turned to look as a small figure crested the ridge.

Richard was at the back, moving steadily. He was having a good trip and I felt pleased for him. He turned and looked back at me, raising his axe in farewell, before trudging over the rise and out of sight on to the glacier. They had all been sympathetic but, as always, Richard was the most emotional when I announced that I couldn't go on. I was feeling low and tried not to show how upset I was to be walking out alone once again.

'Bad luck,' Tat said. 'You know where my first aid kit is if you need it.'

'I won't,' I muttered, staring at the snow.

'Yes, but just in case,' he said, hoisting his sack on to his shoulders.

John walked past and patted my shoulder.

'What a bummer.'

'Yeah. Take care,' I said.

'I wish you were coming with us,' Ray said. He smiled encouragingly. The last time we had climbed together was on Ama Dablam three years before. It had been one of the best climbing experiences of my life and much of that was due to the friendship that developed between us. The summit day had seemed to be a turning point for me, a time when I reaffirmed my love for climbing despite all the problems it had caused me. Two years later a terrible accident on Pachermo plunged me back to the bottom of the hill, with a shattered ankle and a load more fear to carry. It almost destroyed the confidence and self-respect that our success on Ama Dablam had helped to rebuild. It would have been good to have climbed with Ray again.

'There's always next year,' I replied doubtfully. 'There'll be plenty more hills.'

'That's right.' He trudged after the others. 'Don't wait up for us,' he called. 'And don't drink all the whisky.'

'I won't, and you look after Richard.'

'Oh, do I have to?'

And then came Richard. He said nothing. Just walked up to me, put his arms around my shoulders and gave me his version of a Polish hug. He's a great hugger, is Richard. Quite unabashed and unashamed to show his emotions. I tried to shrug him off but he was determined. For a moment I hated him for it. This display was making it harder for me to remain stonily unemotional. Inside I was bursting with childish self-pity and disappointment but externally I wanted to appear calm and matter-of-fact about it all. Now Richard's hug was threatening to undo all my self-control and I could feel myself on the edge of tears. I was glad I was wearing dark glacier glasses. Eventually he let go, straightened up, and with a squeeze of my shoulder, followed the others up towards the snow ridge.

I stood up gingerly and began the long slow descent to base camp, glad of the loan of John's ski-sticks. With each step down a vicious little stab of pain knifed into the left side of my knee, almost making it collapse. I tried various methods – facing in, facing sideways, bum-sliding, hopping – and eventually gave up and just stomped angrily down the staircase of footsteps, gritting my teeth against the pain and hoping the knee would keep working at least until the camp.

The irony of retiring hurt wasn't lost on me. My left knee was the one remaining part of my legs that had escaped injury, and now the meniscus cartilage had chosen to play up. I had spent years weight-training in the gym to get my right leg working again and knew that to prevent further injury to that knee, which was badly broken in Peru in 1985, I would always have to keep it strong. Then I had worked hard on my left ankle, which was severely damaged in the fall on Pachermo. I knew how much muscle mass and strength was lost when a leg was encased in plaster, and simply forgot the advice of the physiotherapist.

After the ankle operation a year before, I had gone on an expedition to Pumori, to see if it was as bad as the surgeons had said. Sure enough, I found that it had only partially healed and the fibula was still sheared off. On my return a four-hour operation with a meccano set of pins, screws and wires saved the ankle from being fused, and I set about working hard to regain flexibility and strength in the joint. At the same time I neglected to strengthen the thigh muscles. These had wasted away after four months without bearing weight while the ankle was in plaster.

On the very first day of the walk-in to Gangchempo base camp John, Ray and I had raced each other down the switch-back road between Dhunche and the village of Syabru, situated at seven thousand feet on a forested ridge. It was a stupid three-hour race that I won by about three minutes, which simply meant that, having arrived at the bar first, I had to buy the beers. While we sat drinking cold San Miguels, the local bus had pulled away from the lodge and set off in a cloud of dust and blue exhaust fumes for Kathmandu via Dhunche. It had not been necessary to walk at all.

That night my left knee began to swell. In its weakened state the cartilage had been badly strained, though fortunately not torn, with the result that I felt pain and instability in the knee joint when walking downhill. The ridiculous thing was that the knee was very strong going up, but still, within hours of the expedition starting, I had ruined my chances of climbing the mountain.

It had been a hard struggle to gain permission to climb
Gangchempo (6400m) since it was not at that time on the list
of permitted peaks. It had originally been named Fluted Peak
by Bill Tilman when he and Peter Lloyd first explored the
unknown and mysterious Langtang region in 1949. They had
been searching for possible routes into Tibet and had received
permission from the Nepalese Government to explore the
area after a refusal to allow them to search the south
(Khumbu) side of Everest for a breach in the great unclimbed
mountain's defences.

Perhaps because of its proximity to Tibet, the Langtang
remained for a long time a rarely visited region and those
who did venture there found the going difficult. In fact,
permission for Gangchempo had cost us considerably more
than other Himalayan peaks of the same height, but we had
felt that it was worth the price since, as far as we knew, the
breathtaking fluted north face – our objective – remained
unclimbed.

The name Langtang derives from the discovery of the
valley, according to legend, by a holy man who had lost his
yak and trailed it from a nearby valley. 'Lang' means yak, and
'Tang' means to follow. When eventually the holy man caught
up with his errant beast, it suddenly died near the snout of the
glacier. He skinned the animal and tried to dry the hide by
spreading it over a large rock. In the fierce sun it became stuck
fast and the lama was unable to peel it from the rock. It is said
to be still there today, immovable from a big red rock by a
lonely hut at the edge of the west Langtang glacier.

In 1976 the Langtang valley (some 1,770 square
kilometres) was designated one of the first National Parks in
Nepal, and it remains the second largest in the country. The
park is home to an enormous variety of birds (more than 150
different species) as well as some thirty mammals including
goral, serow, bear, and the rare red panda. The heavily
wooded lower valley has forests of blue pine, oak, bamboo
and birch and throughout the park there are over a thousand
different recorded species of plants. Despite its proximity to
Kathmandu, barely thirty kilometres to the north of the city

as the crow flies, it is relatively unpopulated. Many of the villages that we passed through on the trek in were predominantly Tibetan, particularly Dhunche, Langtang, and Tamang up near the glacier.

In recent years Langtang has become an increasingly popular trek, especially for inexperienced travellers, and it was a less than pleasant surprise to be awoken by the aggressive noise of Israeli trekkers who seemed to trail us wherever we went. In five expeditions to Nepal I have never met a more consistently loud and abusive bunch and it was not the first time I had witnessed such abrasive and essentially racist behaviour among Israelis. Fellow travellers from all parts of the world have voiced a similar complaint.

Incensed by their rudeness to the women who were trying to feed so many trekkers at one lodge, some of us very nearly became embroiled in a fight with the five Israelis who had trailed us throughout the trek. It was perhaps as well we avoided the punch-up since they all looked as if they had just finished their military service and I suspect that we would have been thrashed. We contented ourselves with muttered rebukes from a safe distance and were glad when finally we managed to shake them off. They probably felt much the same about this furtive group of Brits who kept mumbling into their beers and making odd gestures from behind large conveniently branched trees.

Tat had examined the knee and tried to be encouraging, but he left me in no doubt that the trouble was not merely a twinge that would get better quickly. On the second day's walk we met a young German trekker who accompanied us to the Kyangjin monastery. It turned out that she was a top level sports physiotherapist, and after a consultation with Tat, she brusquely ordered me to lie on a bench while she examined the offending knee.

She seemed delighted to discover two fairly mangled legs covered in scars and bumps and bits that would not bend. I told her about the broken ankle and why I thought the knee was bad, and she immediately reprimanded me for not using two ski-sticks.

'Two?' I repeated as I lay on the bench and looked up at her along the length of my leg. 'I don't use one. What are you talking about?'

'You don't use *any* sticks?' she said, twisting the knee experimentally. 'You are a stupid man.'

'I've never got the hang of walking with them, and anyway I wouldn't want to end up looking like some sort of German trekker,' I said without thinking.

'I am a German trekker,' she snapped, and I realised by the way she was moving my leg that she was also very strong indeed. 'I use sticks always, *always*, and my legs are good. Very strong, not like these.' She waved her hand over them with disdain.

'Well, no, quite, I didn't mean to infer that . . .'

'You must make a strong strapping for this knee.'

'Right. I . . .'

'You have tape?' she asked abruptly. 'You have made this system before?'

'System, eh, what system?'

'Like this, and across, and like this.' She pointed with her finger to show how I should strap the knee. 'You know this way?'

'Well, no actually,' I said, feeling unaccountably stupid.

'You do not know this system and you have such bad legs, no?'

'Well, baddish.' I was going to defend my legs. 'And anyway, I thought they were quite good until yesterday. I was quite proud of them really.'

'Huh,' Heidi snorted. 'And no ski-sticks. This is very foolish. Oh, and this also' – she pointed to the scars on my ankle – 'this needs working on.' She transferred her attention to my foot and began twisting it one way and the other.

'Now, hang on . . .' I said, trying to sit up. She pushed me down. I tried to pull my leg away but it was in a vice-like grip. 'It's been rather badly smashed and I'd rather you didn't make it any worse.'

'No problem. I am good at this job.' She simply ignored my efforts to squirm out of her grip.

'That's as maybe, but I really think we should take this one thing at a time. I mean, it's the knee that's hurting.'

'Yes, I know this. It hurts because this is wrong. It doesn't go up like this,' she said, pushing the top of my foot towards my knee and causing a spasm of sharp pain.

'Ouch.'

'. . . and so you walk like this.' She twisted my knee.

'Whoa.'

'. . . and the muscles are not so strong, and you are stupid without sticks, so this is making the pain. Like so . . .' My knee appeared near my chin.

'Ahha.'

'. . . and the cartilage is catching here where the knee is opening, here.' She prodded the outside of my knee.

'Well, yes. Yes, funnily enough, that is where it hurts, but only going downhill, of course.'

'Yes, naturally.' She looked at me and smiled. 'You have some strong tape?'

'What sort of tape? Elastoplast or bandages or . . .'

'No, no. Strong sticking tape. Zinc tape.'

'Hang on a sec,' I said, deftly recovering my leg when momentarily she had let go. 'I'll just go and ask Tat.'

I went into the lodge where Tat was drinking tea. He looked up and grinned.

'Hello, old boy. And how is the wonderful Heidi?'

'Well, she's bloody strong, I can tell you,' I muttered. 'But she seems to know what she's talking about – I think.'

'Oh, she does that all right,' Tat said confidently. 'In fact, having talked to her these last two days, I reckon she's probably the best physio working on sports injuries I've ever come across.'

'You're kidding?'

'Nope. She's good.' He smiled cheerfully. 'Very good, in fact. What does she think then?' He nodded at my knee.

'Oh, just what you said really, but she thinks the ankle caused it. Oh, and she keeps bollocking me for having no ski-sticks.'

'Quite right too,' Tat said rather smugly. I scowled at him.

'I read somewhere that using two sticks during an average eight hour day on the hill takes something like two hundred and fifty tons load off your lower body.'

'What?' I said incredulously.

'Well, something like that,' he said, 'can't remember the exact figure but it's based on the premise that if you put twenty pounds weight through each ski-stick on each step, then that's twenty pounds off your legs. So, if you call a stride length one metre, then in a kilometre you have saved yourself twenty thousand pounds, that is twenty pounds times one thousand strides, or metres. Or if you prefer it in miles, getting on for thirty thousand pounds. Got that?' I nodded uncertainly. 'Okay? Right, so in say a twenty kilometre day that would be, let's see . . . four hundred thousand pounds, which comes to . . .' He looked up. 'How many pounds are there in a ton?'

'God knows.'

'Call it a bit over a thousand kilos to a ton, so that makes it a bit over two thousand pounds to a ton, which divided into four hundred thousand makes it somewhere near two hundred tons, or thereabouts.'

'Eh?'

'Give or take a ton or two,' Tat added helpfully. 'Two hundred tons is quite a saving on your legs, especially *your* legs. She's not daft, is Heidi.'

'No, you're probably right. Two hundred tons, you say?' I mused, trying to fathom out his maths. 'So why don't you use them?'

'A bit too Teutonic for me. It's a pity you have to look like a German trekker to do it.'

'Ah, yes, I mentioned that. Didn't go down too well, I'm afraid.'

'No it wouldn't, bearing in mind she's from Bavaria.'

'Yes, quite. Anyway, she wants to strap my knee up with zinc tape. Have we got any?'

'I have just the thing,' he said with a suspiciously cheerful grin. He delved around in his rucksack before producing the tape. 'It doesn't half stick though.'

'What do you mean?'

'Oh, don't worry yourself.' He tossed the roll of tape to me. 'It comes off . . . eventually.'

'You know she wants to manipulate my ankle? I'm a bit worried she might damage it. I mean, she really is a strong lass, you know.'

'Don't be daft. She's a professional, and she's very good.'

I lay in the sun precariously balanced on a stone bench while Heidi manipulated my leg and muttered about stupid Englishmen and ski-sticks. An unkempt white donkey wandered into the large dusty yard in front of the lodge. It was painfully thin, with a rack of ribs protruding through its hide, the sharp angular jutting pelvic bones indicating malnourishment. I watched as it ambled towards us on knobbly bow-legs, chewing something with apparent relish. It was only when it came right up close to us that I realised it was chewing a long strip of soiled pink toilet paper which hung from the side of its mouth. The donkey stared at me in my prone position with wide, sad brown eyes and an expression that seemed to plead for help.

'Yearghh!' I yelped and pulled myself away as Heidi reached for a ski-stick. The poor beast turned wearily away, still chewing its pink dinner.

Heidi was an excellent physio, and despite the constant bantering insults among the team, she seemed to find it refreshing to meet climbers who didn't take themselves so seriously that they couldn't have fun on expeditions. I think her experiences with some highly organised, deadly serious and furiously unfunny German trekking groups had led her to believe that this was how things had to be. She couldn't quite believe that we really were mountaineers, and she might possibly have had a point, for on this trip we all spectacularly failed to climb anything.

The knee was firmly strapped in yards of zinc tape. I looked dubiously at the hairs on my legs sticking out from under the tape.

'It is no problem,' Heidi said confidently. 'With soaking in hot water and a small knife it comes off.'

'A small knife?' I repeated, and scowled at Tat's laughter from inside the lodge.

Still, the tape did at least give me enough support to manage the walk up to the base camp, and after Heidi's intensive sessions with the ankle, it did seem as if she had unblocked some major problem inside the joint. What's more, the treatment had been relatively painless.

In the end Heidi came with us to base camp and took part in the puja before setting off on the trek back to Kathmandu. She had hoped to try to cross into the Helambu by the 16,800-foot high pass known as the Ganja La. It was a serious undertaking, carrying her food, fuel and shelter, especially after all the snow that had fallen in recent weeks – a four or five day trek that would involve some scrambling, possibly on ice, and some tricky route-finding, particularly in poor visibility. She was happy and confident in her ability and revelled in the chance to travel alone. If she were thwarted, she hoped to trek back to Kathmandu by way of the lakes at Gosainkund. There would be spectacular views of Langtang Himal, Manaslu and Himalchuli on this route, as well as a chance to visit the three holy lakes – Bhutkunda, Nagkunda and Gosainkunda – where each summer thousands of pilgrims gather to worship the Hindu god, Shiva.

She said goodbye to us after the ceremony and set off walking strongly, quickly settling into a metronomic rhythm with her ski-sticks. I wondered why I was always catching mine and tripping myself up. I was hoping that, once I learned the knack of using them efficiently, it might help me overcome the pain in my knee. Unfortunately the damage had been done, and for this trip the knee simply wasn't strong enough to stand up to the rigours of Himalayan climbing.

3

GIVING UP

When I hobbled into base camp Pemba looked out from the yak shelter, surprised to see me back so soon. He had not expected anyone for at least three days – the minimum time we reckoned it would take us to climb and descend the west ridge. The deep snow laid down by the storm meant that we had been forced to abandon our attempt on the unclimbed north face and settle instead for the west ridge. I muttered something about my leg, went up to my tent and dumped my rucksack down hard.

Glancing up at the mountain, I could just make out the tiny figures of John, Tat, Ray and Chwong moving slowly across the glacier towards a steep rock buttress dropping down from the west ridge. High above them I spotted two dots moving across a small snow saddle on the crest of the ridge. Kate and Brendan had set out one day earlier than the rest of the team. After a while I turned away and looked morosely down into the Langtang valley. I could see no use in staying at base camp. If something went wrong, there was little that I could do. There was no question of my mounting any sort of rescue. I would make a poor runner if help was needed from the valley below. I didn't want to sit and watch their progress up the mountain. It would be a depressing and worrying business.

By mid-day I had packed away the tent and all but a few essential items into my barrel and a large haul bag. I dragged them down to the shelter and handed over a note for Pemba to give to everyone when they got down. I had no doubt that they would be successful. The ridge looked fairly straightforward and the weather had at last set fair. With one last glance at the mountain, now with no sign of any climbers on it, I turned and set off on the three-day slog back to Dhunche. I wasn't looking forward to it. It was downhill most of the way.

If I walked steadily and relied heavily on the ski-sticks, I found that the knee coped quite well. It made a huge difference not to be carrying a heavy rucksack and problems only arose after periods of rest in which the joint seemed to stiffen into a solid lump.

On the second day I descended past the Kyangjin Gompa, where Heidi had treated my leg, and down through a forested hillside now ablaze with the vibrant red of flowering rhododendrons and sweet yellow magnolias. The forest itself smelled strongly of fresh growth, the rich damp reddish soil and scent of pine. Spring had rushed in upon us in the last three weeks and it contrasted strongly with the barren, sterile black and white of base camp.

My knee began to improve with every step I took away from the mountains. Towards the end of the second day I passed a small village where we had camped on the way up the valley. I sat on a fallen tree and drank some water, watching a man run towards me from one of the nearby houses. He looked vaguely familiar and very eager to see me, which was odd. Then I remembered the baby boy on the walk-in. This was his village, and no doubt the man was the boy's father. I fervently hoped that the baby hadn't died, or that if he had the man would see that I wasn't the expedition doctor before venting his anger upon me.

When we had arrived a little over three weeks earlier one of our porters had approached Tat and asked whether, as a doctor, he could help his brother's son who lived in the village. The boy, a month-old baby, was extremely ill. His eyes were sealed shut with mucus and dirt from the smoky atmosphere of the chimneyless dark lodge in which he lived, and he was losing a hard-fought battle against pneumonia. Tat had injected the baby with doses of antibiotics, but he soon ran out and was forced to administer pills that came in adult doses. Using guesswork as best he could, he crushed a pill into a powder and gave roughly an eighth of it dissolved in water to the dying baby. After staying on alone for an extra day, Tat had rejoined the expedition in Langtang village. He held out little hope for the boy's survival. The one thing in his favour was that he had lasted without treatment for so long, which showed that he was a tough little boy.

I felt quite moved by the way Tat shouldered his heavy burden of responsibility as a doctor, something he could never escape from, wherever he was. He had been forced on numerous occasions to try his best, in impossible conditions with inadequate equipment, to treat very sick people in remote areas.

Hurriedly I put away my water bottle as the man approached. As I began to hoist my rucksack on to my shoulders I noticed that the man was smiling broadly and waving both hands at me. I put the sack down and waited for him. He gripped my arms in his hands and shook me in a friendly manner, speaking to me excitedly and looking past me at the trail in the woods from which I had just emerged.

After about five minutes of voluble conversation, of which neither of us understood a word, we parted the best of friends. I waved a ski-stick at him as I went into the woods on the far side of the clearing and he waved back and turned to look up the trail for the others. Although not certain, I guessed that the little boy had survived, and that the man was waiting for Tat to appear from the woods at any moment. I had tried to explain to him that the doctor wouldn't arrive for at least another five days, possibly a week, but had failed miserably to make myself understood. At least Tat was in for a happy surprise on his way down from the mountain. Perhaps the good side of being a doctor is that sometimes, if not very often, it is possible to perform miracles.

By the time I reached Syabru my knee was swollen and on the point of collapse. I had made the descent from base camp in two and a half days, a distance that had taken us more than five days on the way up. And it had involved a descent of

31

almost eight thousand feet, which was the last thing my knee required. The weather had remained clear but for a brief rain shower that morning, and as I wearily ordered my first beer at the lodge I realised that the team would probably have climbed Gangchempo by now and reached the safety of base camp. I felt a sharp pang of jealousy and annoyance at my weakness.

As the sun settled behind the forested hillside I watched smoke seep through the shingled roofs of the houses. Steam rose from the grassy slopes running down from the crest of the ridge to which the village clung precariously. The houses appeared to overlap each other in a chaotic lean-to fashion, as if they were all in a constant struggle against gravity. A criss-cross pattern of shadows rose up above the village to the east, marking out terraced fields of corn and millet.

A mangy dog skulked around the lodge where I sat, searching furtively for scraps of food. A well aimed stone sent it yelping into the shadows. A group of villagers led a bleating black-and-white goat across the yard, followed by a uniformed soldier carrying an unsheathed kukri. The goat stood quietly amid the group of villagers, its stubby tail wagging furiously as it looked around people's feet for scraps of food to eat. After much arguing and laughter one man pulled hard on the goat's tail while another pulled tightly on the rope secured around the animal's neck. There was a surprised bleat, cut short by the *chunk* of the kukri as it sliced effortlessly through the taut neck.

It happened with astonishing speed, leaving me quite shocked – less due to squeamishness than the fact that I hadn't been paying close enough attention to recognise what was about to happen. The man pulling the rope flew backwards and the goat's head arched gracefully over his shoulder. A fountain of blood gushed from the severed neck as the body thrashed and twitched on the dusty road.

Within minutes a woman appeared with a large cauldron of boiling water and the carcass was thrust into it. More boiling water was poured into the pan from a blackened kettle. The mangy dog reappeared from its bolthole in the shadows, unable to resist the scent of fresh blood, and made a belly-crawl towards the head as it lay, momentarily forgotten, in the road. The dog seemed to be quivering and shaking, either from fear or hunger, and it never once took its eyes off the goat's head.

A stone raised a spurt of dust in the ground near the dog's hind quarters but the creature was too close to the blood pooling in the packed earth to pay any attention. Just as it tentatively reached forward to sniff the severed neck the soldier raised the bloodied blade of the kukri and took a step towards the dog which instantly froze. For a second there was a comical expression of lustful hunger and indecision on the animal's face as it glanced rapidly from the gory neck to the kukri before it seemed to make the connection and slunk reluctantly away. The villagers laughed uproariously at the dog's discomfort.

The goat was hauled steaming from the pan and the woman expertly, and with astonishing speed, removed the hair with a sharp knife. The naked white body of the goat was smeared with some powdered spice that stained it to a bright golden yellow. With a deft stroke of the knife, the carcass was cut open and the entrails, liver, lungs and heart scooped, two-handed, into a bucket. Someone produced a set of scales and the carcass was quickly butchered and divided among the villagers. The whole operation had taken no more than fifteen minutes. One moment I was observing a crowd of people and a curious goat and the next there was nothing but a dark stain in the dust, a frantically disappointed dog, and a woman with a bucket of offal.

I finished my beer and went off to buy a bus ticket to Kathmandu. At six the following morning we thundered out of Syabru in a cloud of dust and exhaust fumes and in half an hour negotiated the switch-backs up to Dhunche which had so quickly damaged my knee. Eight hours later I was drinking beer in the Blue Note, listening to John Lee Hooker and watching the sun setting behind the Himalayas.

Some days later the rest of the team arrived in Kathmandu, safe but unsuccessful. Altitude sickness, lack of time, and an impasse on the ridge had forced them to retreat from a high point just seven hundred vertical feet below the summit but a long way from it horizontally. Sure enough, Tat had been fêted as a conquering hero on his arrival at the village where he was delighted to find that the baby had made a full recovery. His medical burdens in Kathmandu were somewhat more prosaic when he found himself treating a young Irishman who, much to our amusement, had been gored in the buttocks by a yak.

Tom and Jerry's Bar was crowded and noisy. Waiters jostled through the throng carrying heavily laden trays of drinks as the rock music blasted out of huge speakers behind the bar. It was more like a scene in some seedy night-club in Benidorm than a quiet drinking venue in Kathmandu.

I had met up with the Gangchempo team for a celebratory drink after their return from an unsuccessful attempt on the mountain. The damaged cartilage in my left knee had almost completely healed.

'Hey Joe,' Tat yelled. 'She wants to know what you do?'

He nodded towards the woman sitting beside him. He had introduced me to her earlier in the evening. She was a school-teacher leading a boisterous group of London kids on their first trek in Nepal and had met the team as they were walking out from the Gangchempo base camp.

One pushy, cheeky lad called Darren had taken on John and Ray at cards. After hours of pontoon and three-card brag, Darren had lost every penny he owned, as well as most of his friends' savings. If he had been less obnoxiously cocky he would probably have been given his money back, but both John and Ray were so irritated by him that they decided to drink their winnings instead. I saw him sitting beside the teacher, grinning insolently and trying to steal Richard's beer when he wasn't looking.

'What?' the woman mouthed, cupping a hand to her ear because she hadn't heard my mumbled response to her question in all the noise.

'How do you make a living then?' she called out, waving

her hand for me to come over and squeeze on to the bench beside her. Reluctantly I perched precariously on the few inches left at the end of the seat.

'I get by,' I said evasively.

'He's a doctor,' she said, smiling at Tat. 'He's a teacher, John's a director of a Stained Glass company, Kate is an oceanographer. Quite a mixed bag you lot are. And Tat says that you're a writer?' I glared malevolently at Tat, who smiled cheerfully. It was just what I didn't want her to know.

'Well, yes. I write a bit,' I murmured. 'I also give slide shows and do a bit of mountain guiding . . .'

'What have you written then?' she asked, ignoring my attempts to change the subject.

I looked around for some sort of distraction. A waiter approached and I raised my hand.

'Right, who's for a beer? It's my shout.' At once everyone became interested in the waiter except for the teacher who kept glaring at me, waiting for a reply to her question.

'Okay, that's six San Miguels, a coke, and what about you, Lorna? It is Lorna, isn't it?'

'You know it is. Why are you being so evasive?'

'A beer. Do you want a beer?'

'Yes,' she said, giving me a level stare.

'Right, I'd better go to the bar and pay.' I stood up.

'He'll come to you,' Tat said with a mischievous grin.

'Thanks a bunch, Tat.'

'My pleasure, old boy.' He was enjoying my discomfort.

'Wot about me?' Darren whined. 'Don't I get a beer?' I could have hugged him.

'Bugger off, Darren, you haven't any money.'

'He's got me money.' Darren pointed at John.

'Correction,' John said. 'The money isn't yours any more. You lost it, remember?'

'You cheated,' Darren wailed. 'Go on, Joe, get us a beer.'

'No, you loathsome little oik,' I replied, and the boy burst into howls of protest.

'You callin' me an oik? I'll have you . . .'

'Listen, you couldn't have any of us in a month of Sundays,

sunshine. And anyway you're too young for beer.'

'I'm old enough to gamble with you, so why can't I have a drink?'

'One. You're under age, and two, you're skint. Oh, and three, we're drinking your money, and it's a hard life,' John said cheerfully, and drained his beer.

'You ain't tough.' Darren bristled. 'You don't know what 'ard is.'

I stood up and went to the bar as mayhem descended upon the table. While I was paying for the drinks I saw Lorna talking earnestly to Tat. He glanced at me and smirked, knowing that I was silently pleading for him to keep quiet.

'So, you write books, I hear,' Lorna said when I returned to the table.

'Er, yes, a few.'

'There's no need for false modesty,' she said sharply. 'Tat says the first one's very good.'

'Stupid old goat,' I muttered as I poured the beer into my glass. 'And it's not false modesty, I just don't like talking about it. Just as Tat doesn't like people announcing he's a doctor.'

'Why not? You should be proud of being a writer.'

'Well, maybe I am, privately,' I said, glaring venomously at Tat, 'but that doesn't mean I want to go round blathering about it all the time. And anyway, it just means I have to tell a story I've told a thousand times, and answer the same questions all over again. I don't want to seem rude, but I am here on holiday.'

'Well, I know now, about this "void" book, so you might as well tell me.'

'It's called *Touching the Void* actually,' I said somewhat sniffily, and Tat laughed. 'And that's as much as I'm telling. If you want to know about it, go and read it.'

'Have you got a copy?'

'I don't carry them around with me,' I snapped.

'Is it good?' she persisted.

'I wouldn't know. I've never actually read it.'

'You've never read your own book?'

36

'Not in one go. Obviously I read my editor's comments on the individual chapters and looked at the proofs, but I've never read it properly all through. Don't think I ever will either.'

'Why on earth not?'

'Oh, I don't know, bad memories, that sort of thing.'

'It can't be that bad,' Lorna said with an incredulous expression.

'It can, you know,' Tat added. 'You should read it.'

'Well, where can I get hold of a copy?'

'Straight out of the front door of this bar, cross the street and go into Pilgrim's bookshop. You should be able to find a paperback copy there.'

'Are you sure?'

'Yes, and . . .'

'Give us a swig on your beer, Joey boy?' Darren said as he reached for my glass.

'Oi!' I slapped his hand away. 'Don't even think it. And don't call me Joey. I'm not a bloody parrot.'

'Okay, Joey,' Darren said with a smirk. 'Do you fancy her, Joey?' He was nodding at Lorna.

'I'm warning you.' I glared at him.

'Would you give her one, Joey? Ouch!' He yelped as Richard clipped him firmly on the ear.

'Christ almighty, are all your kids like this creep?' I asked Lorna.

'No,' she replied, looking wearily at Darren. 'He's unique, is our Darren.'

'Well, he'll be uniquely crippled if he doesn't get the hell out of here.'

'Gi's a beer and I'll go.' Darren grabbed Richard's half full bottle and scampered towards the door.

'You little bastard!' Richard howled as his drink disappeared down the stairs. 'I've had about enough of that child.'

'I've had three weeks of him,' Lorna said with resignation.

'It's at times like these that I should have listened to what my father said.'

'Why? What did he say?' Lorna asked, and we all groaned.

Richard completed his familiar line. 'I don't know, I never listened to him.'

Two days later I was surprised to hear a knock on the door of my room in the Pheasant Lodge. Lorna stood in the doorway clutching a paperback edition of my book. She had a grim expression on her face and her eyes were moist and red.

'Hi, what brings you here?' I said, realising too late that I had only a towel around my waist.

She pushed past me into the room and sat on the bed.

'She wants a shag, Joey.' Darren's grinning face appeared in the doorway.

'Piss off, Darren,' Lorna said with quiet exasperation.

'Go on, give her one . . .'

I slammed the door shut and turned to face Lorna.

'What's the problem?' I asked. She looked up with a bleak gaze. I could see she was distraught and close to tears.

'I read your book last night.'

'Well, it's not that bad, is it?'

'No, not at all. I couldn't put it down. I read it in one go.'

'Ah well, that's because I write quickly,' I replied, trying to keep the atmosphere cheerful. She began to cry.

'Hey, come on.' I sat down beside her. 'It's just a story. What's up?' I didn't know what else to say. I hardly knew the woman. I was perched awkwardly, wondering what to do with my arms.

'I can't explain it very well,' she said, in a tremulous voice. 'What you went through . . . I mean the pain, and the loneliness, and, well, I . . .'

'It all happened years ago,' I put in hastily. 'It's over now and I don't think about it.'

She broke down again. I shuffled awkwardly on the bed.

'I'm sorry.' She wiped her eyes with a tissue. They looked as if she had been crying for some time. I glanced around the mess of gear and clothing littering the room, hoping to find some sort of distraction. The scene was making me feel very uncomfortable.

'You see, I have this problem and there's no way out for

me. It's impossible and I just can't deal with it . . .'

'Well, I don't know what it's all about but I'm sure it's no less real or painful than the trouble we had,' I said, touching her arm. 'Look, what happened to me in Peru just happened. In the end there was really no choice. We were alone.'

'I'm alone. I can't tell anyone and I can't cope with it. I don't know what to do.' She trailed off disconsolately.

'You can tell me,' I said impulsively. 'It won't go any further.' And as I said it I thought, *Why the hell did I say that? I can't deal with a stranger's tears.*

'Can I?' She looked directly at me. I shuffled uneasily. 'You won't tell?'

'No, of course not. You can tell me,' I said again with part of my mind raging furiously. *Get her out of here. You don't need this stuff.* I wasn't qualified to give her advice. *Why has she come to me? What on earth has she seen in my book that as far as I'm concerned just isn't there?* I mumbled something inane about life and the unfairness and impermanence of everything, and then stopped my embarrassed babbling.

'I don't know how to start . . .' She shook her head vigorously and then blew her nose into the tissue.

'Give him a gobble, miss.' Darren's dulcet tones echoed in the courtyard outside. I stiffened and turned towards the door.

'It's all right.' She gripped my arm as I was about to rise. 'It's just Darren.'

'Yeah, I know. Unique, isn't he?' She gave me a faint smile.

'Don't worry.' I put my arms round her and gave her a hug. 'It's good to talk, to share things. Let it out.' *Even if it is with a total stranger who just wants to get out of here and have a stiff drink!* At the feel of my comforting hug she began crying again. *Bloody hell! How did I get into this?*

'I suppose I'd better start at the beginning,' she said, taking a deep breath, bracing herself to tell me.

'Hey Joey? Have you shagged her?' Darren shouted. I heard him shuffling near the door. 'Tits out for the lads, miss,' he chanted crudely. His voice was louder, closer to the door. Before Lorna had a chance to react I had exploded from the bed and threw myself at the door. It banged heavily open and I was delighted to hear a strangled yelp of pain and feel the weight of Darren's body against the wood.

As I burst into the courtyard I saw him scrambling to his feet and then set off in a crouching sprint. I lunged after him, trying to get hold of his collar. He side-stepped and sprinted for the gate. I watched as he reached the alleyway where he turned to give me the finger and then fled down the dusty road. I returned the gesture. *Forget it*, I told myself, *he's just an oik with a viciously tight perm. He's not worth it.*

'Did you catch him?' Lorna called through the doorway.

'No,' I almost shouted.

'I'm glad,' she said with a smile. 'He's a good kid really. Lots of spirit, if he is a bit trying.'

'Trying! I was going to strangle the little bugger,' I snapped.

'And that would have been unfair.' She was right. I knew that if I had caught Darren I would probably have hurt him. I was so angry that I would have hit him as if he were a man rather than a pestering child, and that would have been unfair.

'I'll still give him a clip when I next see him.'

'Yeah, that's about right,' Lorna said brightly. The tears had gone. She stood up suddenly and smoothed her hair nervously with the palms of her hands. She had told me nothing.

'Look, I'm sorry I came . . .'

'It's okay. Don't worry about it,' I interrupted her, feeling the adrenalin still pumping. My attention had switched to Darren and wouldn't settle back on whatever it was Lorna had been trying to say. 'Are you sure you're all right?'

'I'll be all right,' she said, looking down at her feet. 'It was unfair of me to bother you. Look, I'd better go and find Darren.' She left, quietly saying thanks. I didn't understand why.

I was angry at my uncontrolled reaction to Darren's infuriating behaviour, and even more frustrated over my helpless inadequacy in the face of Lorna's despair. Why did some people expect me to have special psychological and emotional insights just because I'd had a bad time in the mountains? I had even received letters from strangers insisting on God's role in my survival on Siula Grande. There had also been letters thanking me for the help my book had been in dealing with physical and emotional injuries of a different sort in other circumstances. It confused me. My experience and injuries were often small compared to what many of these people were going through, and nothing when put beside the visitation of extreme cruelty and violence endured by the innocent, the powerless and the deprived in Tibet, in Cambodia, Bosnia, Rwanda and elsewhere. At least in Peru we were responsible for our own pain and difficulty.

I didn't like how close I had come to attacking Darren. I knew that if I had caught him I would have taken out my frustration on him, been unduly vicious. Why do something I despised? Because I could. He was smaller than I was. I had an excuse – I could get away with it.

Perhaps that was the truth of humanity's instinctive barbarity. It happened because in certain circumstances it was allowed, it was possible to get away with it. Was the veil of civilisation really so thin and fragile?

4

BODY LANGUAGE

I watched his shaven head as he bent over the pool table and cued to break the pack. He was all tattoos and muscles and swaggering machismo, and he exuded menace. He wore jeans, a grubby white tank top and a denim jacket. He had crudely cut the arms off the jacket and it hung unevenly on his shoulders with ragged tatters of white thread fringing the arm holes.

There seemed to be a rehearsed violence in his behaviour, as if he had practised each mannerism separately and was now putting them all together to create the image he wanted to project. It produced an oddly dislocated appearance, almost puppet-like. I suppose it worked in a crude sort of way, but there was something suspicious about it, something that didn't ring true. I had noticed the way he walked, a chest-forward strut, and held his cue, biceps clenched, tattoos bulging. There was an aggressive thrust to his chin and the shaven bullet head was cocked to one side, ready for the head-butt. He was declaring his hardness, stating his power, his idea of manliness. I thought he looked bloody stupid.

On a couple of occasions he had caught my eye as I watched his performance with the previous player. He had immediately raised his chin and stared back. The set of his jaw and the raised questioning eyebrows said it all. *You staring at me or what? Do you want some then? I'm hard, I am.*

I quickly averted my eyes as he swaggered to the table, all rolling shoulders and thrusting crutch, and played an arrogantly casual shot. The balls cannoned around the table and the white dropped into a pocket. He had fouled and given away two shots. I tried not to laugh as he shrugged his shoulders dismissively, jerked his head back in a twitchy threatening manner and strutted back to his stool by the bar. His opponent cleared his remaining four yellow balls and potted the black. The white ball rolled inexorably back from the shot and, just when it looked as if it would stop, it dropped into the middle bag.

The hard-man's demeanour changed. For that split second, when the black ball dropped, he realised that he had lost. For a moment he seemed to deflate, and then the white ball rolled into the middle bag and he pushed himself off the stool, spilling his beer on his jeans as he raised his fist to the table and uttered a primeval howl, straight from the football terraces, but sounding ludicrous in a half-empty pub. He had won by default. The loser looked relieved to have no more to do with it and walked away with a rueful grin. They didn't shake hands.

I studied the back of my opponent's head as he swung his cue back and forwards. The recently shaved skull had a bluish tinge of stubble showing through the pale white skin. It was covered in bumps and a few clean white lines revealed old scars. I saw his shoulder muscles tighten as he paused at the top of his back swing and then he crashed the cue forward into the white ball, his elbow jerking down and his head lifting with the power of the shot.

There was a loud, sharp crack as the triangle of balls scattered, reds and yellows zig-zagging violently around the table. The white ball flew into the top right pocket. He glared accusingly at where it had disappeared. He'd fouled on the break so it was two shots to me. Nothing unusual in that. It was common to smash the balls as hard as possible when breaking and anything could happen but, as far as I could tell, this man made all his shots in exactly the same way. He was a terrible pool player. He wasn't so much playing pool as showing off his manhood.

The balls had broken nicely for me – all in the open, off the cushions, four of the seven in easy potting positions, two nestling together and offering an easy plant into the middle bag, and the last could be developed into a better position. His, on the other hand, were a mess. Five lay against the cushions, two were in the open but blocked from any of the pockets. He slammed his cue down hard on the edge of the table in petulant annoyance and swaggered to the bar. He was an ugly man. I smiled to myself as I bent over and addressed the first red ball. I was going to enjoy beating him.

The red went cleanly into the middle bag. The white stopped where I wanted it. Another middle, hit soft, then I took a shot along the cushion to drop one into the top right and position the cue ball for a pot into the top left pocket. I chalked my cue and looked at the pattern of balls. My opponent shouted something which I didn't hear above the roar of music from the juke box. I looked up and found him glaring at me. I looked quickly back at the table, anxious not to antagonise him. I could feel his eyes on me as I cued the white ball. The red dropped but I had jerked the shot and lost position on the next ball. I heard a derisive laugh from the corner of the bar.

I missed the next pot, a difficult oblique angle into the middle bag, and the white rolled past the position for the next shot. He was getting to me. I could sense his anger. He was making me angry, needling me. I walked around the table to see if I could recover the position. I had hoped to clear up from the break but I had made a mess of it. I tried a speculative shot, unlikely to succeed but worth the risk. The black was in the open, pottable from any angle. There was still a chance to whitewash him from the break. I wondered what that would do to his manhood.

As I bent to address the cue ball a hand slapped into vision on the side of the table.

'Oi!'

'I've still got two shots,' I said, straightening up and facing him. He pushed his face close to mine so that his head jutted forward from his neck. He had a tattoo on the side of his neck. It was crudely drawn, home made, probably done with a compass point and some ink.

'You fouled on the break,' I said calmly and met his glare. He glanced at the table, then turned away.

'Watch it,' he said menacingly as he swaggered to his stool. *Watch what?* I thought. *What have I done? This guy's a moron.*

I bent over and tried to concentrate but I could feel him staring at me. As I took the shot it occurred to me that he was just the sort to have L.O.V.E. and H.A.T.E. tattooed between the knuckles of his fists, and probably had 'I love Mum' on a heart with an arrow through it on his bum. I missed the pot and the white ricocheted into his yellow balls on the side cushion, breaking them into good open positions.

He pushed himself off the stool and approached the table. The position still wasn't very good for him and he scowled as he chalked his cue. I watched him as he bent down and potted an easy yellow with excessive force. He straightened quickly, flicking his cue up from the table in studied disdain. The white ball powered around the baize, bouncing off the cushions, and came to a halt tight against the knuckle of one of the pockets. The black kept rolling, heading towards one of the bottom corner pockets, and I saw his shoulders sag slightly. It stopped an inch from the edge.

He dropped the next yellow, again with maximum force, and the shot looked good. It was a difficult angle to cue the white ball and a long pot as well but the yellow had thunked satisfyingly into the pocket. He stood and posed for a while and strutted his stuff. I knew it had been a lucky shot and so did he, but he strutted all the same.

I watched him walk round the table, all clenched up, face set hard and tight, and felt mesmerised by the effect. Surely he realised how ridiculous this pathetic parade made him look. Unless, of course, he was too dumb to see it for himself. I looked across at the man who had lost to him earlier and he raised his eyes and shrugged. I smiled at him, reassured that I wasn't the only one thinking this was an absurd performance. The skinhead potted another yellow with an extravagant flourish but, when everything had come to rest, the white ball was nestled up close to one of my reds.

He bent down to address the ball and I moved to the side to get a clear view of what he was doing. As he lined up the shot, sliding the cue back and forth, one of his bridging fingers clearly nudged the red to one side. It moved about an inch. It was a clear foul. I expected him to stop his shot and stand back from the table, but instead he hurriedly struck the white in an effort to conceal the foul play. I looked across at the player by the bar to see if he had noticed. He nodded in a resigned sort of way and turned to get his drink.

I walked to the table and stood by the skinhead as he admired his handiwork.

'Two shots,' I said in a calm matter-of-fact voice.

'Yer what?'

'Two shots, mate,' I said. 'You just moved the red with your hand.'

'Did I fuck,' he snarled. I looked over at the bar for confirmation. The player had his back to me.

'Come off it, it moved about an inch . . .'

'You calling me a cheat?' He thrust his face into mine. I stepped back.

'The ball moved,' I replied, wishing I had said – no, my mistake. Carry on.

'Right then – outside – *now*,' he shouted, jerking his thumb towards the door. 'I'll take you. I might have a bad neck and a bad arm but I'll fooking batter you.'

I didn't move. What was this about a bad neck and arm, I wondered, as he poked a finger into my chest, making me step backwards off balance.

'I can do you with one fucking arm, I can.' He was shouting now, working himself into a rage. His face had turned red. I noticed as he pointed his finger accusingly at me that there were tattoos on his knuckles. *Why do I always get the nutters?*

'It's just a game . . .'

'You fucking wanker,' he yelled, spraying spittle in my face. 'I'll have you, yer ponce. Come on – outside.'

He kept ranting at me as I stared at him, wondering when he was going to punch or butt or kick. I could see the previous player looking at us from the bar. A Rolling Stones track was blaring out from the juke box. People standing round the snooker table were looking at us in that disinterested way people do when they see something exciting about to happen but don't want to get involved. I could feel myself reddening. It was embarrassing to have this idiot bawling at me in front of everyone. I stepped back again and felt the wall press against my back.

He was all pumped up now, believing his act, playing the part. I wondered why he hadn't hit me. I tried to think what I could do. Resort to Martial Arts? Adopt the stance of the alarmed butterfly and if he grabs me I can try the Aikido grip on his wrist and break his arm? I couldn't for the life of me remember how to do it. Do I use the left hand on the wrist and right on the elbow?

'Come on yer poof!' he yelled. 'You a fucking student, eh?' He added as if it were the ultimate insult.

'No, I'm not actually.' I kept my eyes fixed on his. 'Look, just forget it, okay? It's not worth fighting . . .'

'Come on, yer bastard poof – OUTSIDE!' he screamed again. He was becoming repetitive.

'Look, mate,' I said as firmly as possible, 'there's no way I'm stepping out there with you. I'm not daft. If you want to fight, then do it here, in front of everyone. Otherwise, just piss off, will you?' I said, alarmed at my own boldness.

The truth was I didn't have the first idea what to do. I wanted him either to shut up and go away or do something, hit me, anything, rather than just stand there yelling at me. I wiped his spittle from my face and felt myself shaking. My hand trembled and I wondered whether he could see it. He would think I was scared. I wasn't scared. He was intimidating right enough but there wasn't a great deal I could do about that. I felt resigned, in a weary sort of way, to the fact that I was about to have my head punched in. It never occurred to me that I might be able to punch his head in.

Oddly enough, I found it embarrassing. There were all these people watching us as if we were some strange sort of sideshow. It seemed so pointless and ignorant, and I worried that they might think I was as dumb as my opponent.

I stared back at him, holding his angry glare, and tried to look impassive. He didn't take any notice, which was strange. If I were threatening someone, and they remained calm and unflustered, I would begin to think I had bitten off more than I could chew. His level of verbal abuse just seemed to increase in volume and rage.

Perhaps he really was mad. Or maybe he was just one of those idiots who stomp people to death outside night-clubs or on football terraces with no idea what damage they might be doing, never stopping to think of the consequences, of how a mindless boot can rupture the spleen or haemorrhage the brain – the ones who stand dumbly in the courts in their Sunday best and say they never meant to kill him, your honour, and whose friends look on aghast when they are sentenced for murder and just can't understand the injustice of it all. I was briefly tempted to ask in as haughty a voice as possible whether he was irredeemably thick but decided against it.

More than anything I wished he would stop shouting in my face, and preening and posing and doing his he-man thing. I realised that I was shaking with anger. It was the adrenalin surging through me in anticipation of the violence and the pain that was coming, but I wasn't scared. It was the mindlessness of it all that was making me angry – that and the sense of helplessness. I wanted to hit him, to get him down on the ground and hurt him, make him cry like a child, but I knew I wouldn't.

I have always been useless at fighting. The few confrontations I'd had were scrappy confusing brawls from which I had failed to extricate myself. I don't think I have ever hit anyone first. Usually I have become embroiled to help a friend who is being attacked, or trying to calm things down. If my primary aim of running away has been thwarted, I just try to defend myself. The few times when I have attempted to hit an assailant the result has been fairly ineffectual. Either I miss completely or I hit the other man in the wrong place, and so make him hopping mad. I once tried to knee a man in the groin as hard as I could but only caught his inner thigh, and after that things got very bad. On another occasion a drunk head-butted me in a Sheffield night-club and then collapsed on the floor at my feet with tears streaming down his face. Being smaller than him had meant that he had simply smashed his nose into the top of my head. I watched in bemused surprise as the bouncers dragged him to the exit and, after some hefty blows of their own, hurled him out into the street. I never knew why he had decided to hit me in the first place. I had not set eyes on him before.

If I am with a group of friends and some gnarly drunk comes up spoiling for a fight, he'll pick on me every time. I'd lay good money on it, and then when it's all over everyone would come up to me and ask me what I'd done. I sometimes wonder what it is about me that makes these people so angry. Perhaps it's because I am small, an easy target. Maybe they don't like my appearance, the way I look, my hair, my accent, my body language, just the look in my eyes.

When I was a young teenager, I used to cold stare my reflection in the bathroom mirror. I practised having the meanest look in the world, slitting my eyes, clenching my jaws to make the muscles stand out, and snarling ferociously. Inevitably, after a while, a nervous tick would develop in my upper lip and it would start twitching. My cheeks and jaws would be wracked with painful cramps and I would go all dizzy and nauseous from trying to outstare the mirror. Sometimes I'd go downstairs and try out a few stares on my sister, Sarah, but most times she wouldn't even notice. Once she asked me if I was feeling poorly, and on another occasion, when I felt I had got the contemptuous sneer and the flint-eyed stare just about perfect, she came over and hit me with a book and told me to grow up, cheer up and get outside.

I abandoned the hard staring technique and instead took up swaggering in an impressive, buccaneering sort of way. For a while I had the rolling gait of some old sea-dog and the bow-legged stance of a man who had spent his entire life on a horse. It might have been effective had I been six feet tall and weighed seventeen stone. At five-feet-one and eight-and-aquarter stone, it looked pretty silly. Ironically, I managed to achieve a swagger of sorts years later after smashing my right knee while climbing in Peru and shortening my leg. When the weather was cold and damp, I limped as well, but it wasn't exactly the effect that I had had in mind. Seven years later I broke the other leg and shortened that one as well, so I lost the swagger and just occasionally limp now.

I spent a long time trying to raise one eyebrow, hoping to achieve what I thought was a refined sardonic demeanour. Even when holding one eyebrow down with my finger, or else using some elastoplast, the other brow remained resolutely at the same level. Then there was the agony of tearing the plaster off my eyebrow. I still occasionally try it, for old times' sake, when I'm shaving, and my face still creases up in some awful grimace and I drop my head to one side and get shaving foam all over my shoulder.

I did, however, perfect the sneering look-away. The idea was to close the eyes slowly, having looked contemptuously down at one's rival (which is awkward if you are short), and then to look away, turning the head up and to the side in a haughty, disdainful manner. It must have been pretty good because the one time I tried it in earnest in the midst of an angry quarrel, I was punched painfully on the side of the head.

These were desperate prepubescent attempts to be an adult, to behave like a rough and ready no-messing tough guy. I might have been better off if I had learned how to fight. When I started smoking at fifteen and was retching behind various bike-sheds, feeling distinctly unmanly, it struck me that it would look pretty neat if I could learn to roll a cigarette with one hand. It took me a year to master the technique. I persevered only because I had seen some cowboy do it while riding his horse on the High Chaparral and knew it could actually be done.

In the end I could roll them effortlessly, and did so with studied nonchalance whenever I thought a girl might be impressed and fall for my charms. They never took the slightest bit of notice and the ciggies were rolled so tightly that it made you go blue in the face trying to suck any smoke out of them.

Eventually I gave up and took up looking aloof and mysterious at parties, leaning with my back to a wall and feigning studied indifference. This wallflower method of manliness made me appear dull and boring, which I suppose I was, and as a result I always felt lonely at parties when no one talked to me. In the end I grew up and discovered I was an adult anyway.

I can't roll cigarettes with one hand any more, and I don't sneer as a rule, but apparently I do still stare quite well. I am totally unaware that I'm doing it. I had asked my friends why it was always me that the nutters picked on and several of them commented that I could look pretty nasty when I was staring at people. I was quite amazed to learn this about myself. As far as I could tell, it was just how I looked when I wasn't smiling, and I couldn't very well be expected to go around with a dumb grin on my face all day. So now I've learned that when I'm just sitting there, trying to work out some problem, feeling serious but nevertheless quite happy, I'm all the time giving out these terrible signals.

I still can't figure out whether it's just how I look or a throwback to a childish time when I used to make myself feel giddy staring at mirrors.

'I could have you any fucking day, yer poncey git.' The thug jabbed his finger at me and spattered me with spit. I cold stared him as hard as I could and felt my jaw muscles begin to twitch. He turned abruptly away and swept his arm across the pool table scattering the balls. The sound of Jagger singing seemed suddenly very loud now that someone wasn't screaming in my face.

The music rose to a crescendo of drums and bass. I looked around as the song faded. Everyone had gone back to their drinks and conversations as if nothing had happened. The phoney fight seemed to have gone on forever but I realised it had taken less time than the song.

I walked over to the snooker table and marked my name up on the board below the long list of people waiting to play. My ploy of coming to the pub early to get a game seemed to have backfired. I turned to watch the next game and saw the thug glaring at me from his position at the bar. I looked away, still shaking from the fury and the embarrassment.

I wondered how close we had come to fighting. I'm never very good at working out whether it is all bravado and boastful words or if it is for real. I naturally assume that anyone prepared to be that violent verbally is likely to back his words with actions. It seems a risky strategy not to do so.

Within half an hour the pub's clientele had trebled and the music had been cranked up to full volume. At least it helped to swamp the baleful glances I was receiving from the bar. I sat on a bar-stool watching the snooker and trying to calm down. I couldn't get the thought out of my head that from now on I was going to be confronted by a deranged skinhead every time I came into the Broadfield.

It was a depressing prospect. I went to the pub most nights – it was my one chance to escape from the house and relax over a game of snooker or pool. While I was writing, it was often the only time I got to meet and talk with other people during the entire day. I didn't want to be forced away to some other pub just because of a bullying idiot.

I was livid with myself. I felt that somehow I had failed. I had been weak, a coward even, for not standing up to him. It was altogether irrational, and I knew it, but that didn't help. I hadn't backed off and I hadn't resorted to violence. At least I had avoided sinking to his level, or more likely, the level of the floor to which violence would have soon reduced me.

For a while I wondered whether I could have taken him, whether I still could. I toyed with the idea of following him into the gents and battering him with a pool cue when he wasn't looking. Not exactly Queensberry Rules, but effective. I wondered whether the Aikido moves would have worked. The one I had in mind would have dislocated his shoulder, and broken his wrist, if not his elbow as well. Yet I knew I was incapable, unless absolutely desperate, of that sort of viciousness. I also guessed that I would probably have got the moves wrong and broken my own wrist and shoulder in the process.

It has always struck me that most people shy away from violent confrontations, partly out of fear, but mostly, I suspect, because it is outside of their experience and training. It doesn't seem to have a great deal to do with size, or strength, or confidence. I know several friends who are small and do not appear threatening in any way but who are quite ferocious fighters when they are forced into a corner. I have never been able to understand the mentality required for such violence. It is almost as if you must become a different person, switch suddenly into an utterly focused and cold state of mind, and launch the attack with absolute and ferocious commitment. There is no room for doubts, no time for questions about what you should or should not do, only your opponent and how you intend to beat him. I don't mean knock him back with a well-aimed punch, or restrain him in some arm lock until he calms down. I mean the sort of attack that stops him in his tracks, that incapacitates him before he has had the slightest chance of hitting you. Any weapon will do, a cue, a bottle, a boot or a fist – and once he's down, make him stay down.

Years ago, in a pub in Llanberis, a similar sort of thug had a go at me. Ostensibly it was another argument over a game of pool, but I could see immediately that this was simply an excuse. The man, a tall powerfully-built local labourer, liked to fight, and particularly liked attacking English climbers. At the time I had a Stevie Wonder hair-style with fifty tightly woven plaits adorned with multi-colour beads chinking around my shoulders. This was perfect ammunition for the bully, who naturally assumed it must mean that I was gay, and since I was also English and a climber, he felt morally obliged to batter my head in.

I managed to back out of the situation and make myself scarce, but I heard later that he had tried the same thing with a friend of mine the following week. My friend was half his size and presented an easy target. Unfortunately, if you live by the sword then you tend also to die by it. What the bully didn't know was that behind a mild-mannered exterior his victim was capable, when roused, of the most horrifying violence. The bully had his leg smashed in five places.

I can remember feeling elated that he had got his just desserts and at the same time disturbed by the uncompromising viciousness with which he had been dealt. On one level it made sense. There was no point playing at it; half measures could have had disastrous consequences. Yet I knew that, however angry, impotent and belittled the man might have made me, I simply could not have finished him off by stamping on his leg as it rested across a step. Secretly, however, I was pleased.

Running away, backing off, defusing the crisis with reasoned conversation, even bursting into tears or offering your opponent money, might well be the better way to deal with such situations, the most civilised and rational approach, but it doesn't do much to assuage the feelings of frustration and resentment, the sense of hurt pride and loss of face that comes with such a retreat. It is just as annoying to discover that, despite myself, I also harbour the same banal images of manhood and machismo; that however logical I am about it all I still feel as if I have wimped out, been the weakling once again.

It's strange how deeply it affects me. Superficially I think such notions are idiotic, but when pressed into a corner, I find myself mourning the fact that I couldn't behave like a proper man, fight the good fight, look tough in front of my friends, be the same sort of arsehole as my attacker. Perhaps it is in all of us, conditioned into us somewhere along the line, and however hard we try to deny it and behave in the correct, socially acceptable and civilised manner, the aggression is still there just beneath the surface.

We will always be savages at heart. We have an innate capacity for violence, a primeval inclination towards mindless brutality, however much we try to distance ourselves from this uncomfortable fact.

I sat brooding on the bar-stool, working myself into a rage about the thug's apparent victory. He'd made me feel stupid, and weak, and cowardly. I resented him for that. He had made me want to be savage, to smash him up and break his bones, and I hated him for that, for making me something I was not, something I never wanted to be. I stared furiously at the snooker table, unnerving the man addressing his shot.

'What's wrong with you then?' I turned to find Richard Haszko by my side.

'What?'

'You look like a bulldog chewing holly that the cat's just pissed on,' he said cheerfully. 'Who's bitten your bum then?'

'Oh, it's nothing,' I lied, and took a swig from my glass.

'Well, I wouldn't like to see you upset if that's the case.'

'Oh, some guy's just called me out,' I said morosely. 'That jerk over there in fact.' I scowled at the back of the thug's bald head.

'Charming,' Richard said, looking at him. 'You certainly know how to pick the easy ones, don't you? What did you do?'

'Nothing,' I shouted indignantly. 'That's exactly it. I didn't do anything.'

I told Richard what had happened and he nodded sympathetically, but I knew from the twinkle in his eye that he found it all highly amusing and didn't seem at all surprised that it had happened to me. This made me all the more incensed and I began venting my pent-up rage on him in a stream of frantic explanations. He grinned and offered to buy me a pint. As he approached the bar I noticed that he was careful to go to the opposite end from the thug.

'What's new then?' he asked as he returned and handed me the glass.

'Oh, not much,' I said. 'Mal's invited me to Cho Oyo, but I'm not sure I want to go.'

'Why not? Too expensive?'

'Well, yeah, it's a lot to pay for one hill. Especially with such a high chance of failing.'

'Why should you fail?' Richard asked. 'I thought it was supposed to be one of the easiest of the highest peaks?'

'Well, it is, along with Shishapangma, but it's still eight thousand metres, and I'm not sure that easy is the right adjective to describe any of them. I mean, I know it's technically easy. From a climbing point of view, it's more like hill walking than climbing, but at that altitude I don't reckon anything's easy.'

'No, you're probably right,' Richard conceded. 'But if your leg is strong enough, you should be all right.'

'Maybe,' I said dubiously. 'I've never been that high before. I have no idea what it would be like.'

'Painful, I should imagine.'

'And not very interesting,' I said. 'Not from a climbing point of view anyway.'

'Yes, it could be hell,' Richard agreed. 'All that load-carrying and trail-breaking. It was bad enough on Gangchempo.'

'None of us got up that either.'

'There's also the altitude,' he added. 'The chances of a pulmonary or a cerebral are pretty serious. Will it be without oxygen?'

'Of course. They all are now, except perhaps for Everest. Forget ethics, oxygen is just too damn expensive.'

'How high is it anyway?'

'Twenty-four thousand six hundred feet,' I said. 'It's the sixth highest, I think. Yeah, Makalu's the fifth, Cho Oyo's the sixth. Eight thousand two hundred and one metres. And the idea is to do it from Nepal.'

'I didn't know you could do that any more.'

'Apparently, you can. The German team that was caught crossing into Nepal by the Chinese last year and fined were done by an errant group of soldiers in the area.'

'But they paid a fine of thousands of dollars?'

'I know, but Mal says the Nepalese authorities have assured him it's okay. I think the route we're trying, the original Swiss route, lies on the actual border.'

'No, it's definitely in Tibet,' Richard said firmly.

'Higher up it is,' I agreed. 'We're going to make a base camp in Nepal and then cross the Nangpa La pass and join the route at Camp One. We sort of traverse up on to the route and then – okay, you're right – we're in Tibet.'

'It would be a lot of money to pay just to get arrested by the Chinese.'

'Tell me about it,' I said testily.

'And it is in Tibet, however you look at it,' Richard persisted. 'It's all a bit dodgy, don't you think?'

'How do you mean?' I asked in surprise.

'Well, you know, the Chinese occupation of Tibet, the human rights issue, all that stuff. Puts you in a bit of a moral dilemma, don't you think? You'll be seen to be supporting the repression, just by going there.'

'Yeah, I'd been worried about that. I was reading something the other day about whether you should stay away on principle or go just to bear witness to it. You know, to see what has happened and add your voice to the call for freedom in Tibet.'

'Sounds like a convenient little argument to me.'

'How do you make that out?'

'Well, for a start, what on earth are you going to see of Tibet halfway up Cho Oyo?'

'That's not the point,' I protested.

'That's exactly the point,' Richard said smugly. 'You won't see anything. You'll just go in, climb the hill or not as the case may be, and then bugger off again. You won't have borne witness to anything. Just had a good time at the Tibetans' expense.'

'No way,' I snapped. 'At least by going through Nepal we're not paying the Chinese for the peak permit, and all the costs of travel and visas and so on. If we did that by going through Tibet then we would be giving direct financial support to the regime. This way we pay the Nepalese instead.'

'Well, maybe so, but you're still not giving the Tibetans anything, are you? You're still going into their country, climbing their mountains, and then pushing off again. And however good it makes you feel, I don't think being moralistic about it all and bearing witness and all that stuff is going to help the Tibetans one bit.'

'It's not as simple as that.'

'Isn't it?' He gave me a searching look and then grinned mischievously.

'You're winding me up,' I said. 'You're just playing devil's advocate.'

'So, it's too expensive. The risks of high altitude are scaring the tits off you. You don't know whether you can climb an eight thousand metre mountain. The climbing's boring. You're not sure how strong your legs are and you're in a moral dilemma about Tibet. Right?'

'Well, yes, I suppose you could say that,' I replied uncomfortably.

'Are you going?'

'Yes,' I said without hesitation.

'I knew it,' Richard laughed gleefully. 'From the minute you mentioned Cho Oyo I knew you were going. Have you ever been capable of saying no?'

'Yes,' I said sharply.

'When?'

'Oh, I don't know.' I was looking round for a distraction. 'That Gangotri trip, for instance. Anyway it's rude to refuse things.'

'But you went on that trip, for God's sake!'

'Well, I know I did, but I did say I wouldn't go. I definitely said no.'

'Fat lot of good it did you then.'

The skinhead suddenly lurched into view and glared at us both. Richard started trying to shuffle round behind me. I shoved him away and gave the thug a stony-faced stare.

'Don't *do* that!' Richard hissed in my ear.

'Do what?'

'Stare at him like some homicidal maniac.'

'I just gave him a look . . .'

'Some look. You might as well have called his mother a prostitute and his father a child molester. He'll bloody kill us.'

'No,' I said quietly. 'Somehow I don't think he's as hard as he likes to look. He's all mouth and no trousers, that guy.' I gave him another quick stare and got the jutting chin and raised eyebrow look in return. He thrust his chest forward with his chin and did a few menacing shoulder rolls. I wondered whether he practised in the mirror.

'Look, just get away from me, will you? I don't want to be here when your little theory gets violently discredited, thanks all the same.' Richard moved away. 'Oh, and go to the bar. It's your round,' he said over his shoulder.

As the bell for last orders rang Pete Cranwell, the landlord of The Broadfield, came up to me and reminded me of the pint he had won from me at pool the previous night. He was a jovial, powerfully-built man who had been the driving force behind changing the pub into an increasingly popular venue. He had a strong Glaswegian accent that, on first hearing, I had barely been able to understand. Conversations with him above the roar of the juke box and the clamour of people enjoying themselves had been a matter of desperate guesswork, frantic mental translating and enthusiastic nodding, despite taking in only one word in five. I had managed to develop an ear for it over the years, which was rather like getting the hang of Urdu after years of prolonged exposure to Asian music during uncomfortable bus rides up the Karakoram Highway.

While we were away on the Gangchempo expedition, the pub had undergone a complete refurbishment and, more important, Pete had convinced the brewery to go along with his plans to serve many different brands of keg beer. At any one time there were ten different hand-pulled bitters on tap, all kept in excellent condition, so that deciding which one to have became a complicated task.

'Right, then. A pint of Heineken for Pete,' I said to the barman, 'a pint of Directors, and a pint of Butterknowles, thanks.' Out of the corner of my eye I spotted John Stevenson slip through the door.

'Get us a pint of Flowers, will you, Joe?' he shouted from the back of the scrum of people waiting at the bar.

'Oh, Rambo here is trying to start world war three,' Richard announced to John as I handed out the glasses. 'Is this Butterknowles? It looks a bit dark to me.'

'Eh, yes I think so,' I said. 'Here give us a taste.' I grabbed his beer and took a hefty draught. 'Well, it might be Flowers actually. Can I try yours, John?'

Having had a good drink of both I announced that I had no idea which was which but that I knew mine was Directors and no one needed to taste it. Richard scowled at me and held his pint protectively in both hands.

'What's this about world war three?' John asked, and I told him about the thug's behaviour. Pete looked suddenly grim at the prospect of trouble.

'Oh, him!' John said when I pointed out who it was.

'What? Do you know him then?' I asked.

'Well, sort of. He was pretty aggressive to Eileen the other night and tried to have a go at me.'

'I've never seen him in here before.'

'You have,' John said. 'You just don't recognise him. He had his head shaved in here for charity a few weeks ago, when you were away.'

'Well, I don't remember him,' I said dubiously examining his profile as he scattered the pool balls with customary violence, 'and I'm sure I wouldn't forget that in a hurry.'

'You would,' John said. 'He never used to look like that before he had his head shaved. Steve, the hairdresser, was telling me he's been doing it to everyone – all this mouthing off and asking people outside and the like.'

'Then I'm surprised he hasn't had his lights punched out by now.'

'I think it might happen if he's not careful,' Richard said grimly. Pete nodded in agreement. It wasn't something he liked to hear about in his pub.

'He used to wear suits and jackets and fairly straight gear before he started showing off his tattoos and muscles and pratting around,' John added.

'You're kidding?' I said incredulously, and stared at the shaved head as it straightened from the pool table.

'Yeah, it's weird, isn't it?' John agreed. 'Apparently he's all mouth, and if he tries it on, you should call his bluff. Threaten him back or agree to go outside and he'll just fold up. It's all a front.'

'Well, it looked a bloody effective front from where I was standing.'

'Joe Heally had a go at him the other day. He said he was terrified it wouldn't work, but he was so sick of being intimidated all the time that he decided to go up and call him out. Apparently the guy was all apologetic and back-tracking like mad. That's what you should have done.'

'Oh sure. It was the first thing that occurred to me when he started poking me in the chest,' I said. 'So I should've said, fine, let's do it. Just pop outside with him and demonstrate how well I bleed.'

'You could have groined him viciously on the knee,' Richard interrupted.

'Well, that's grand. Thanks for the advice,' I muttered.

As I walked back to my house, hunched up against a cold rain-laden wind, I saw the thug walking in the same direction on the other side of the road. *Oh God*, I thought, *he probably lives on the same street.* I turned my face away, momentarily alarmed that he might recognise me. In the pub, safe in the security of numbers, we had made no secret of the fact that we had been talking and laughing about him. Suddenly the idea of it being all bluff didn't seem so convincing any more.

I felt another surge of resentment and anger. It seemed the height of lunacy to change your behaviour simply because you've had your hair shaved. What on earth did he really think of himself? Did he ever think at all for that matter? Anyone dumb enough to believe in his own hair-style deserved everything that came to him. I had had any number of unusual hair-cuts - beaded dreadlocks, peroxide blond flat-tops, Belisha-beacon orange mops, even the shape of a mountain razored into the surface of a skinhead cut – and not once had I behaved at all differently. I had always been the same person inside despite what others may have thought of my appearance. The idea that someone can revert from being relatively mild and placid to a mindless bully seemed altogether illogical to me. I decided that the man must have always been that way. Inside he had always been full of rage. Maybe a chance encounter in a charity head-shaving had shown him his real self. Or he was looking for some image to hide behind.

In truth, I should have pitied him, seen his basic insecurity, his vulnerability protected by bragging and posturing, forgiven him his imbecility. However, I had been exposed to gratuitous violence in the past and had seen friends with fractured skulls and stab wounds as a consequence of other people's shortcomings. I have never had much sympathy for the idea of looking at the real causes of it all. It could well be due to poverty, or poor education, or a childhood exposed to parental violence and abuse. There are no doubt any number of explanations, but in reality, when violence is being forced on me, I choose to see it as mindless thuggery. Reasons and explanations are all very well but they are not excuses. They don't make it disappear. The violence was there to be despised in myself as much as in him. His actions had made me want to be violent. I hated him for making me realise that, despite my disdain of him, I also had the same potential for brute violence, and if I wasn't capable of meting it out I would be quite happy to watch someone else do it instead. The only difference between us was that I wasn't dumb enough to wear it like a hair-style.

He turned off to the right up a steeply curving hill. I watched him attack the incline with characteristic aggression. It was almost funny.

When I arrived home I looked at the black-and-white photograph of Everest on my kitchen wall and remembered my conversation with Richard about Tibet. He had touched a raw nerve when he talked about the guilt of going there, and the photograph made me realise how much I wanted to at least try to climb Cho Oyo. After all, the Chinese invasion of Tibet took place almost fifty years ago. There was nothing anyone could do about it now. Why decide not to go when everyone else will go anyway? And maybe there is some truth in saying that if you don't go you'll never really know? Hadn't the Dalai Lama himself encouraged people to go to Tibet for those very reasons?

I argued with myself all the way up the stairs, trying to assure myself that I was right. There was no harm in going; all that stuff was in the past. I dialled Mal's number and got his answering machine.

'Mal Duff here of Ascent Travel . . .' I waited for the tone and then left the message.

'Hi Mal. It's Joe. About Cho Oyo. Count me in. Give us a ring tomorrow. Bye.'

I replaced the receiver. There had never really been an argument. Ever since reading Heinrich Harrer's book, *The White Spider*, I knew that if the opportunity ever came to climb one of those high Himalayan mountains I would go. I would make any excuse in the world to do so. It was still a mysterious land of fabled mountains, a place of beauty and mythology and adventure.

I went to bed with the uneasy feeling that perhaps I too was choosing to believe in my own hair-style.

5

THE BURNING GHATS

The early morning mist drifted through the serried ranks of shrines hugging the ground. Wood smoke hung in the still air, clinging to the branches of high trees that formed a back-drop to the temple complex of Pashupatinath. It was eerily quiet after the bustle and clamour down by the burning ghats.

A man, hunched with age, carried a large bronze pot to the small doorway of one of the shrines and, squatting down, began to brush dust from the stone steps. I watched as he reached up and pulled open the iron grill of the door. He gave a few perfunctory sweeps with his small handbrush of bound twigs and a cloud of dust and ashes billowed from the dark interior. The feeble light from a small oil lamp flickered in the disturbed air inside the shrine. He set some offerings from his pot neatly in the dark recess, closed the grill, rose to his feet and moved slowly to the neighbouring shrine.

The shrill sound of a car horn echoed in the distance and the dull rumble of traffic noise had already begun to reverberate through the mist and wood smoke. The Hindu temple of Pashupatinath, situated to the east of Kathmandu on the road to Bodhnath, has a peculiarly hypnotic effect on me.

It is typical of the easy relationship between Buddhist and Hindu in Nepal that two such important religious centres, Bodhnath and Pashupatinath, should be so close to one another. Bodhnath is the site of a six-hundred-year-old Stupa, supposedly one of the largest in the world, under which the bones of Kashyapa Buddha, who preceded

Gautama Buddha, are believed to be buried. It is also the centre of Tibetan culture in Nepal, with a monastery, or Gompa, and a large population of Tibetan refugees.

Pashupatinath is probably the most famous temple in the country and has an enthralling, eerie ambience. There is an unworldly atmosphere to the place; a sense that spirits are at work, that quiet voices echo from the temples and shrines and whisper as you pass. Some people have likened it to Lourdes in France, as if they sense a power in the place, a chance that marvels could happen here; the feeling that unreal portents from an ancient time could abruptly change their lives. I always have a vague sense of foreboding when I visit this place, as if I am an intruder and there is a presence that knows it.

Whenever I have been in Kathmandu I have visited the temple, usually early in the morning when the light is soft and the funeral biers are being built on the ghats by the Bagmati river. Up high above the ghats, on a tree-ringed hill, the shrines and temples stand silent in the morning mists. Monkeys roam through the trees, occasionally scavenging from the offerings at the shrines.

They were not as numerous as those at Swayambhunath, the great Buddhist temple to the west of the city, where the monkeys seem to run amok around the huge central Stupa with its all-seeing eyes of Buddha and colourful prayer flags. They too scavenge for food, stealing the offerings of the devotees and sometimes terrorising the tourists. The steep steps climbing the hill to the Stupa and the pagoda-style temple are often swarming with monkeys, sliding down the handrails, chasing each other in mock battles with fierce bared teeth, and snatching bags and parcels from the unwary.

I dislike the animals, fearful of the diseases they might be carrying and well aware that they are capable of inflicting a vicious bite.

In many ways, Swayambhunath is the more striking temple, with its impressive Stupa, standing on top of a hill above the city. Where the Stupa rises from its great white dome-shaped base a forest of small white shrines cluster busily around it, like a sea of minarets. The eyes painted on the plinth of the Stupa have become the famous symbol of Nepal and are seen everywhere, embroidered on t-shirts, baseball hats, and jackets, staring from the covers of menus, advertising treks and river-rafting tours, even painted on the back of rickshaw shades. Prayer flags stream down in long lines from the gilded spire of the Stupa like Maypole ribbons. The panoramic view from it of the city and the valley is breathtaking on a clear evening with the sun setting behind the distant snowy mountains. Yet the temple seems to lack the eerie spiritual atmosphere of Pashupatinath. There is no sense of the frailty of life and the oppressive closeness of death that infuses everything at the burning ghats. There are also too many sightseers and tourists for my liking, which is hypocritical since that is exactly what I am.

On the hill in the quiet morning mist above the ghats there is an ageless tranquillity, a deceptive feeling of permanence. The visitors that I have met there seem subdued and contemplative. It has a timeless feel. The dull stone of the shrines, blackened by the smoke of countless offerings, and the vague shapes of monkeys moving in the shadows of the trees contrast strongly with the bright white and orange of the golden pagoda down by the river. There, in the bright sunlight, the flower-sellers jostle the crowds, hawkers sell offerings and incense, and stalls offer countless statues of the Hindu deities in wood or brass – Ganesh the elephant-headed son of Shiva and Parvati, Lakshmi, goddess of wealth, Durga the terrible form of Parvati; Kartikiya, Shiva's son, and the God of War, and Shiva in his various forms. Bhairav the frightful one, Nilakantha with his blue throat from swallowing the poison that would have destroyed the world, and Pashupati in his incarnation as Lord of the Animals.

It is best not to know what they were and to ask the vendor and listen in delighted confusion as he recounts how and why the images are so strange. It is a story-teller's delight.

The westerners who walk among the shadowy trees, admiring the shrines on the hill, seem relieved to have escaped the clamour and the urgent business of living that surrounds the temple and the ghats below. The sanctuary of the hilltop lends them the opportunity to reflect on what they have just seen. The spectacle of a body being cremated publicly has a sobering and mesmerising effect. It is perhaps not as disturbing as watching a traditional Tibetan air burial, in which the remains of the departed are ceremoniously cut up and fed to circling vultures, but nevertheless it is an arresting sight to the western sensibility. Every time that I have watched a cremation I feel trapped between conflicting emotions. There is a feeling of remorse that I should be such a morbid voyeur, intruding on people's lives, and a genuine sense of admiration and respect, as if I am privileged to be able to witness someone's ritual departure from this life.

Caught between a gruesome fascination and a realisation of my own vulnerability, I am always amazed at the way death is so casually accepted and open for public display in eastern countries. Far from being a grisly macabre scene, it is something that adds an immense sense of perspective to living.

When at last I walked slowly down the steps to the ghats I saw that the men attending to the building of the biers had brought a body down to the edge of the muddy grey river bank. They laid it carefully on the lowest step, with its feet touching the water. The corpse was wrapped in a white shroud which clung to the contours of the body. I could see from the shape that it was a woman. The men, wearing soot-stained dhotis, reached under the shroud and removed the clothing, careful not to reveal the body. They threw the clothes into the shallow water of the river, where they floated slowly downstream.

I watched a man wade across the river and retrieve the clothes. No one seemed to be offended.

When the body had been prepared it was lifted gently, a foot momentarily exposed as it rose from the water. The toenails were painted vermilion red. The attendants placed the shrouded body on top of the bier, reaching up with outstretched arms to secure it on the layers of faggots and stout split-wood logs. Despite their ragged dress and impoverished appearance, they managed to be both respectful and efficient at their grisly task. I knew that they were out-castes, known as chandal, and it seemed strange that, despite having such a lowly position in society, they were deemed fit to perform this last important ceremony for the people.

I sat on some steps leading down to the river and watched as the bier was lit on the opposite bank. The golden pagoda rose majestically in the background as the smoke began to seep from between the layers of the pyre. A small bridge arched across the river to my right. It was crowded with people, some stopping to watch the cremation, some tourists snapping away with their cameras, others looking bemused. A large white cow, dewlap swinging heavily, pushed its way through the crowd. An old woman squatted on her haunches in the mud at the foot of one of the bridge supports and vigorously pummelled her washing in the filthy water. A dog nosed around in the shallows for morsels. Further downstream a monkey fastidiously shook its wet paws as it too scavenged for food in the river. It ran away in a cringing crab-like scuttle as the man who was clutching the woman's wet clothes recrossed the water.

There were several biers prepared on either side of the now burning woman's pyre. Attendants carried armfuls of wood down to each one. Looking downriver, I could see where people, too poor to afford enough wood and the help of the chandal, had built their own biers on the mudbanks in the middle of the river. Pathetic mounds of ash and charred wood and what appeared to be bones that had escaped the flames lay on the mud waiting for the cleansing rush of monsoon flood waters to sweep them away. Another monkey approached one of these blackened barrows, and I realised with a sudden stab of revulsion what it was scavenging for.

Close to where I sat a group of some twenty young men were playing a boisterous game of cards. The players slapped down their cards with great force and elan, uttering loud shouts of triumph when they won. Coins and notes were scooped up and just as quickly thrown dramatically back into the pot as the next hand was dealt. They seemed unaware of the flames consuming the dead woman no more than thirty yards away across the river.

I felt oddly separated from my surroundings, as if I were observing the proceedings from some invisible point high above. Each event seemed to be quite independent of the others, almost as if they were not happening, and the participants hardly acknowledged the existence of other groups.

The old woman washing her clothes crouched in the shadow of the bridge. She seemed to be so absorbed in her work as to be completely divorced from the jostling crowds of devotees and tourists above her. Thirty feet away from her, smoke rose into a windless sky from the funeral pyre.

The corpse being consumed in flames and the out-castes concentrating on the cremation appeared frozen into their own separate world. No one stopped to look around, to see what was happening nearby, to acknowledge that there was anyone else in their world. It was so commonplace to them as to be unremarkable, yet for me it was extraordinary. I felt continually distracted, forced to look from one scene to another to confirm that they were still taking place.

Beside the unlit pyres two white-shrouded bodies lay ignored by the men busily stacking the firewood. The card players hollered and laughed and threw in their cards as if they were gambling in some smoky lodge. The monkeys and the dogs scavenged with such starved intensity that they seemed oblivious to all but what they were looking for. I sat in my own cocoon watching the progress of each spectacle, feeling as if I were invisible.

When the pyre began to collapse in upon itself, the attendants used poles to push the charred logs back into place. At one moment I saw to my horror a foot protruding from the end of the blackened glowing embers. It was quite untouched by the flames. I thought I could see the red varnish on the nails. It was attached to a black stick of charred bone. I watched one of the men try to flick it into the centre of the flames but it remained stubbornly attached to the stick of bone. He reversed the pole, and holding it at arm's length above him, he thrust it down hard into the pyre. The foot jerked upwards and remained pointing at the roof of the pagoda in the background, like some macabre sign post. When the man again flicked at the foot with his pole, it folded back neatly on itself and disappeared into the flames. Belatedly, I realised that the blow had broken the connection at the knee and enabled the leg to bend up and back upon itself. Feeling slightly nauseous, I rose to my feet, walked away from the card players and joined the crowds crossing the bridge.

As I stumbled into the dusty square outside the temple complex a young boy at the wheel of an auto-rickshaw waved enthusiastically for me to climb aboard. I hesitated for a moment before abandoning my plan to walk back towards the city and search for the man who lifted boulders with his penis. I had heard that he had been seen near the temple performing his act to crowds of appalled onlookers and wanted to get a photograph of him. I had been told by witnesses that the rock he lifted was of considerable size and weight and that as far as they could tell there was no subterfuge involved. I was curious to see how he did it and reckoned it would make an excellent picture for a slide show. It would also be a salutary lesson to watch and remember that, however hard I sometimes thought my profession was, there were other ways to make a living that I would definitely not take up. However I had seen no sign of him, and decided that he was probably having a rest day, sitting in a mountain stream somewhere and cooling the tool of his trade. I climbed into the back of the black and yellow auto-rickshaw.

'Ten rupees,' I shouted above the demented whine of the engine as the boy gunned the rickshaw around in a tight circle. He stopped and looked over his shoulder, giving me a dazzling white smile and a characteristic rolling nod of the head.

'Fifty rupees, if you please, sir.' He said it with a straight face.

'Fifty!' I cried with a derisive laugh. 'No,' I said as I started to dismount.

'Forty, sir.'

'Ten,' I said, stepping out of the small cab.

'Twenty.' He beamed. 'Twenty is best price.'

'Fifteen, best price.' I smiled at him and turned to walk away as he hesitated.

'Okay, sir, good price,' he cried as he revved the scooter to keep up with me.

'Durbar Square,' I yelled as I flew back into my seat and we accelerated in a cloud of dust down the rough road towards the city. It might have been healthier to walk, but it was a damn sight more exciting dicing with death in these little hornets of the road that are affectionately called *tuc-tucs*. Auto-rickshaw drivers universally seem to be convinced that their own particular vehicle is at least ten times more powerful and half the size it actually is. They have an assumption of immortality which is almost beyond belief, but they all tend to be the most skilful of drivers.

I once proposed to Mal Duff that one day we should buy a couple of tuc-tucs at the southernmost tip of India and drive them all the way to Kathmandu. We wondered whether we could get sponsored by the Indian company that manufactured them and, although it was mostly beer talk late at night, I still harbour fond hopes that I could yet find myself buzzing merrily across the plains of India, dodging elephants and jousting with sacred cows.

I was shaken from my reverie by a cacophony of deep horn blasts from a large bus that loomed over us as we hurtled into the first corner and the boy replied with the manic squeaking of his own horn. I lurched sideways, sure that the wall of brightly-coloured metal and glass would run us down and saw that he had deftly squeezed his tuc-tuc between a bus and an overtaking lorry. As we erupted from the crushing gap into their exhaust fumes we side-slipped a couple of tourists who were wobbling uncertainly on their hired bicycles. The boy turned to beam happily at me.

'Cigarette?' he asked, still looking over his shoulder.

'No,' I yelped. 'Look at the road, for God's sake!' I pointed to two large cows that were sitting in the middle of the road, chewing pieces of garbage. My driver sped confidently between them, pulling in his knee at the last moment to prevent catching it on a horn. I sat back and wished I hadn't given up smoking. It was nine months since I had agreed to go to Cho Oyo and had decided to quit the habit in a moment of mad enthusiasm.

I paid the boy twenty rupees when we reached Durbar Square, relieved to have got there in one piece. I had hoped to meet a man called Jesus for a game of chess but, despite a long search, I couldn't remember where his shop was situated. A year ago he had thrashed me at chess every day for a week. He sold me a beautiful Mandala, and traded in Tankas, the rectangular Tibetan paintings on cotton, as well as intricate astrological and geometric representations of the world and the heavens.

I wandered around the temples and statues in the hot sun, entranced by the mixture of styles and cultures, gazing admiringly at the pagoda style roofs and intricate erotic carvings on the wooden roof beams. Pigeons in large numbers sat on the clay tiles of the three-tiered roof of the Taleju Temple. The high steps and brick walls were painted brightly in a wash of crimson, and the sun reflected starkly off the light stone-slabbed courtyards and streets, casting dark shadows inside the temples and shrines. I walked towards Freak Street past a statue of Kal Bhairav, a huge stone image of this fearsome-looking creature. A couple were busy taking photographs.

'It's a lie detector,' I overheard the man say and moved closer to look over his shoulder.

'If you touch its feet and swear not to have committed a crime when in fact you have, you will immediately be struck dead,' he read from a travel guide.

When they had moved on to document and record some other innocent artefact I went up to the image and placed my hands on its feet. I thought I'd quietly tell a lie, but for some reason I decided against it. I felt a chill of superstition run through me as I hurried away. Being in the old part of the city is like being transported back to medieval times; but for the honking of horns and the clatter of bicycles I suspect that little has changed here for centuries. I preferred to stroll purposelessly through the maze of narrow streets, delighting in the unexpected rather than take a book and make a disciplined search for every listed site.

Until I had overheard the couple at the statue the only thing I had recognised was a frightening wooden statue of what appeared to be a face riddled with nails. Apparently, if you have a toothache and you simply walk up and hammer a nail into the statue, the pain will go away. I was never convinced of the efficacy of this cure, but I supposed the distraction of battering your anguish away with a hammer might help just a little bit. I was sure it was preferable to visiting a street dentist any day. Then again, thinking of the bicycle-driven drills, the lack of hygiene and painkillers, it might have been a better idea to hammer the nail into the dentist instead and tell him it's in lieu of payment.

I saw two saddhus approach another saddhu who was resting on the steps of a temple. One man, tall and rangy, was wrapped in a dusty brown blanket. A small monkey perched on his shoulder with a paw gripping the saddhu's tangled dreadlocks. His companion was dressed in long black robes with a red blanket worn like a sash across his chest. He carried a small metal bowl on a chain. The third man was an extraordinary sight. He wore a long-sleeve shirt, covered by a jacket that trailed below his knees, partly obscuring his trousers. His turban was tightly woven around his head. Everything was of the brightest reds and scarlets you could imagine. Three white rice paste stripes ran across his brow and he wore garlands of bright orange flowers around his neck. Behind him, leaning up against the carved crimson-painted wooden door of the temple, was a staff draped in red scarves and more garlands, all topped with a pair of white horns. He looked for all the world as if he were the guardian of the temple.

None of the three was looking at me when I raised my

camera to take a discreet shot but as the shutter clicked they all turned abruptly and stared at me, as if they had heard it above the clamour of the square. It was uncanny. The scruffy pair took a step towards me and shouted something. One held his hand out as if asking for money. I wasn't sure what to do, so I turned away with a friendly smile. Suddenly I heard a shout and, glancing back, saw the one with the monkey rush towards me. The monkey leapt from his shoulder and scampered towards me, screeching in a high-pitched alarming manner and barring its teeth in a vicious snarl. Luckily it was tied to the saddhu by a long cord which jerked it back by the neck and into the air, distracting its owner long enough to allow me to melt into the crowds of a nearby street.

I decided I'd seen enough for one day and headed towards the Thamel area of Kathmandu where the expedition was staying. We were due to fly to Lukla early the next morning to start the walk-in via Namche Bazar and the Thami valley to Cho Oyo base camp. A ferocious savaging by an irate monkey was the last thing I wanted. What I needed was a few cold San Miguel beers and a relaxing afternoon on the roof-top terrace of the Blue Note, my favourite bar in Kathmandu, which served popcorn free with the beer and played superb Blues songs at maximum volume.

As evening gathered over the city I sat playing chess with a small computer on the terrace of the Blue Note. The first notes of 'I'd rather go blind' made me look up in pleased recognition. It was one of my favourite tracks, especially when sung by Etta James, and I sat back, hoping it was her. As her voice pierced the hubbub of voices and the street sounds below I relaxed and looked at the sun sinking below the surrounding hills.

The music triggered a wave of confused emotions. I knew that I was in the process of losing something. I was letting it happen. Once again a relationship was disintegrating and once again I was running away. I wondered whether it was still possible to save it, and then I dismissed the idea. I had been selfish and disloyal and no amount of patching together would ever mend the rift. Well, it wasn't as simple as that, but there was some truth in the thought.

I wasn't at all sure that I wanted to be there. The climbing was technically unexciting but nevertheless dangerous. The mountain was too big, and too expensive. It was also in Tibet. There were other reasons for not being here. Perhaps I had come only as a convenient way of escaping an impossible situation, a way of avoiding betrayal. I loved the adventure of it all, the setting off to unknown futures, the excitement of being in this wonderful land, of stepping out of mundane home life for a while. Yet at the same time there was a nagging sense that something was wrong. Perhaps Richard had been right to laugh at my inability to say no.

I would accept all offers of trips simply because I was scared that some day in the future the damage inflicted on my legs would force me to stop going to the great mountains, possibly to give up climbing altogether. It was almost ten years since the doctors had said I would never climb again, never walk without a limp, and that I would have to be content to lead a sedentary life. I had believed them. Yet this was the tenth expedition I had been on since then. Given that three of those years had been occupied with recovering from injuries, I couldn't help but smile at how wrong the doctors had been.

Yet deep down I knew that there was truth in what they had said. Every winter's morning I could feel the threat of their words and it haunted me. I had tried to face the possibility of giving up climbing without much success. To be forced to abandon the high peaks would be like bereavement. I couldn't imagine being unable to go back to them. I had accepted that I would never climb with the same degree of commitment again, never achieve my more outrageous ambitions. It had forced me to be honest with myself and admit that I had not been as good as I had wanted to be and probably could never have achieved those aims.

It was a hard thing to admit – shaming in a way – that I had been so conceited, but it had been a turning point and had opened a different door for me. There was so much more to life than climbing. And now, without the acid burn of youthful egotistic ambition, I was still as much in love with being here, being part of it all, as I had ever been.

I also knew that with no mountains I would be lost, quite utterly lost. *What on earth would I do? What could replace them? Nothing.* I listened to Etta James singing 'Baby, baby, baby . . . I'd rather go blind boy, than see you walk away from me' and it made my heart turn over.

I have never forgotten the vow I made to myself as a teenager that I would never look back and regret. There would be no room for concession. If I wanted to do something I would do it totally, not just when circumstances allowed, when my job or my family permitted, but completely and without compromise. I felt that I had embarked upon a mission, that I was driven on by some other force. If it required a narrow-minded and selfish course, then so be it; it was for the greater good. I hadn't fully realised then that the vow had only been for the greater good of me.

Whatever span of life I might be allotted, thirty-five years or one hundred, it seemed imperative to do everything now, when I still could, physically and mentally. I may yet discover that I made the wrong decisions, that there were so many other things, better things, I could have done with my life, that I can only look back and regret.

I am afraid of the passing years betraying all that I once was and did. Time is cruel like that. I once heard a famous novelist talking about time and age and the passing of life. He described growing old as an arc of disappointment, of falling short, like an arrow that has ended its upward flight and now dips inexorably back down towards the earth. He talked of how it was the ultimate sadness, a realisation of loss and of failure; a wish to have had so much more. He was looking back, regretting, observing what could have been, seeing those chances missed. Perhaps it was an impossible vow that I had made.

'Who's winning?'

A voice shook me from my reverie. I looked up to see Mal standing at my shoulder.

'What? Oh, it is,' I said, peering hopefully at the flashing lights of the chess board. 'I tried the Nimzo Indian defence but it seems to like it.'

'What's the Nimzo Indian?'

'Ah, well, that's the problem really,' I said sheepishly. 'I only know the first seven moves and it seems to know the rest.'

'Best not to do any of the openings and then it hasn't a clue what you are up to,' Mal said. He turned and ordered two beers before sitting down and examining the chess board.

'What are those flashing red lights?' he asked, pointing to the left side of the board.

'Oh, it means it's my go.' I moved a piece and pressed its peg down into the board. There was an electronic beep and two lights flashed, indicating the new position.

'Why is that one flashing?'

'It's thinking,' I said. 'Depending on what level you're playing, it has a certain length of time to analyse which would be the best move. I can override it and this forces it immediately to make the best move it has so far come up with. But that's cheating really, and it doesn't stand a chance if I do it. Here, I'll show you.'

I pressed the button marked play. The light stopped flashing and two more indicated its required move. I lifted the black queen to its new position and pressed it into the board. There was a double beep and lights flashed everywhere.

'What does that mean?' Mal asked as he handed me a bottle of San Miguel.

'I think it means it's won,' I said dubiously, scrutinising the position. 'It seems to have check-mated me.'

'So much for cheating,' Mal said, laughing as I turned the machine off and closed the lid.

'So, are we all set for tomorrow then?' I said as I poured the beer.

'Yeah. We're all sorted. We fly to Lukla in the morning, which should get us to Namche for the Saturday market. We'll spend Sunday there as well, just to acclimatise, and then set off for Thami on Monday.'

'Great. How long is the walk-in to base camp?'

'Oh, about five days, I think,' Mal replied. 'It's a short day to Thami, about four hours last time, wasn't it?'

'Yeah, or less even.'

'Right. Then it's another day to Ari, a day to another place, can't remember its name. Actually, I don't think it has a name. Then a longish day to base camp.'

'That's four days,' I said.

'Yes, but we'll probably have a day at Ari acclimatising. The base camp's pretty high, over five thousand metres.'

'So is the mountain. I wonder whether I can go that high?'

'Of course you will,' Mal said airily. 'It'll be a doddle.'

'I doubt it somehow. Anyway how is the team shaping up?'

Mal gave me a break-down of the other eight members of the expedition. It was an international mix: two Americans, a New Zealander, a Venezuelan, five Englishmen and a Scot.

Clive Jones, the Kiwi, and Delgado José Antonio both looked impressively fit. Clive was a tall rangy man who was obviously very serious about training and personal fitness. He had dazzled me with a list of pulse rates, recovery times, and what he could do on a mountain bike. He'd also announced that he had given up beer, much to Mal's and my horror. José had climbed Ama Dablam the previous autumn and had been travelling around India and Nepal for the last five months, trekking and staying fit.

R.J. Secor and Rick Novak both came from California. Rick was a big man with a ready smile and an open friendly attitude. He had been working as a dish-washer in California to save money for the expedition which seemed to me to be a fearsome feat given how expensive the trip was and my memories of slaving for a pittance as a *plongeur* in Chamonix years before. He had climbed with Mal many times before, especially in Scotland where Mal ran guided ice-climbing courses. I'd seen a photo of Rick climbing the vertical icicle of Elliott's Downfall in Glencoe, stark naked but for his boots, harness and mitts.

R.J., as he likes to be known, was seriously Californian.

He was a personable type but I wondered whether some of his mannerisms might cause friction, particularly with the British climbers. However well meaning he appeared to be, I suspected that some of the more 'right-on', politically correct aspects of his character might come in for some cruel satire. The culture of British climbing is about as far apart from California as one could possibly imagine.

David Horrox had worked as a guide on previous trips to Nepal with Mal and was a quietly determined man. On first meeting he didn't strike you as the hardened mountaineering type but he proved to be one of the strongest members of the team, calmly forging ahead on the mountain, carrying big loads without complaint, and in a typically British understated and calm manner arriving on the summit without fuss or difficulty.

Dave Hall and Geoff Pierce quickly teamed up together. Geoff had hardly any climbing experience and the mountain was to prove to be too big and psychologically overwhelming for his first attempt in the Himalayas. Dave was to suffer dreadfully from the altitude and would have to abandon the expedition with Geoff shortly after reaching base camp.

The last member, Neil Lyndsey, was also the oldest on the team but he was strong on the mountain and had plenty of experience in the Himalayas.

'Have we got an early flight then?' I asked Mal as another couple of beers arrived at the table.

'Yup, it leaves at nine, weather permitting, and some of our gear is coming up in the second plane.'

'Good. Well that should be fun,' I muttered. 'Nothing like an hour of terror to get you going in the morning.'

6

FEAR OF FLYING

To put it mildly, I dislike flying. Since I spend a lot of time travelling around the world, this is rather inconvenient. Once, when flying from Islamabad to London, I was so overcome with anxiety that shortly after take-off I found myself locked in the lavatory, braced across the seat with my legs jammed against the sink unit, in a state close to hysteria. I believe this irrational fear stemmed from a terrifying landing in Germany on a rainswept windy night in 1974. I was fourteen, and sitting by the window with my eldest brother, David, beside me as we approached the runway. I watched the wing dipping and yawing alarmingly as we flew through gusts of crosswind. David seemed quite unperturbed by the conditions and calmly read his book. Up to then I had happily accepted that flying was the safest way to travel and that the probability of ever knowing someone who had been involved in an air crash, let alone experiencing it myself, was so small as to be not worth worrying about.

I watched the runway lights appear out of the gloomy darkness. They were fixed to box-shaped metal poles at intervals along the edge of the tarmac. As the ground rushed up towards us I sat back and waited for the smooth rumble as the undercarriage met the concrete. Suddenly we dropped with a stomach-emptying swoop and hit the runway with shocking force. I felt the impact of it thudding up through my seat. There was a loud bang and the aircraft bounced back into the air before lurching drunkenly down again on to the tarmac. After we struck the second time we seemed to be tearing along on two wheels, canted steeply over on my side. The overhead lockers flew open, the lights went out, and many of the passengers started screaming and shouting. Flight bags, coats and bottles of duty free gin and whisky cascaded down from the lockers.

I remember staring fixedly out of the window, watching the wing tip dipping towards the runway lights that were flashing past with frightening speed. I was convinced they were going to hit the wing, and I knew enough about wings full of fuel and high velocity impacts to guess what would happen if they did.

I didn't scream, and nor did David, but in the brief moments of darkness I clearly heard adult males yelling in panic. Frightened as I was, I remember thinking that men were not supposed to scream; at least, they never did so in films. It was unnerving to hear. Suddenly the plane righted itself, the reverse thrust of the engines began to brake our hurtling charge, and the lights came back on. Within seconds we were taxiing down the runway at walking speed.

As the lights came on a scene of chaos was revealed. All the lockers on one side gaped open and passengers struggled to get bags and coats off their heads and shoulders. Some were still frozen in silent terrified screams. As the roar of the engines diminished the cabin filled with the sound of taped music; that bland tinned Musak that is played everywhere now that some research has revealed how calming it is, despite the fact that it clearly seems to do nothing but irritate most people. Then came the wonderfully unflappable and beautifully modulated voice of the stewardess.

'Good evening ladies and gentlemen. I hope you have enjoyed flying with us . . . please remain seated with seatbelt fastened until the aircraft is at a standstill and the engines are switched off . . .'

There was not the slightest acknowledgement that anything unusual had happened. It made me feel as if I had imagined the screams in the darkness. But for those screams, I might have been able to dismiss the whole thing from my mind. David was pale and wide-eyed.

'What happened?' I asked.

'I think we got caught in some wind shear as we came in,' he said hesitantly. 'Thank God we were so low at the time.'

'Why were they all screaming? You weren't screaming.'

'I was too bloody scared to scream.'

It was strange to see how well behaved everyone was after the lights came back on. It was almost as if they were all frightfully embarrassed by their loss of self-control, and now that the music was on, and the lights nice and bright, they thought it best to behave as if nothing at all had happened. People politely returned bags and coats to each other, and laughed nervously as they handed back bottles that only minutes before had come crashing on to their heads, and generally gave a fine display of stiff-upper-lip British reserve. I remember Ma saying as she watched us streaming into the arrivals lounge that she had never seen so many people who all looked as if they had just seen a ghost.

I reckon that was the start of it all. Nagging questions began to creep into my mind with each successive flight. *How does this thing work? Could I get out of here if something went wrong? What if an engine falls off? How do they get three hundred tons of metal to leave the ground?*

It was take-offs and landings that I couldn't cope with. I was so totally aware that I was in a vast tooth-paste tube full of aviation fuel, belting along at hundreds of miles an hour, that all I could do was to grip the hand rests with manic intensity and stare fixedly out of the windows, trying to will the thing to stay in one piece.

Once, as we soared into the sky above Edinburgh, I was distracted by the urgent prodding of the passenger next to me. I was surprised to see an old lady desperately trying to get me to release the vice-like grip I had applied to her painfully swollen arthritic knuckles as we launched off down the runway. Oddly enough, my fear seemed to be worse on the big jets. I've flown in small light aircraft, been buzzed around Alpine and Himalayan mountains in helicopters, and even took up propeller-powered paragliding for a while. None of these induced in me the sort of blue funk that the jets did.

Helicopters are by far the most dangerous flying machines. The maintenance on them has to be scrupulous. If any one moving part breaks then the whole Heath Robinson whirlygig immediately goes crashing to earth. There's only one engine and no hope of gliding. Auto-gyration landings are pretty dodgy in the mountains. Yet, in a perverse sort of way, I quite like flying in them. It's almost as if the notion that they can actually get into the air in the manner in which they do is so outrageous that passengers simply suspend their belief and decide that it must be safe. The fact that they have also plucked me from some pretty terrifying climbing situations probably also accounts for my irrational fondness for helicopters.

No matter how many safety statistics are thrust my way, I can't get it out of my head that, if anything is to go wrong in a big jet, it will be the one I am on board. I don't care if there are only one point two passengers per million flown that get killed; I'm convinced I will be in that statistic. When a Pakistan Airlines airbus crashed into the hills on its final approach to Kathmandu in 1992, killing everyone on board, it simply confirmed my worse fears. These things do happen. The fact that some of my friends were on board that fateful flight belied the comfort of statistics. Perhaps I should have thought that, since my friends had been killed in such an air crash, then the probability of it happening to me must be even more unlikely; lightning doesn't strike twice, as the saying goes. Unfortunately I'm well aware that it quite certainly does strike twice, and the reality of that disaster has only increased my nervousness.

Approaching Kathmandu airport, particularly in bad weather, or when there is a build-up of cumulus, has always been a nightmare for me as I stare out at the close terraced red-earth hillsides and the huge white mountain walls on the horizon. When thermal up-draughts cause the plane to dip and yaw suddenly I feel my body tense into a tight compact quivering mass. So it was with mixed feelings that I boarded the Twin Otter, a small twin-engined STOL (short take-off and landing) aircraft, capable of carrying about fifteen passengers, for the flight from Kathmandu to Lukla. The team was in boisterous mood. Only a few of us had made the flight before and the others were keenly anticipating views of the Himalayas. I was gloomily contemplating the far more dramatic mountain landing at the other end, for I knew Lukla to be one of the most terrifying places to put down that could possibly be imagined.

I sat at the back next to the door. The stewardess pulled up the steps and closed the door as the propellers roared into life. I couldn't understand why a stewardess was needed. All she did was to get on, give everyone a boiled sweet, and get off at the other end. It wasn't boiled sweets I needed; two or three valiums might have been more to the point.

The flight to Lukla is probably one of the most spectacular air journeys in the world and not only because of the stupendous views. The smallness of the plane with its racing propellers, the crude unpressurised cabin with the open view of the cockpit and the pilots juggling with the controls, and the mountains rearing up on all sides increase the sense of vulnerability as the plane scrapes over high passes and its tiny shadow flits across the steep forested hillsides that loom high into the cold morning air.

Once it has gained sufficient height, circling above the Kathmandu valley, the plane turns and sweeps north-east towards the great mountains of the Khumbu. As the foothills of the Himalayas begin to rise in height the plane seems to edge closer to the earth. Soon the red terraced fields and the meandering footpaths along the crests of rocky ridges disappear beneath a canopy of birch, oak and blue pine forests.

Flying across the grain of the land the view down varies between the summit ridges of steep wooded hills and the yawning dark drops into deeply cut valleys which the early morning sun has not yet reached. The fish-tailed summit of Gaurisankar and its formidable icy ramparts slide past the port windows. Passengers strain to peer out, cameras clicking and fingers pointing. Far below, slivers of white mark the roaring progress of powerful rivers cutting deeply through mountain gorges.

At times the aircraft crossed familiar stretches of the trek into the Khumbu region from the village of Jiri which I had walked four years earlier. I caught glimpses of the trail weaving in zig-zags up to high ridges, some adorned with prayer flags. The highest point of this ten-day trek is the Lamjura pass (11,580 feet, or 3,530 metres). I remembered hearing the distant drone of planes struggling to gain height as I had trudged up the long oak-forested ridge above Sete towards the pass. At the time I had wished I was up there flying comfortably into Lukla in forty-five minutes instead of wretchedly staggering up and down tens of thousands of feet of deep-cut valleys. By the time you reach Everest base camp by this route from Jiri you will have climbed and descended something approaching twice the height of Mt. Everest.

Once you reach the Lamjura pass and descend into the valley of the Dudh Kosi river it is a long steady climb up to Namche Bazar, the Sherpa capital (11,300 feet, 3,446 metres). Despite weary legs and a desire for flat paths and no more knee-hammering descents, it is a superb way of gradually acclimatising and slowly absorbing the ambience of the mountainous country. The trail is well travelled by porters, villagers and trekkers alike and along the way hospitable lodges sell tea, or jugs of the traditional Tibetan rice beer *chang* with apple pie, spicy omelettes and cinnamon rolls.

It is especially beautiful in springtime when the rhododendron forests are ablaze with red blossom and creamy magnolias garland the hillsides. The intense heat of the sun at such altitude seems to release all manner of aromas as the forests heat up and the moist dark soil exudes steamy mists which cling to the wooded ridges.

I have been into the Khumbu four times since trekking in from Jiri and have flown in on every occasion. Saving ten days walking allows more time on the mountains, and in any case I cannot afford to put my legs through so many hard battering descents any more.

As we crossed the Lamjura I looked out of the window and saw a group of trekkers making their way out of the rhododendron grove and up on to the rocky open ground of the pass itself. Ahead of them lay the long descent through damp lichen-draped fir and rhododendron forests to the town of Junbesi. I saw a woman look up and wave at us as we skimmed over their heads. I could clearly see her beaming smile and hoped she was enjoying her adventure as much as I had done.

The plane banked to the left and then straightened quickly, crossing Junbesi as it headed for the Dudh Kosi. I tried to spot the monastery above the town. It was a vibrant community of more than one hundred monks, and its abbot, Tulshig Rimpoche, was formerly at the Rongbuk Monastery in Tibet on the north side of Everest from where all the pre-war attempts on the mountain had started. (The title *Rimpoche* means 'Precious One' and indicates that the abbot is believed to be a reincarnation of a previous lama.) I wondered if he had been there when the Chinese army invaded Tibet, or whether he had fled when it was reduced to rubble. I imagined he must have been a young novice then and perhaps this allowed him to escape the worst excesses of the tortures perpetrated on the older venerated lamas. I wished I had known about him when I had stayed in Junbesi four years before. I would like to have talked to him.

While we were approaching the deep-cut valley of the Dudh Kosi – literally, the milk river – I peered anxiously at the clouds massing above the hillsides. There were only a few isolated small clusters of cumulus above and visibility was excellent. Looking down the aisle, I could see the pilot and co-pilot adjusting the throttles and correcting the trim as we flew through pockets of turbulence. The engine note changed as the nose began to tip forward into a steep dive and the hillside above Lukla suddenly filled the windows of the cockpit. The thin white line of the airstrip came into view, perched three thousand feet above the river on a shelf jutting from the face of the looming hillside.

I knew it was the steep incline that helped to slow the plane after landing, but it was also frighteningly short. Once again I fought the surge of fear that rushed through me and tried to convince myself that everything was fine and we would land safely.

I saw a couple of the lads mutter curses of alarm and glance around with questioning looks. I tried to grin cheerfully, hoping to hide the tension building up inside me. I glanced at the air strip growing bigger in the window and then quickly looked away. To all intents and purposes, it looked as if we were flying straight into the centre of a huge steep hill. It didn't feel right somehow.

Two years earlier I'd flown in with Mal on the way to climb Lobuche and Pachermo's unclimbed east face. There had been the usual delays before take-off while weather conditions in the mountains were reassessed. Then, as we approached the mountains, the cloud cover had increased until we were making detours around the larger towers of cumulus. These massive anvil-shaped thunderheads are lethal flight dangers. Inside their boiling fluffy cotton wool columns huge forces are at work with immense wind shear creating tremendous turbulence. Winds of over a hundred miles an hour could be blasting upwards and a few feet to one side the same speed of wind would be slamming down towards the earth. Such forces could destroy an aircraft, even a big jet, as if it were a balsa wood toy.

In the time I had learned to fly paragliders and qualified as a pilot I had learned a good deal about the weather and flying conditions. The air was a fickle thing, a slippery inconstant fluid possessed of immense power. There seemed to be countless names for all the different perils of flying; wind shear, wind gradients, washboard air, wake turbulence, and rotor.

Worst of all were the thunderstorms, the aerial monsters. These towering black-headed cumulonimbus, dark tumbling storm clouds, could suck you up to fifty thousand feet in hundred mile an hour winds inducing vertigo and loss of consciousness, taking you to such heights you die due to lack of oxygen. They could freeze you to death, batter you with huge hailstones, kill you with lightning strikes and slam you into the ground with horrendous unstoppable force, or simply shred your pathetic craft as if it were rice paper. I never forget the lessons learnt about the vagaries of flight and the knowledge simply increased my fear of flying.

Now, as the plane began to nose into bigger and bigger banks of cloud and it lurched from side to side, wing tips pitching violently, I felt my hands go clammy. I saw the co-pilot casually reading *The Rising Nepal* newspaper. He didn't appear to be alarmed.

'It's looking pretty bad,' I said to Mal who was peering out of the side window.

'Yeah, it's socked in all right,' he said. The plane lurched drunkenly to one side and I bit back a yelp of alarm. 'I reckon he'll turn back.'

'Thought as much myself,' I said, half-relieved at the prospect of safety and half-depressed at the thought of waiting another twenty-four hours for a flight.

'Those guys look pretty worried.' Mal pointed to a young German couple near the front, clutching their ski-sticks and glancing nervously from the side windows to the view through the cockpit windows.

'Doesn't look as if they have made this flight before,' I said with a nervous laugh. 'Good thing too. Guess what state they would be in if they had seen the landing strip?'

'No chance today,' Mal said confidently. 'I've never seen them get this far in such cloud cover before.'

'Well, I wish they'd hurry up and make their minds up. And I wish that pilot would stop reading his bloody paper.'

'Don't worry,' Mal shouted above the din, 'they've probably already confirmed it with the control tower at Kathmandu. No way are we going down in this.'

Almost as he spoke the words the plane nosed forward in a steep dive. A small circle appeared in the white cloud layer blanketing the cockpit window. There was a glimpse of a distant pencil-thin white river, a huge wall of rock and the green shade of forests far below.

'Christ almighty!' I yelped. 'What is he doing?'

'Going for it I think,' Mal said with a grin. 'At least he's stopped reading the newspaper.'

I grabbed the back of the seat in front of me and stared at the small gap in the cloud into which we were diving. It seemed to be closing up as we got nearer.

The German couple had become even more agitated. The man looked back down the plane with wide eyes as if trying to confirm to himself that we really were in a Stuka-style dive. I had to brace my knees against the frame of the seat in front of me, so steep was our angle of attack.

The woman let go of her sticks and uttered a panic-stricken scream. The man tried to calm her and then, catching sight of the view ahead, joined in the screaming. It sounded thin and reedy above the din of the engines. Wind buffeted us to one side and for a moment the hole in the cloud was replaced by impenetrable whiteness. *Oh God, I hope there's something down there,* I muttered to myself, which was pretty dumb since I knew exactly what was down there; mountains, forests, cliff faces, and extremely hard unfriendly terrain.

The hole suddenly reappeared and we seemed to dart down into it. For a few seconds we arrowed through a tube in the clouds with fluffy tumbled walls looking strong enough to stand on, and then with shocking abruptness we erupted into clear air beneath a lowering ceiling of dense cloud. The Lukla airstrip sprang into view, filling the cockpit window.

The couple who had calmed as we had threaded the eye in the cloud began screaming again. They probably didn't recognise the white strip on a seemingly vertical hillside for what it was. For a moment I thought the man was going to grab the controls but I quickly realised that he was too mesmerised by the view to do anything. I laughed happily. My fear had been dissipated by the sheer terror of the German couple.

Just as it seemed we would plunge into the hillside the pilot smoothly pulled the plane's nose up into a sharp stall as we bounced down hard on to the runway. There was a loud roar as the wheels pounded over rocks the size of tennis balls and the plane rushed up the angled slope. There was a squeak of alarm from the German couple as the sight of a wrecked plane on its roof flashed past and the rock wall at the end of the strip filled the window. Then with a last roar from the engines we slowed to a halt. The couple slumped exhausted in their seats. It was probably the best value for money theme park roller-coaster ride they would ever experience.

The crashed plane had apparently tipped over when landing in crosswinds a couple of weeks earlier. Of the sixteen passengers one woman broke her forearm. The aircraft land here at such slow speed and brake so quickly that fatalities were reported to be rare.

This time the weather was clear and relatively cloud free and the landing was smooth and uneventful. We quickly disembarked and helped unload our rucksacks from the belly of the plane. In the distance we could hear the droning of a second plane as it approached Lukla. Within an hour we had gathered all the barrels, rucksacks, boxes of food, stoves and hardware and portered them to a lodge nearby. We ordered drinks and sat in the shade trying to recover from the breathless effort of load carrying at nearly ten thousand feet.

The ugliness of the village of Lukla makes it a cheerless place even on a bright sunny day. The name means 'place of many sheep and goats' and, but for the airstrip, it would have remained a tiny farming hamlet. The huge influx of trekkers and expeditions requiring accommodation and porterage had transformed the place. There were often ugly scenes of angry chaos at the tiny airport as flights were cancelled due to the weather and passengers were trapped for days on end in the village. There are never enough flights out and at times hundreds of passengers get caught in the backlog of cancellations when planes – which arrive only in the early morning – are grounded and then everyone is condemned to another long wait and yet another furious scuffle at the check-in desk the following day. Having good contacts and knowing who to bribe can be very useful, but the resulting pandemonium in the waiting list queue lends a tense and frenzied air to Lukla, as if it is unwanted and only to be got out of as quickly as possible. It also has an odd feeling of being at the end of treks and expeditions; many people's dreams finish here and the road back home begins.

Camp II on the Garganta col, Huascaran, before the night climb to the summit.
(Photo: Simpson)

Dam bursts and the scars of an alluvion at the head of the Ishinca. *Below:* The grey alluvion scar at the foot of Huascaran seen from Yungay cemetary. (Photos: Simpson)

Mountains on my mind. (Hair by British Hairways; photo-montage: Ian Smith)

Street crowds where Joe was mugged in Lima, and a police presence outside the Church of San Francisco, which stood above the catacombs. (Photos: Simpson)

Joe near the top of the North Spur on Ranrapalca, Peru.(Photo: Ric Potter)
Below left: Joe at the top of the North Spur of Ranrapalca. (Photo: Potter)
Below right: Ric Potter after the ascent. (Photo: Simpson)

The lake below Laguna Churup and Nevado Churup in the Cordillerra Blanca, Peru.
(Photo: Simpson)

A shattered bus is all that remains of the once prosperous town of Yungay. The four palm trees mark the buried Plaza de Armas in the town centre. (Photos: Simpson)

The cemetary at Yungay where 240 survivors sought refuge.
Below: Ric negotiating the 'shark's-fin' *penitentes* – ice formations that turn to slush in the sun – at the start of the last climb on Ranrapalca. (Photos: Simpson)

It also seems to be permanently under construction. The one stone-paved street is forever blocked by piles of stones and timber. Men swarm over the building debris, hammering at half-built walls with empty window sockets framing the sky. Yaks and porters laden with the expensive trappings of rich climbers and trekkers trail up the hill towards the airstrip. The impermanence of the place is palpable, despite the frenetic building work. Down the hillside, below the terrace on which the village is perched, the main trail up into the Khumbu links a whole series of communities in an ancient passage of traders taking fresh produce and meats to market and bringing back luxuries from the distant city, connecting families and villages. Lukla itself seems to be in a separate world far above these scenes of real life, there for a transient population that passes through like shadows in a ghost town. I often wondered what would happen if for some reason the planes stopped coming. The whole village would disintegrate. There would be a mass of unoccupied expensive lodges and the skeletal remains of half-constructed buildings looking incongruous in what should be simply high grazing pastures for sheep and cattle.

'I'm going down to Phakding,' I said to Mal as I finished my tea.

'Fair enough,' he said. 'We'll catch you up tomorrow. We have to wait to see if José's rucksack is going to turn up. It didn't arrive on the second flight.'

I stood up and shouldered my rucksack. 'Right. I'll see you tomorrow, on the trail, if not in Namche. I'm in no rush.'

I set off along the track that twisted down towards the Dudh Kosi, contouring above the prosperous village of Chaunrikhaka, an area of pleasant pastures and fields of crops. Looking down the valley, I could see where it narrowed and the forested slopes hemmed in the river. I remembered the steep climb up a spectacular path through a gorge that reverberated to the thunder of huge waterfalls. Shortly beyond Chaunrikhaka I arrived at the junction with the main trail up the valley at the newly built village of Choplung.

It was mid-day, the sun was burning down from a clear

blue sky, and it was good to stretch my legs and relax after the tension of the flight. I quickly got into a rhythm with my ski-sticks matching the music from my personal stereo. It took a couple of hours to reach Phakding, passing on the way through small hamlets, fields and forests on the broad well travelled path.

At Ghat, which straddled both sides of the Dudh Kosi I had crossed to the east bank and followed the familiar path, gradually feeling more and more at home. I loved seeing all the signs of Buddhism – the tall straight poles with prayer flags fixed down their length, sending forth their prayers on the wind, boulders carved with the Tibetan chant 'Om mani padme hum', which literally means 'Hail to you jewel of the lotus'. It is a prayer to the spiritual leader Guru Rimpoche, who was said to have been conceived in a lotus flower in the centre of a turquoise lake. Before long I was muttering the chant to myself as I walked past these impressively carved monoliths, which are sometimes painted in bright colours.

The people in this region follow a form of Buddhism known as Lamaism, which is based on the teachings of one of the oldest sects called Nyingmapa, or 'Ancient Ones'. It is a mixture of the ancient Tantric Mahayana Buddhism of northern India and the pre-Buddhist religions of Bon, the worship of ancestors and gods as well as inanimate objects such as rocks, fields, sources of water and a wealth of wrathful demons and spirits. The sense of the land, their whole world, being an essential, living evidence of their religion is very powerful. Delightful legends abound, of saints flying into the region from Tibet, using their mystical powers of flight and commandeering the rays of the sun to defeat local gods and evil demons. The sites where these holy ones touched the ground, marking it with their heels or hands, become village temples, as at Thangboche and Pangboche – 'teng' means heel and 'pang' means hand.

The prayer wheels must be passed on the left and spun clockwise. The very action of doing so is both a mark of devotion, an affirmation of faith, and bestows spiritual merit both on the passer-by and the person who erected the symbol.

They affect how you travel through the land. Nothing seems to be done by chance. Shapes and colours, everything bears some significance. On the fabric of the prayer flags and painted mani rocks the colours are also symbolic; green for water, blue for sky, red for rocks, yellow for earth and white for clouds. Inside the spinning water-driven prayer wheels and printed on the flags are mani prayers. The wind and water, rain and sun speeds their invocations throughout the world. Even the design of the chortens, or stupas, reflect abstract Buddhist concepts. The square lower plinth represents the earth, the rounded dome is water, and the spire is fire, often in thirteen circular segments to indicate the thirteen steps to enlightenment. On top is the symbol of wind and sun.

Rocks, trees, streams and springs are believed to be the dwelling places of secret spirits. Even the mountains have Gods. Each of the twenty-one Sherpa clans has its own mountain or area as its deity. Pumori, Kantaiga and Tamserku are all sacred mountains, as is Chomolungma, the Tibetan name meaning Goddess Mother of the World, or Sagamartha, the Nepalese name meaning Mother of the Universe. It is also and less impressively known as Mount Everest, named after the Surveyor General of India who never even saw it.

When I arrived at Phakding I settled into a friendly lodge on the banks of the Dudh Kosi and was again entranced by the sense of mysticism, the exciting feeling that anything could happen. I sat in the sunshine, drinking chang, and admired the display of flowers on the balconies of the lodge. A cooling breeze came up from the icy surge of the nearby river. I knew why I kept coming back, kept saying yes.

7

A WALK ON THE WILD SIDE

I heard shouts and shrill whistles and looked up the trail to see what was happening. The ochre-coloured beaten earth path twisted out of sight as it curved around the forested hillside ahead of me. The track ran along the east bank of the Dudh Kosi river which boiled past in a surge of swirling green and white water several hundred feet below. In places landslides had swept across the track and poured down to the river. Shattered branches and huge boulders were testimony to the destructive power of these slides. I was walking peacefully through an area of blue pine forests when I heard the warning cries ahead of me. There was little room for manoeuvre. I guessed what was coming and quickly hauled myself up the steeply-cut earth bank and held on to the trunk of a pine tree.

At that moment four panic-stricken yaks came charging round the bend and swept past where I had been standing. Two of the animals had shed their loads which hung by their sides or under their bellies. The triangular wooden frames which held these loads were placed on top of thick yak-blankets and tied tightly with a single stout rope under the animal's chest and close to the back of its forelegs. This was obviously what had enraged them as the girth slipped back and dug tightly into their loins.

A man came running down the track after his stampeding beasts. He was uttering piercing whistles and strange guttural cries which had no effect whatever on the animals. They thundered on, tossing their heads and colliding with each other. I watched as they disappeared round the lower bend

94

before cautiously lowering myself back to the path and peering warily into the trees to check that no more hairy monsters were coming. I was in little doubt that I could have been killed or badly injured if I hadn't leapt up the bank.

As a rule I walk on the inside edge of paths, keeping well away from the often precipitous drops on the outside. There is a purely practical reason for this beyond lacking confidence in the strength of the edges of the paths. Any yaks (or the hybrid dzos, a cross between a yak and a cow) coming down the trail, especially if heavily laden, present a very real danger. Most are docile enough and appear scared of strangers, but when a load slips and an enraged beast stampedes its companions, the panic and fear transforms them into the thundering monsters of nightmares. I have never trusted the yak in particular, with its vicious swept back horns and squat long-haired body. The animal is a formidable sight, and the bad tempered ones are dangerous. Unwary trekkers have been gored and killed by them in the past. The most common peril, however, is simply being nudged off the trail by passing animals.

It sounds like common sense to stand on the inside away from precipitous drops, but I have seen any number of western trekkers step neatly to the outside as a caravan of these large beasts swayed past them with the clanking of brass cattle bells swinging from their necks. Sometimes the animals accidentally knock victims off the path with part of their wide and heavy loads, unable as they are to judge their width, and then the poor traveller can suddenly find himself plunging to his death down a vertiginous hillside or falling into a raging icy river. There is almost no hope of survival in a river such as the Dudh Kosi.

I have heard accounts of trekkers who have managed to fall to their deaths from high paths all by themselves without the helping nudge of passing beasts of burden. I knew of one man who was killed on the trail to Thangboche because he stepped back to frame his photograph better without looking behind him. He fell hundreds of feet into the ravine below. I find it quite astonishing that people can be so careless. After all, no one would consider stepping out into a busy road without looking to see if there were vehicles bearing down on them, and the paths in Nepal are exactly that, ancient trading highways, busy with the flow of passing traffic.

There are of course unavoidable incidents, the equivalent of a juggernaut losing its brakes, where only a quick reaction can save the day. Several years ago Mal had been extremely lucky to survive being charged by a runaway yak. He and his wife Liz had been striding contentedly along a trail some distance apart from one another when a yak had come charging down the trail. Mal was trapped on the narrow path between a steep drop to one side and a high bank on the other. Fortunately Liz had already turned a corner and seen the crazed animal in time to leap out of the way. She had yelled a warning to Mal but he hadn't heard the alarm above the music on his personal stereo.

He looked up as he strode towards the bend in the track to see that the yak was suddenly upon him. The animal probably didn't see Mal as it galloped head down, blinded with panic and rage. Mal had no time to leap aside and was hit full in the chest by the yak's lowered head. Luckily the wickedly sharp horns were widely spaced and he found himself thrown forward across the animal's head and carried at breakneck speed down the path.

For a moment he clung on hoping that he could save himself from being gored, but he soon realised that the yak was now totally blinded by his body and could plunge off the side of the path, hurling both of them to their deaths. The creature made frenzied attempts to dislodge its unwelcome human baggage, throwing its head from side to side as it continued to charge forward. Mal had the presence of mind to grab the flailing horns in his arms and try to lever himself to the side while at the same time pushing the animal's head down and away so as to keep the lethal horns out of reach of his soft vulnerable belly. More by accident than design, the plan worked and he found himself thrown up and clear, on to the wooded bank above the path, as the yak slewed its head round with a vicious curving swing of its horns and thundered off down the track. Mal swiftly scrambled up into the treeline, desperate not to repeat this display of bullfighting bravado.

The way ahead looked clear, and I was about to step out when I heard cattle bells jangling in the trees at the bend in front of me. The man who had been chasing his yaks round the corner returned and began a loud, excited conversation with the yak herder at the back of the second group.

They hurried back down the track with concerned expressions and I followed, curious to see what had happened. Two hundred yards along the path I found the two men looking over the edge and pointing to something on the rocky bank of the river hundreds of feet below. Looking down, I could see the black squat shape of a yak lying amid the boulders. It kept lifting its head, as if trying to get up. The rest of its body remained ominously still. It had broken its back in the long tumbling fall down to the river. Parts of the load lay strewn around, and I could just make out the sounds of mournful bellows coming up from the river.

I turned and left them to the task of retrieving the load. The carcass would probably be butchered there and then before being hauled up to the path. I wouldn't have been surprised if it had turned up for sale in Namche later that day. It was still early and there was plenty of time to reach the bustling Saturday market. The Yak herders didn't seem unduly upset about the loss of their animal. I found this surprising, and would be more than annoyed to lose my car in such a random manner. I've never managed to find out exactly what a healthy yak costs although I know that they are insured in some parts for twice as much as a porter. This seems a disturbing reflection on the value of human life, but then a yak can carry twice as much as a man.

Mal and the team had not yet caught up with me since I had decided to make an early start so as to avoid making the final gruelling two thousand feet switchback climb up to Namche in the full heat of the day.

The yak had fallen just outside the village of Phakding where I had spent the night. I hurried on through the small village of Benkar, crossed the river by an impressively carved and painted boulder and then climbed steadily up to Monjo, where I decided to wait for the team and ordered a beer. Mal had the expedition permits. I knew that just past the next village of Jorsale, a cold and shadowed place, was a guard post which marked the start of the Sagamartha National Park. Entry fees were paid here and trekking permits examined at a small building beyond the village.

Monjo is an attractive village set amid pine forests on the banks of the Monjo Khola. This stream is fed by the snows of the sacred mountains Tamserku and Kantaiga which are hidden from sight by the steep wooded hillside. The houses hug the right bank of the stream, nestling into the pine forests, and thin lines of smoke from cooking fires rise straight up from them into the cool morning air. Small fields have been cleared from the rocky ground, where the lush green of barley crops contrasts with a clear blue sky.

The air was redolent with the fragrance of pine needles, the sharp aroma of wood smoke and the sweet smell from stacks of freshly sawn timber that lined the path up to the village. Stonemasons were busy working on piles of the hard grey local rock, dressing it into rectangular stones and putting up the first walls of a new house. Judging from its size, I guessed that it was to be yet another lodge to accommodate the increasing number of visitors to the area. There was a prosperous atmosphere in this typically neat and tidy Sherpa village.

At the head of the valley, framed by the steep pine-covered cut of the valley walls, the triangular rocky mass of Khumbi-yul-lha dominated the view. This was the most sacred mountain in the Khumbu; inviolable and never to be climbed. Named after the region's most important mountain god, it towered above the villages of Khumjung and Khunde which are perched high on the hillside overlooking Namche Bazar. From Monjo, which was still a good three hours' walk from Namche, the mountain seemed to be watching over the valley, a formidable wall of dark grey rock streaked with snow. The Sherpas believe the mountain is their watchful guardian. Monjo is the lowest point in the park, and beyond the guard post there is a steady climb up through a cold and shadowed ravine until you reach the junction of two gorges where the Dudh Kosi and Bhote Kosi rivers meet. Here the cold intensifies as the wind is funnelled down the gorges into this sunless rocky confluence. A precipitous climb, undulating through woods by way of rocky shelves and steep, slippery paths, leads to a spectacular suspension bridge which hangs hundreds of feet above the Bhote Kosi.

With the expedition together again, I watched as porters and yaks, both carrying immense loads up to the market, slowly made their way across the undulating and swinging bridge. Prayer flags attached to the wire handrails streamed out in the cold river-borne wind. On the far side the path zig-zagged up through sparse dry forests in a lung-burning climb of two thousand feet.

I turned up the volume on my Sony Walkman to maximum, put my head down, and tried to keep up with Mal's steady stride. It was best to make this hot and dusty ascent in one go, overtaking the slow-moving porters and yaks as they kicked dustily up the switchbacks.

Namche is the Sherpa capital, and on Saturday, market day, the town is full of the noisy clamour of villagers who have come from all over the region to trade. Unlike the other smaller villages the houses here are huddled together in a crescent, clinging to the steep amphitheatre shape of the hillside that hangs above the Bhote Kosi river. On the opposite side, high above the river, the ice-draped flanks of Kwangde pierce the sky like a white shark's fin. From the summit a long knife-edge ridge forms a continuous mountain wall up the Bhote Kosi valley towards Thami.

I wandered through the chaotic throng of stalls on the wide level terrace in the middle of the town. Porters lounged in the sun by their empty baskets after the hard climb up to the town. There was a festive air and people were wearing their best clothes. It was a chance to meet up and exchange gossip, drink tea and chang and make the most of the social day of the week.

Baskets of maize, wheat, rice and millet brought up by the

traders are quickly sold to people who come down from the higher villages to stock up. Namche used to be a centre for trade between the caravans of yaks bringing salt and carpets from Tibet and the porters carrying in foodstuffs from the lower valleys. The salt trade has gone now but there were still a good many Tibetans milling through the jostling crowds. With the increase in the tourist business Namche is now a centre for mountaineering and trekking equipment as well as countless souvenirs – yak-hair blankets, long brightly coloured aprons, woollen socks and sweaters, Tibetan horse blankets, and all manner of precious stones and necklaces and bracelets carved from yak-bone and wood.

Many of the Sherpanis – wearing the distinctive ankle-length wrap around dresses called the *ingi* – were adorned with their best jewellery, some with waist-length necklaces of bright stones and distinctive ear and nose rings. The necklaces were strung in long heavy strings of blue turquoise, red coral and bright yellow amber.

We settled comfortably into the Sherpa Co-operative lodge in the centre of the town where we planned to stay for two days to get accustomed to the sudden height gain. Flying in to Lukla inevitably meant breaking the golden rule of not gaining more than one thousand metres in a day. There are avoidable deaths every year in the Khumbu because people do not heed the advice which is widely available. I've seen them on their hands and knees, vomiting by the side of the path leading towards Everest base camp, clearly showing advanced symptoms of high altitude mountain sickness. Pulmonary and cerebral oedemas quickly strike victims who become as ill as this and they are often fatal. To avoid spending a day or two resting on the walk-in they are prepared to risk their lives, and on reaching their Holy Grail, they are too sick with thunderous frontal headaches and nausea to appreciate either what they have achieved or the view.

I, for one, am terrified of the insidious dangers of oedemas. They have already killed too many highly experienced and talented mountaineers, some of whom were friends. I am justifiably alert to the slightest symptoms and always listen carefully to my body for the smallest indication that something is wrong. Perhaps I'm too cautious, but I am still here. The mountains will always be there. If you retreat for uncertain reasons, you can always return another day.

In April 1990, on the way back to Namche after climbing Ama Dablam, I was horrified to learn that a Japanese woman had been found staggering along the path just above the town. Her two male companions had been so fixated on climbing Kala Patar, a 17,000-feet pile of rocky scree near Everest, that they had abandoned her near Pangboche when she developed symptoms of advanced altitude sickness. Almost blind through the effects of cerebral oedema, she had struggled back up to the heights of Thangboche monastery and on towards Namche where she died twenty-four hours after being found nearly comatose on the trail. Her companions did not lose face. They scaled what to all intents and purposes is an insignificant slag-heap with a good view of Everest. One of them was so ill during the ascent that I doubt he saw anything and only survived climbing the rocky pimple because a Canadian woman virtually carried him back down again.

Fortunately none of the Cho Oyo team were suffering any ill-effects from the flight to Lukla. That evening Mal outlined the itinerary for the five-day walk to base camp. The next morning was spent resting and sightseeing. The keener members of the team climbed the hill above Namche to visit the relatively unspoilt villages of Khunde and Khumjung while I chose to read and relax over beer and chess in PK's Khumbu Lodge.

'Checkmate, I reckon,' I said with quiet satisfaction.

'Ah, yes, so it is,' Mal said as he examined his denuded forces. 'The Scottish defence, or Highland frontal assault ploy fails again.'

'That makes it two all in the series,' I announced. 'Do you want another beer?'

'Are bears Catholic? Does the Pope . . .'

'Yes, stupid question.' I grinned. 'How are you feeling?'

'Pretty good. I've managed to shake off that cold.'

'Yeah, on to me,' I said ruefully. I had begun to feel blocked up and full of cold the night before and now my suspicions were confirmed. 'I only hope it doesn't get to my chest.'

'Oh, you'll be all right,' Mal said confidently. 'I got rid of it pretty fast.'

'I know but you didn't have it at this height. It will be just my sort of luck to get a chest infection now after giving up smoking for the last eleven months.'

'You can always take some antibiotics,' Mal suggested.

'They don't work so well up here,' I replied. 'And they certainly won't work at all at base camp. It's over five thousand metres, for God's sake.'

'Yeah, you have a point there,' Mal admitted grudgingly as he poured beer into his glass.

We left Namche on a fine day with the sun beginning to burn away the morning mists. As we climbed steadily up the maze of streets towards the village *gompa*, a large herd of unladen yaks and dzos were being driven down to the lodge we had just left. The main bulk of our supplies had yet to be sorted and loaded under the direction of Chwang, who had been our Sirdar and a friend on most of Mal's expeditions. He was an accomplished mountaineer. Two years before, when Mal and I had made the first ascent of the East Face of Pachermo, and then possibly the fastest descents of the North Ridge, it was Chwang who swiftly and efficiently organised my painful evacuation on the backs of two Sherpa porters after our 600-foot fall.

I received a disturbing reminder of that accident in the lodge on my return to Namche when a large haul bag was presented to me. Because of weight limitations, much of my equipment had been left behind at Thengbo with Chwang and the boys. I gingerly unzipped the bag and a damp musty smell washed out. Emptying the contents on the floor, I began sifting through the mess of clothing, hardware and personal effects. There was a single crampon. I pulled out a pile jacket and some Gore-Tex mitts, mouldy with damp and heavily stained with crusty brown blotches. I realised with a shock that they were blood stains. I hurriedly pushed the filthy, mildewed and bloodied gear back into the haul bag and zipped it up before dumping the lot.

On the first day we were following the same route as we had on the Pachermo trip, climbing up out of the village to gain a trail high above the east bank of the Bhote Kosi valley. As we passed the monastery with its long lines of prayer wheels set into the ochre-red walls, I spun each one, muttering the Tibetan chant 'Om mani padme hum' under my breath. With light day sacks the walk to Thami is a delight wending through forests of mixed pine, fir, birch and rhododendron high above the dramatic canyon of the Bhote Kosi.

I looked down into the bowl of the town and noted how few trees were left. Namche means 'place shaded by forests', yet apart from tall specimens on sacred land near the monastery there wasn't a tree to be seen.

The small gompa at Pangboche, the oldest in the Khumbu, has a very impressive stand of old black juniper trees. The story goes that the trees sprouted from the hairs of an old and venerable Lama which he had torn out and spread around the monastery. Legend has it that the patron saint of the Sherpas, Lama Sangwa Dorje, stamped his palm print in a rock as he made his leaping flight to the Khumbu from Tibet and the site with its grove of ancient tall trees has been a revered place ever since. The height of the junipers reveals their great age, and they are the last remnants of what was once an extensive forest covering the now bare hillsides.

The massive demands for firewood created by the influx first of climbing expeditions and then trekking parties had denuded huge areas of forests in the mountain regions and created serious environmental problems. As more and more visitors demanded bigger hotels and lodges, hot showers, varied meals, and porterage, so the problems got increasingly out of hand.

The Sherpas' traditional trade with Tibet had stopped when the borders were closed in 1959 and they had turned instead to the rapidly expanding tourist trade which used up vast forest resources to provide fuel and building materials. For those in affluent centres, such as Namche it was not such a problem since they could more easily afford to pay people to fetch the daily requirement of fuel. In the scattered remote villages it became harder and harder to find the vital firewood for their own domestic use.

Fortunately steps have been taken to halt the destruction of the forests. Small hydro-electric plants have been installed and more are planned. The increasing use of solar panels to heat water and charge batteries has helped reduce the pressure on the land. New Zealand has been at the forefront of a reafforestation programme and there are now at least five tree nurseries in the Khumbu, each capable of producing 100,000 seedlings every year. Sir Edmund Hillary's Himalayan Trust has opened schools, hospitals and dental surgeries, improved bridges and water supplies, built airstrips and hydro-electric plants, and these have all greatly benefited the communities. The National Park is now a World Heritage Site and as a result grants and funds are available through UNESCO to help with the preservation and upkeep of the monasteries and numerous religious and cultural sites.

Clearly the damage done cannot be entirely mended and the lives and landscape of the Sherpas' world has been changed for ever. Still, it is good to know that now there is some sort of control on the runaway destruction that commercial pressures brought to the region. I feel a sense of guilt that our desire to pursue purely selfish ends, to go on fabulous treks or climb great mountains, should have led to such destruction.

Climbing mountains may well seem highly significant to me, but to the people living a hard life in a hard land it must appear an absurd way to spend one's time. For the most part the Sherpas only climb mountains for the income. They act as porters and high altitude guides and are frequently exposed to great dangers. It is acceptable for me to put my own life at risk: that is my choice. It now seems morally dubious to create a situation where others can get sucked into the maelstrom. The Sherpa population is not large and male fatalities have a devastating effect on the small communities. Mountaineering exacts a heavy toll and it is not uncommon to find an unusual number of widows left to bring up children, look after the home, and try to earn the missing husband's wage. The high cost of a funeral frequently leaves the young widow destitute.

As I followed the path to Thami I couldn't reconcile my deep affection for the town and its people and fascinating culture with the sense that I was really just a passer-by, someone fortunate enough and rich enough to be a travelling voyeur, a stranger who came and took and went, nothing more than a credit card adventurer. I reminded myself that there were many other countries I had visited to play my foolish games which had far more serious reasons to make me feel guilty. Places where people fought simply to survive from day to day, where human rights abuses were widespread, where poverty was endemic and life was cheap. I remembered as I walked pleasantly in the spring sunshine that I was walking towards Tibet. I felt uncomfortable at the thought of my hypocrisy, but it was a bit late to start examining my conscience.

The land became more open and less forested as I headed up the valley past long lines of *mani* stones towards the junction of the Bhote Kosi and the Thengpo Khola rivers. A steel box frame bridge crossed a dramatic gorge hundreds of feet deep where the multi-coloured rocks were carved into fantastic swirls and undercut by the thundering icy water. The noise in this narrow canyon was deafening and a cold wind rushed down with the river, making me shiver as I waited for some yaks to cross the bridge. There was no sun in the shadowed rocky defile. I edged back against the rock walls to let the animals pass. A stand of prayer flags on thin whippy branches bristled and waved in the wind.

Once out on the bridge, I peered over the steel handrail at the boiling green and white water funnelled by the narrow constricting walls which squeezed it into a raging torment. It hurled itself down in a dizzying series of s-shaped tubes and the sight of it and the thunder of its passage mesmerised me. It had that same hypnotic effect that looking down precipitous drops can have, the feeling of being pulled inexorably towards it despite resisting – as if some force was beckoning me. *Come on in, come on down,* it seemed to whisper, and I felt myself press against the cold steel handrail. I could imagine its deadly spell on wavering suicidees. The hollow stomach, a sickening cold dread in the chest, a moment's denial and then the easy embrace of the whispering spell of the fall. I pushed myself away and shook my head as if to break the enchantment of the green surge below me. The walls echoed louder with the roar of the water. I turned and quickly crossed the bridge to the far bank. I had no doubt about how long I would survive should I fall in. It would be no more than seconds after I hit the water and I knew that my body would never be found.

I remembered a story I had heard about a man who had decided to swim the Dudh Kosi river armed with a five-minute supply of oxygen, a small mask and a buoyancy aid. He had floated down a couple of rivers in Europe and reckoned it would work just as successfully. There was even a film crew there to record his feat of lunacy.

When they reached this spot, where the man intended to enter the water, the film crew took one look at the horrifying thunder of white water and baulked at the idea of letting him jump. They did their best to dissuade him, even insisting that they would not film him, but he was adamant – whether from madness or a compelling belief that he could survive. In he leapt, to the utter horror of the film crew, and that was the last anyone ever saw of him. He simply disappeared, snatched instantly down below the surface as if some monstrous ogre had devoured him. Not a sound, no screams, no instant of flailing resistance, just *whoomph* and he was gone, as if he had never existed. They never found his body. I stood at the point where he had jumped and stared incredulously at the water tearing past. It was suicidal.

He was probably jammed under some huge boulder, and the life instantly crushed out of him. His oxygen would only have prolonged his death even if the thundering of tons of water hadn't immediately battered him senseless, ripping away the small cylinder and mask. It would have made a very short film. A sight of the raging torrent, the heavy knocking sounds of boulders tumbling ominously beneath the surface, a millisecond shot as the man dropped through the air, the raging torrent again, and the mutterings of *'ah merde!'* as the film crew peered morosely into the river – what a dumb way to die.

Not far from the scene of this act of insanity, within sight of the water-worn boulder from which he had jumped, was a suspension bridge swaying in the wind. Mal had told me that this was the bridge from which Sungdare had jumped five years before. He was an exceptional man. He had climbed Everest five times. He was strong and brave and successful, much in demand by big expensive expeditions who wanted his experience and help to get them up the mountain. Mal described how he had left his clothes on the bank, walked to the centre of the bridge, and jumped into oblivion. Perhaps he couldn't cope with the unexpected fame, the wealth and the pressure. Maybe there were such conflicting forces bearing down on him, the great gulf between his traditional Sherpa upbringing and the brash money-fuelled stress of big expeditions, that he felt forced to run away. Whatever the reasons, and however sad, his jump was a deliberate choice with a clearly understood consequence. Even with the help of strong liquor it is a courageous thing to do, and despite the apparent futility and despair that it revealed, it was in the end perhaps the bravest thing he ever did. It was not a dumb way to die.

Once across the bridge I began to climb the path which switch-backed steeply up a dry dusty hillside until it contoured out over its summit dome and the lower fields of Thami came into view. I looked down from a point halfway up the hill and saw the awesome drop down into the river. If I tripped and started falling, especially down near the bottom of the hill where the angle was steepest, there would be nothing to prevent me from plummeting straight into the river gorge.

After a cold beer at a small friendly lodge in the village of Thami I joined the rest of the team in the final grind over a huge wall of moraine and descended past the chortens and prayer flags of the Thami monastery down into the terraced fields of the upper Thami valley. The massively thick walls buttressing the monastery leant into steep bluffs high above the Thengpo river. The red ochre walls of the monastery itself, with its gleaming gold spire catching the flame of a low sun, was visible high up, sheltered by the sweep of water-streaked cliffs.

The fields were brown and bare, dotted with piles of fertiliser, ready for planting. I watched the women sitting outside their houses in the sunshine, selecting seed potatoes which had been dug up from deep pits.

We huddled in the shelter of a low earthen wall trying to keep out the biting cold wind and the dramatic drop in temperature once the sun had finally dipped below the jagged rocky ridge of the horizon. It was a long cold wait for the yaks to arrive with the tents and camping equipment. I shivered convulsively and cursed myself for wearing shorts and leaving my warm clothing with the yaks. Just as I was preparing to wobble off to the nearest lodge on goose-pimpled white legs I heard the welcome jangle of cattle bells coming down on the wind.

8

An Eye for a Tooth

As usual, my gear was the last to arrive and I fumbled through my sack for warm pile clothing. By the time I had put the finishing touches to my tent and laid out my inflatable mattress and sleeping bag I had warmed up again. I sat in the doorway of the tent looking across to where the moraine bank loomed above the drystone walls of the potato fields. From here onwards I would be in unknown territory, and I felt a tingle of excitement run through me.

Suddenly I was caught in a spasm of the violent coughs which had plagued me all day. It was the sort of retching cough that seemed to start from a dry tickling sensation at the back of the throat. It didn't trouble me while I was walking or climbing strenuous hillsides, but the moment I stopped the tickling sensations began. So far there had been no sign of serious bronchial infection and I hoped it was due to the dusty trail and a slight altitude cough. I still hadn't shaken off the cold that I had caught in Namche and felt blocked up with catarrh, but at least it hadn't gone on to my chest.

Leaning into the back of the tent, I scrabbled around for my first aid kit and swallowed the fluorescent red capsules, knowing that at the present altitude the effect of antibiotics would be negligible. I wondered if I should return to Namche until I had shaken off the cold but dismissed the idea. I didn't want to find myself too far behind the rest of the team, unable to keep up because they were so much better acclimatised. Besides. I didn't know the way up to base camp and doubted my ability to find it alone.

'Hey Joe, are you there?' I heard Mal call.

'Yes, what is it?'

'Can you give me a hand here? I've got a problem.'

'So have I,' I muttered to myself as I pulled on my boots and crawled out of the tent. One of the pills seemed to be stuck halfway down my throat and no amount of swallowing would shift it. As I rose to my feet I started coughing again, and putting my hand over my mouth, I felt the pill bounce off my palm. It landed in the dust at my feet. I picked it up, rubbed it on my shirt and popped it back into my mouth. 'Bit of dirt never hurt anyone,' I said to myself. I was running short of erythromycin. By the time I reached Mal's tent the pill was lodged in the same position, but this time it also felt gritty.

'What's up?' I asked as I saw Mal crouched in the doorway of his tent, examining something inside.

'It's Chwang,' he said as he ducked out of the tent and I saw Chwang lying on his back with his head near the door. 'He's lost his teeth.'

'That's a bit careless,' I said facetiously. 'I didn't know he had false teeth.'

'They've been knocked out. At least his front ones have, and he may have broken his jaw.'

'Bloody hell! How did he manage that?'

'It was a yak.' Mal was searching through the large expedition box. 'Have you got any Superglue?'

'Er, well, yes.' I was struggling to understand how a yak came to knock Chwang's teeth out. 'Why, do you need it?'

'We might do. This stuff is a bit old,' he said, showing me a small glass jar.

'What is it?'

'It's instant filling. You can use it for emergency repairs if your fillings fall out.' He opened the jar and poked at the contents dubiously. 'I think it's gone off. Must have been left open too long.' The contents looked hard and dry, like flaky old putty.

'Does it work?'

'Oh yes,' Mal said brightly. 'It's great stuff. Usually you can just press it in and it quickly goes hard. There's some chemical reaction goes on when it's exposed to air. It will last a few weeks which is better than nothing if you are miles away from a dentist.'

'Yes, I suppose it is,' I replied, looking with concern at Chwang's upside down pain-wracked face. There was a livid swelling along his jaw line and blood on his cheek and lips. 'How are you doing, Chwang?' I asked. He nodded his head and mumbled something unintelligibly.

'He looks in a bad way,' I said to Mal. 'What happened? Did it kick him?'

'What?'

'The yak. How on earth did it knock his teeth out?'

'It damn near killed him actually,' Mal said cheerfully, and went on to describe the accident.

Chwang had been late leaving Namche after a lot of haggling about load weights and the usual time-consuming business of organising the equipment into balanced and categorised loads. When he reached the steel bridge below Thami, he had waited to ensure that there were no stragglers and then followed the last of the heavily burdened yaks across the bridge. As he started up the steep twisting path on the opposite side there was the faint sound of shouting from far above him, barely audible above the thunderous roar of the river. Glancing up, he saw one of the yaks, several hundred feet above him, struggling to maintain its footing after it had slipped on the dusty scree-covered slope.

At that instant a rock kicked down by the animal's hooves smashed into his upturned face. The impact knocked him backwards. The drop into the river was just a few feet behind him and he fought to remain conscious and keep his balance. The rock had struck him across his lower jaw and chin and the lower teeth had cut through the inside of his bottom lip, causing a nasty two-inch gash. One of his front teeth had sheered off just above the line of his gums and another was flapping loose in its socket. When he had regained his composure after the concussing impact, he had climbed stoically up after the disappearing yaks.

'But he's been here in camp for ages,' I said incredulously as Mal finished telling me what had happened.

'I know,' Mal said. 'It was only after he had dealt with all the cook tents and our gear and everything was sorted that he came up and asked me if I could take a look.'

'I wondered why he was wearing that scarf across his mouth,' I said, remembering how Chwang had been wandering around with a green silk scarf wrapped around his lower face, covering his mouth and nose. 'I thought it looked very piratical, quite dashing in a weird sort of way.'

'It was to keep the cold air off his teeth,' Mal said with a laugh. 'You should see it. There's this horrible red worm hanging from the stump of his tooth. I think it's the nerve.'

I gulped and the pill suddenly slipped down from where it had been lodged.

'I'm worried that he might have broken his jaw as well,' Mal added. 'Can you give me a hand while I examine him. I need you to hold his head – oh, and a torch if you've got one.' I fumbled in my pocket for my torch. Mal got down on his knees in the cramped doorway. 'If you hold his head steady, I'll try to manipulate his jaw. Okay?'

'Yup,' I said, holding the sides of Chwang's head. Mal moved his jaw gently.

'Does that hurt, Chwang?' There was an odd sound in reply. 'I can't feel anything clicking,' Mal muttered as he moved the jaw up and down and then from side to side.

'Whoarr erroom, huh!' Chwang replied vigorously.

'How about that?'

'Warroom.'

'Yeah, I thought so,' Mal said, looking at me. 'It's not broken. Chwang says he can move it.'

'Really?' I said in amazement. 'Is that what he was saying?'

'Well, something like that,' Mal said. 'Let's have a look in his mouth. The jaw's pretty swollen. If it was broken I'm sure it would have clicked and even Chwang would have complained about that.' I thought his mumbles had sounded distinctly unhappy as it was.

'Can you shine the light in here?' Mal asked as he slowly

prised Chwang's mouth open. 'Ooohh, nasty,' he added as the long deep cut was revealed in the torchlight.

'God, that's deep.' I winced at the thought of how painful it must be. 'It might need stitches.'

'That's what I'm thinking.' Chwang's eyes widened perceptively and he shook his head.

'Uh roor umm erth,' he spluttered emphatically.

'Says he doesn't need it. Thinks it will heal on its own.'

I stared at Mal in astonishment at his quick translation. I had no idea he was so fluent in Nepali, or Sherpa dialect.

'I'm not sure that I can stitch it,' Mal mumbled. 'It's right along the bottom of his gums and his lip. Looks a bit tricky. How's your sewing?'

'My what?' I yelped, peering at the bloody mess. Chwang's gaze switched from Mal to me. 'I think it would be better left alone.'

Chwang nodded.

'Yeah, perhaps you're right,' Mal said reluctantly. 'Well, what should we do with this tooth then?'

I shone the torch beam upwards.

'Oh Jesus!' I said in horror. 'That must really hurt.' The pulpy red nerve protruded from the neatly sheered tooth and was lying across the loose neighbouring tooth. I stared at it with repugnance.

'The pain will be unbearable while it's exposed like that. That's why I thought we should plug the hole with this filling stuff.'

'Can't we just get him down to Namche? There's a dental clinic there now. They could do something. I heard that PK's daughter has performed root canal surgery there.'

'The trouble is he doesn't want to go. Not until base camp has been established.'

'But that's days away,' I said, staring at the mess of Chwang's teeth and trying to imagine what it must feel like.

'Come on, let's have a go with this filling stuff,' Mal said decisively. 'I've given him a couple of pain killers.'

'I thought you said it had gone off?'

'That stuff has' – he nodded at the glass jar on the grass –

'but I found this in the first aid kit.' He held up a white plastic tube.

'Does it do the same thing?'

'Yes, but it has to be really dry. And I mean bone dry.'

'I don't fancy trying to dry that,' I said with a shudder. 'You'll never be able to avoid the nerve.'

I couldn't see what Mal was doing as he bent over close to Chwang and seemed to be pushing at something with his finger.

'It's no good,' Mal said at last. 'It just won't take. It's too wet.' I opened my eyes and peered at Chwang. He didn't look at all happy.

'Have you got that Superglue?'

'Er, yeah, it's here.' I handed Mal the tube. 'What are you going to do with it?'

'Stick his tooth back on.'

'Which tooth?'

'This tooth,' Mal said triumphantly as he held up the remainder of Chwang's front tooth. 'He almost swallowed it after he was hit.'

'Are you sure you can stick teeth together with Superglue?' I asked hesitantly. 'Won't you have the same problem with the moisture?'

'Probably, but what else can we do?' Mal looked at me with a grim expression. 'I know you can glue caps back on. Maybe this will work.' He didn't sound convinced.

'Okay then, if you're sure,' I said, and regretted it at once. I knew Mal had no desire to hurt Chwang. They were good friends. He was doing the best he could, trying hard to save the man any further pain, and although it was turning my stomach over to watch his efforts, I knew he cared deeply about Chwang. I also knew that Chwang would never have asked Mal for help, or endured such treatment, if he hadn't trusted Mal implicitly. I had as much sympathy for Mal as I did for Chwang.

After fruitless efforts to glue the tooth back on to the stump, which mainly succeeded in gluing fingers together, we abandoned attempts at dentistry and tried instead to persuade

Chwang to go down to Namche.

'If he left now he could be there by nine,' I said to Mal. 'He could be treated and catch us up tomorrow. We would probably only miss him for one day.'

'Well, he won't have it,' Mal retorted. 'He doesn't trust the other guys to get everything sorted and it's not in his nature to back down. He won't be seen to lose face.'

'Getting your teeth repaired is hardly losing face.'

'Not to us it isn't,' Mal said as he stood up, 'but Chwang's a proud man, and he knows how important his role as Sirdar is. He can't be seen to be weak.'

'But that's not weakness, it's practical,' I protested. 'He can do a better job if his teeth don't hurt.'

'Oh, don't worry about the pain. He'll deal with that okay. Any of the porters would, and he knows it. Chwang's not from this area. He comes from the Kanchenjunga region, so it's all the more important to show that he can take it. My guess is that he won't go down until we do.'

'How is it now, Chwang?' I asked. 'Have those pills started working yet?'

He mumbled something inaudible and came out of the tent, wrapping the silk scarf around his mouth and turning his back to the icy wind.

'Do you fancy a cup of tea?' I said without thinking.

'No.' Chwang shook his head. 'Too hot.'

'Ah, yes, of course. How about a cold beer then?'

'No, no.' Chwang said decisively with a forced grin and hurried away to his own tent.

'Well, I fancy a beer after that,' Mal said firmly. 'Come on. There's a good lodge in the village.'

The lodge was situated on a steep earth bank overlooking the Thengpo Kola. It was an old solidly-built traditional house with thick clay-sealed rock walls and the typical roof of wooden shingles held down by small boulders. Ducking through the low doorway, I followed Mal up a flight of broad wooden steps to the upstairs room. Yellow lamplight filtered down between the joints of the floorboards and the rustling of heavy animals in the darkness below betrayed the presence of cattle. The downstairs rooms of these houses are used as cattle byres and for storage of firewood and fodder. They provide welcome warmth and insulation from the bitter winter cold.

We emerged through the open trapdoor at the top of the stairs into the smoky atmosphere of the kitchen. As usual there was no chimney and the smoke was left to find its way out through open windows and the cracks in the ceiling timbers that were burnished black with the soot and tar from countless fires. A young Sherpani, holding her infant on her hip, was tending to the hearth as we arrived. An older woman, probably the grandmother of the house, sat drinking tea from a chipped glass. They both smiled in welcome. The gold of the older woman's front tooth flashed in the firelight.

I was relieved to find that there was an adjacent room to the kitchen with tables and benches, the far walls stacked with old plastic barrels from past expeditions and the glass windows plastered with stickers from numerous big foreign expeditions to Everest and Cho Oyo. In the darkness at the far end of the long room there was a small altar facing one of the windows. Some offerings were arranged on a shelf and a large vividly coloured scroll painting hung in pride of place. The grimy red fringes of silk gleamed as the grandmother carried in a brightly burning Tilley lamp. Mal ordered two beers and the woman gave a beautiful gold smile when he called her 'didi'. It meant sister and was a polite greeting for a woman slightly older than oneself. The old lady chuckled as she returned to the kitchen to fetch the beers.

This place reminded me of the lodge in which Mal and I had stayed on the way to climb Pachermo. I had wanted to buy some cigarettes and, finding that there were none to be had in the lodge, I went in search through the village for another lodge that I had been told might have some. No lights came from the houses and the moonless night sky was covered with thick low cloud. Groping down narrow alleyways, I came by chance to the lodge where our porters were spending the night. A glass was promptly filled with thick chang brewed from millet and a packet of Yak cigarettes were produced from an old wooden chest. I had nearly finished the chang, which tasted disastrously strong, when the lady of the house promptly filled my glass up again before I could refuse.

The men laughed and their smiles glittered in the smoky gloom. By the time it had been refilled four times I could feel myself becoming dizzy and light-headed with the effects of the crude alcohol. However much I protested the glass was filled to the brim.

I couldn't for the life of me work out what to do. I didn't want to offend anyone by boorish refusal, but equally I didn't want to throw up in the fireplace and collapse unconscious in the corner. When eventually I managed to escape three glasses later I could barely walk and tottered around in the labyrinth of passageways, bouncing off walls and sleeping yaks for what seemed like half the night.

I stumbled into the lodge where we were staying and staggered up the stairs. It was only then that Mal told me about the traditional Sherpa custom of hospitality by which you had to make three ritual refusals. If you made only one or two refusals your glass would still be filled. Since I had no knowledge of this custom, and after numerous failed refusals was barely able to speak, it was a wonder that I had made it back at all.

There is a strict observance of etiquette beside the fireplace at the centre of a Sherpa house. Seating for the owner of the house, seats of honour and behaviour around the hearth are considered very important. I never know which seat is which and try to avoid sitting near the fire unless invited to do so. I have seen tourists shoving and bustling for the warmest vantage point quite unaware of the offence being caused. In their easy-going and tolerant nature the Sherpas ignore such displays of rudeness and consequently people never learn what they have done.

I was mortified to discover that I had transgressed countless traditional customs and obviously caused offence, however innocently, when Al Burgess, who spends half his life living in Nepal, told me about some of the peculiarities of Nepalese behaviour. Feet are regarded as unclean and shoes in particular are seen as the most degrading aspect of clothing.

They should always be kept on the floor, if not removed, and the soles must never be pointed at people. Outstretched legs are offensive and should be drawn up since a Sherpa will never step over them. However accidental, it is an insult to touch someone with a shoe, and to kick someone is the gravest of offences. It made me wonder how many fatal accidents had occurred in the mountains through Sherpas attempting to accomplish dangerous manoeuvres on cramped, precarious terrain to avoid breaking these rules of conduct.

In most houses there is a space set aside for the spirit of the land, the *Lhu*, and there is a tradition of not burning rubbish or throwing spent cigarettes and foods scraps into the fire. All smoke is a prayer, and the smoke from such unclean fuel would be an offence to the *Lhu*. I learned something of the culture from Al and could appreciate it all the more when I opened my eyes and could watch these sensitivities at play.

'What do you think Chwang will do?' I asked Mal as we poured the beers into thick glass tumblers.

'He'll tough it out,' Mal replied. 'I've seen him do it before. He'll be okay.'

'Good. It would be a pity to lose him.'

'It would be a complete disaster,' Mal said as he pressed down on a black knight which was threatening my king. The board beeped and flashed red lights. 'Check.'

'Mate,' I added.

'Is it?' Mal said in surprise. 'Oh yes, so it is.'

'A well planned move, eh?' I muttered. 'It's good to see someone who knows exactly what they're doing,' I added sarcastically.

'Aye, well, it's the Highland gambit again.' Mal grinned.

'I can't see the point of playing openings with you. I mean, there I am desperately going through the first eight moves of the Sicilian defence and you just do anything that comes into your head. The whole point of openings is to respond in a series of pre-planned moves. You know, develop the pieces, castle, control the centre, that sort of thing, not just charge headlong through the middle of the board.'

'Maybe, but it worked.'

'Yes, but I had a much stronger position,' I protested.

'And lost.'

'Yes, but there is the aesthetic side of the game you know.'

'You still lost.'

'Yes, but . . .'

'Attack, always attack, that's the key,' Mal said emphatically. 'Straight into the middle and rip his throat out. That's how to play chess.'

'Not very subtle though, is it?'

'You don't need subtlety. You just need to win.'

'So how come you are now six three down in the series?'

'Am I? I thought we were all square.'

'Nope.'

'Ah, well then, attacking does of course have its risks. You know what I mean – nothing ventured, nothing gained, better to live a day as a lion than a life as a lamb, that sort of thing.'

'It's a board game, not philosophy!'

'Could be both,' Mal suggested defensively. 'How you play the game is just as much a reflection on how you live your life, don't you think? It's all about style, about attitude . . .'

'It's about winning, for God's sake, which at the moment you are unstylishly failing to do.'

'Yes but when I win, I win well.'

'Hang on, you didn't even know that move was checkmate until I pointed it out.'

'Instinctively I did,' Mal said with a mischievous glint in his eye.

'Felt it in your waters, did you?'

'Yes, sort of.' Mal stood up. 'And talking of waters, I need a pee. Come on, let's get back.' He drained the last of his beer.

9

ARM AND A LEG

The stony track was hemmed in by steep walls of scree rising up to black broken rocky ridges. At the head of the narrow river valley a huge rock buttress partially obscured the lower slopes of a dramatic mountain pyramid whose flanks were sheathed in ice. Vertical cliffs, looming darkly from the shadow of gauzy clouds, were sprinkled with dustings of the night's snowfall. We had decided to call it the Matterhorn peak since none of us knew its name. It had dominated the last few miles of the approach to the small settlement of Ari where we planned to spend a couple of days acclimatising. As the clouds lifted I framed the view and took a photograph. I bent down to replace the camera in my rucksack and heard the distinct sound of cattle bells and distant short cries of encouragement. Yaks were approaching slowly, drifting off the track in search of morsels to eat. Occasionally a rock whizzed by them, expertly thrown by their handlers, and they veered back on course. They were not our animals, and I was surprised to see that they were unladen. The empty wooden load frames swayed atop the thick tasselled blankets on their backs. A few were adorned with faded red pieces of cloth sewn into the thick black hair of their ears. The animals looked ill-kempt and weary.

The leading yak was an unusual grey and white colour, its large wet black eyes prominent in the whiteness of its face. They were all pure bred yaks, no hybrid yak-cow crosses among them. At these high altitudes the traditional thick-set long-haired yaks perform better than the dzos, but they are susceptible to both disease and heat in the lower valleys. Except in winter, these yaks are rarely taken below ten thousand feet and their ability to endure the harsh mountain conditions have made them indispensable to the Sherpas and Tibetans alike. They are sure-footed and for the most part easy to domesticate. I've heard that there are still small herds of wild yaks roaming the high border regions between the two countries.

As the train of animals swayed past me with steam rising from their flanks in the high cold air I saw that the handlers were Tibetans. They had obviously made their trade in Namche and were returning to Tibet over the Nangpa La pass. I had seen blocks of whitish pink rock salt on sale in the market as well as Tibetan carpets and wondered why these traders were going home unladen. Maybe currency was more valuable than trade goods. Even so, given the wealth of goods available in Namche, it seemed strange to see nothing at all going back across the border. Then it struck me that there might be Chinese border controls at or just beyond the pass. It was a worrying thought since there was that German expedition which had been heavily fined the previous year for attempting to climb Cho Oyo by crossing from Nepal into Tibet at 19,000 feet, just as we hoped to do.

I followed at a leisurely pace behind the yaks, watching the men giving occasional abrupt whistles and sharp guttural cries to chivvy the beasts along. As we swung away from the claustrophobic shadow of the Matterhorn peak we emerged on to a snow-covered hillside above a wide open valley. Ahead lay a dazzling horizon of snow peaks etching the blue sky with their jagged white ridges and summits. In the valley below I could make out a flat cultivated area and the patchwork patterns of dry stone walls built on the floor of the u-shaped glacier valley. We were moving along a natural shelf, remnants of lateral moraines banked up when the glacier had reached further down the valley in colder periods. There was no sign of the glacier yet but the terrain was becoming noticeably more barren and rocky.

As we traversed above the valley towards the distant peaks

I saw a small building, more a hut than a house, nestled up against a circular dome-shaped hill at the head of the lower valley. I could just make out tiny figures working in the fields nearby, bent over their hoes in rhythmic digging movements. I saw three people approaching the hut and could make out the bright colours of western clothes and the rucksacks that they were carrying. It was Mal, Clive and José.

By following the Tibetans I had nearly missed the campsite at Ari in the valley below. It was an understandable mistake since I had expected it to consist of more than one small dilapidated dwelling and a few sparse fields. If the clouds had not rolled clear of the valleys quite so quickly I would have found myself wandering towards Tibet without a clue as to where I was. Since I was carrying only a small day sack with a camera, a water bottle and a warm jacket, it would have been a cold and miserable night out in the open if I had gone on without spotting the others below. Hurriedly I began to descend the scree slopes in long jumping strides, letting my feet slide with the scree and hoping that I wouldn't set any larger boulders in motion. The thought had barely crossed my mind before I found myself running headlong downhill chased by some very large and ominously fast boulders.

As sometimes happens, a small rock avalanche had been triggered as I crossed the bed of a gully where the stones had accumulated in deep layers. I might have felt more confident if I had not been wearing shorts. My bare legs felt painfully vulnerable as I made ill-judged leaps down the river of stones. The thought of tripping over, or of being hit by one of the flying behemoths from behind, made me take more and more desperate bounds down the gully, which only set larger masses of rock on the move.

I was soon surrounded by masses of rocks and boulders and loose earth sliding past me at different speeds and condemned to keep frantically hopping and leaping with it like a barefoot madman dancing on a sun-scorched road of bubbling tarmac. The forward tilting lunge down the hillside meant that I had no time to look up and see where I was running. I hoped there were no unseen cliffs ahead of me.

At the moment when I thought that I was going to receive the sort of gravel rash that only schoolboys can dream about, I spotted a large rock slab protruding from the bed of the gully. I made a despairing leap for it, hit the slab with considerable force, and breathed a sigh of relief when it chose not to go tobogganing off with the rest of its enthusiastic comrades. I perched on the slab, breathing heavily, occasionally forced to jump up and down to escape the more eager boulders bounding towards me. After executing a few nifty skips and hops to avoid the shrapnel of the passing rock avalanche I waited for things to calm down. From far above me I heard the raucous laughter of the Tibetan yak herders who had witnessed my moment of insane rock-skiing and were cheering and whistling, and clearly wanted to see more. I scurried furtively out of the gully and angled down towards the valley at a more reasonable pace, glad of the comforting shelter of the dust cloud that hid me from my audience. At least I had cheered them up. Watching a rich foolish westerner in shorts playing hopscotch with a hillside was obviously just the tonic they needed.

'How's it going?' Rick Novak asked as I put my pack down in the field by the hut.

'Oh, fine,' I said, examining the cuts and scratches on my calves. 'Just doing my bit to amuse the natives.'

'Have you seen our yaks?'

'No. There were some empty ones with those Tibetan guys, but ours can't be far behind. They left well before me this morning.'

'Gee, wasn't that just a great walk?' Rick said with his usual infectious enthusiasm.

'It was until the end,' I answered ruefully. 'Do you fancy some tea? Is there a Sherpani in that hut?'

'Yeah, but should we go in? I mean, heck, it might be rude or something.'

'Oh, I wouldn't say so. She'll be glad of the business I imagine. Where's Mal?'

'He's in the lodge with José,' Clive said, nodding towards the lone hut as he passed by in search of a good flat tent site.

123

The single room above the cattle byre was dark and cramped. There was no glass in the windows which had been shuttered against the icy wind. Smoke hung in thick layers and caught in my throat as I ducked in through the doorway. It swirled in the sudden breeze and I caught sight of Mal and José sitting cross-legged on the wooden floor at the far end of the room. There were no benches or tables. Large bales of rolled-up mattresses were stacked against the wall behind them. A woman was tending the small fire at the base of the hearth. It was a typical square of dried clay and mud, just under waist high, with two holes on its work surface. A large blackened pan covered the central hole and flames licked up the sides. There was a bright red glow from the open hole beside it. The woman paused from blowing into the base of the oven where some small sticks protruded. She smiled shyly and gestured for me to sit anywhere I chose on the floor.

I moved over towards Mal in a crouch, convinced that the ceiling was lower than it was. The smoke was so thick at head height that I could barely see anything.

'At least it's warm,' I said as I lowered myself to the floor and rubbed my goose-pimpled bare legs.

'It's excellent, isn't it?' Mal said.

'I'm not sure about it being excellent,' I muttered, peering dubiously at shadows and shapes lurking behind the smoke.

'She's got some wonderful gear here,' Mal said, pointing to an intricately-carved wooden vessel by the fireplace. Firelight glinted on old burnished brass inlaid into the tall cylindrical object.

'What is it? A butter churn?'

'I'm not sure. It might be for making tea. Tibetan tea with salt and butter.'

'Oh, right. Is that how they make it? What's it like?'

'An acquired taste,' Mal said with a grin.

'Pretty disgusting then.'

'Aw, I thought it was pretty neat,' Rick said cheerfully. 'Do you want some?'

'Er, no thanks. I'll stick with lemon tea, or chang if it's any good.'

'It is.' Mal raised his glass of warm greenish liquid. 'She makes good chang. Not as good as Ma Chang, but good.'

Ma Chang, as we had dubbed her, ran a lodge in Pheriche, a village that lay a long day's walk from Everest base camp. Her excellent chang had been responsible for some mighty headaches in the past. Each household makes its own chang, a form of millet or rice beer, and the quality and strength varies from house to house. I got the impression that each family recipe was carefully guarded. Sometimes it is thin and clear and sharp, and sometimes - especially if made from millet – it is thick and speckled with a grainy texture.

I waved to the woman of the house and she came over. I greeted her with the word *'namaste'* and held my palms together, fingers steepled as in prayer. She responded in the same way and smiled. I have always been charmed by this traditional Nepali greeting which means literally *'I praise the god within you'.*

'And have you seen these blankets?' Mal said while the woman was pouring chang from a big Chinese thermos flask into my glass. 'They're good quality. Tibetan, I'm sure.'

I glanced at the horse blankets and rugs draped over the rolled up mattresses. They were grubby, darkened by years of smoke and soot, the patterns barely visible after years of wear and tear.

'How do you know that they're any good?' I asked. 'They look old and worn out to me.'

'Exactly,' Mal replied forcefully. 'That means they are not the sort of thing sold to tourists. These are the genuine article, and if you got them washed properly you would be amazed at how all the designs and colours would come back.'

'If any of those Tibetans come across the Nangpa La I'll bet you could buy a decent rug from them,' I said.

'Yeah, and you'd get a good price as well,' Mal added. 'Cut out the middle man. They'd be worth three times as much in Kathmandu.'

'I just met some guys going back empty,' I said, and I told them about the yak train. 'You know, it might be a bit of a problem having a base camp on a trade route.'

'How do you mean?' Mal asked.

'Well, it's some temptation, isn't it? All that gear lying around and us up on the hill.'

'It'll be fine. There will always be staff at the camp, cookboys and that.'

'Did you hear about that guy who had his boots nicked last year?' I asked, fuelling my distrust and paranoia.

'Hey, no shit, he lost his boots? Heck, that's no place to lose your boots,' Rick said with a cheerful laugh.

'Yeah, he was a Yugoslav, or was he a Czech?' Mal said. 'Anyway, they only took the outer plastic shells but it did for him all the same. He was just preparing for a summit bid when they were taken.'

'I suppose you can't blame them really, can you?' I added. 'It's like that man who was asked why he liked robbing banks saying because that's where the money is.'

'Too much of a temptation, you mean? Heck, we must seem sickeningly rich to them with all our expensive gear, and they have a hard life,' Rick added.

'They could just be natural thieving little scrotes,' I muttered into my chang. 'Those guys looked distinctly dodgy to me. Wouldn't trust them further than I could throw them.'

'The gear's arrived.' We looked up to see Dave Horrox peering into the smoke from the door.

'Right,' Mal called and swilled down the last of his chang. 'I'll get these.' He handed some rupees to the woman by the fire as I heard muttering in the smoke behind me, followed by a thump, a yelp, and the sight of Rick emerging from the gloom rubbing his head where he had collided with the door frame.

The yaks were tethered in the camping field surrounded by the handlers and our Sherpa staff. Girth ropes were unhitched and the heavy double-sided loads lowered gently to the grass. A few yaks had been tied down to heavy rocks so that their nostrils were pressed to the stone, the nose rings stretching the nostrils painfully and preventing any chance of them lashing out angrily with their horns. I made a note of their features and decorative coloured tassels so as to remember to avoid them in future. I had been told that the red tassels sewn into their coats indicated that they were dangerous. I found this out when I was innocently approaching a magnificent specimen with an abundance of red cloths hanging round its horns and backed away hurriedly, but the petite Tibetan girl who was loading the beast seemed quite unconcerned. With brisk efficiency she reached high over its shoulders to pull on the girth ropes exposing her soft belly to the threat of the yak's horns. Perhaps it liked her. It was certainly in fine condition, with its coat groomed and combed and a pretty display of red and yellow cloths sewn into its coat.

I have since learned that some of these adornments are to do with various rituals. Cattle are decorated with ribbons and coloured strips of prayer flags, and blessings are made and prayers said over them in the hope of good harvests, plenty of strong calves and bountiful milk production. Despite this knowledge, I'm still highly suspicious of red-flagged yaks, perhaps because of matadors, red capes and fighting bulls, and I give a wide berth to any that I see with nose rings.

We spent the following day resting at Ari. The more enthusiastic team members stomped heartily up the surrounding hills to gain precious acclimatisation. I hacked and spluttered my way up a twisting rocky gully that cut up the hill opposite our camp site. At my high point I thought I could just make out the distant summit of Cho Oyo. It looked huge. A plume of snow streamed from the summit, indicating high winds despite the sunny weather. The rocky bulk of Dragkya Chnulung partially obscured the view. I watched Clive and José, the two strongest climbers after Mal, high on one of the mountain's subsidiary ridges.

I sat in a grassy hollow overlooking a range of hills to the east. There was a notch cutting a high pass through these hills and I thought I could make out the faintest line of a path. Beyond lay the beautiful and much visited lakes at Gokyo. The Ngozumpa glacier ground its way down in a river of ice and jumbled moraines fed by the glaciers and ice fields of Cho Oyo and Gyachung Kang. Beyond this valley, by circuitous passes, lay the Khumbu itself and the mighty bastions of Everest, Lhotse and Nuptse. I knew that the busy trail crowded with trekkers and expeditions lay no more than a dozen miles as the crow flies from here yet it might as well have been a thousand miles away.

'Hi, Joe,' Geoff Pierce called as he came round the hillside. 'How are you feeling?'

'Oh, pretty good,' I said. 'A bit breathless, but that's to be expected.'

'Yeah, I feel quite strong. It looks big doesn't it?' he said, nodding in the direction of Cho Oyo.

'Yes, if that's it.'

We relaxed in the warm spring sunshine, talking about the mountain and the forthcoming climb. Geoff was understandably cautious and doubtful about his first attempt at Himalayan climbing.

'Well, you've certainly leapt in at the deep end,' I laughed. 'Didn't want to try anything too big for your first attempt at climbing, eh?' He looked a bit crestfallen and worried. 'Don't fret,' I added. 'Just take it steady, nice and slow, listen to your body, and do as much as you want to do. It might be technically straightforward but there's no such thing as an easy climb at that height, so be careful.'

'Is there a route through to the Khumbu?' he asked, looking at the notch in the hills.

'Yeah, but it's not done very often and I think it's a bit necky.'

When clouds blocked out the sun the temperature plummeted and what had been a refreshing breeze quickly stripped the heat from our bodies. We hurried down towards the warmth of the tents, small dots of colour against the backdrop of the fields far below us. By mid-afternoon the cloud covering had thickened and snow began falling from a leaden sky.

Huddled in the warmth of the hut I peered at the chessboard in the smoky gloom. The red lights blinked sharply in the half-darkness but it was almost impossible to distinguish one piece from another.

'Do you know I found a leg today,' Mal said, apropos of nothing in the silent gloom.

'What sort of leg?' Dave Horrox asked.

'Human, femur, with a broken hip joint.'

'Are you sure it was human?' I asked.

'Absolutely, and I'm pretty certain it was from a European, judging by the length of it.'

'What, just a leg bone? Nothing else?' Geoff asked.

'Yeah, odd that. I found it in the stream bed coming down from that notch in the hills.'

'So where the heck did half a man's leg come from – if it was a man?' Rick wanted to know.

'Maybe he was eaten?' I suggested.

'That's a possibility, but even so there would be plenty of evidence lying around. Bone chips and fragments and so on.'

'You said the top of the femur was broken?'

'I'm no pathologist, so I can't really tell whether it happened before or after death, but I have this theory about how it got there.' Mal paused and raised his glass to the Sherpani who was offering more chang. 'Whoever that leg belonged to is presumably dead, right?'

'Unless he was just this extraordinarily careless sort of bloke and lost it, you mean?' I said with a smirk.

'Aye.' Mal grinned at me. 'So what is the significance of the fracture in the head of the femur? An avalanche is one explanation. It might have killed him outright, or smashed his hip and crippled him so that he couldn't rescue himself.'

'We're presuming that he was alone then?' Geoff prompted.

'Makes sense,' Mal said, glancing up at him. 'If he had been in a group, there would have been people to rescue him, or recover the body.'

'Not if he was buried,' I pointed out.

'We'll never know,' Mal conceded, 'but I reckon he was on his own, and got himself killed, but not at the spot where I found his thigh. It's too low to be swept that far in an avalanche.'

'Why would he be alone up here?' Rick asked.

'Maybe he was trying to cross over to Gokyo to avoid having to go back down through the police post at Thami.'

'If that's the case, how did he get up here past them originally?'

'Oh, any number of ways,' Mal replied confidently. 'Chwang says that Tibetans seeking exile sometimes come over the Nangpa La and cross over to the Thengpo for that very reason. If you look at the map he could even have come from the Rowaling by crossing the Tashi Lhabsta pass at Pachermo and then over those cols. You know where I mean, Joe?'

'Yes, but it's a hell of a trek. Wouldn't fancy it on my own.' I said.

'No, nor me,' Mal agreed. 'Anyway, so he gets stuffed somewhere up towards that notch, a lot higher than I went, hence no body. Now the bone was picked clean, so it's obviously been exposed to the elements and scavengers for quite some time. And it's not uncommon for birds to carry big bones up to great heights and then release them over rocky ground in the hope that they will break open and let them get at the marrow.'

'It would have to be a big bloody bird.'

'There's plenty of them around. Lammergeiers could do it, or the Himalayan griffons. There were some above the valley today. You know it's thought that many of these birds use the high passes such as the Nangpa La, or even the South Col, as migration corridors through the mountains? They found some dead eagles on the South Col in the sixties.'

'Okay, so what about the fracture?'

'Well, it could have been a cause of death, I suppose. He could have bled to death if he had ruptured his femoral artery, or just been made crippled and helpless.'

I shuddered at the thought of the pain and loneliness of such a death.

'But it's an odd looking fracture site,' Mal continued. 'More consistent with an impact than a twisting break. That's what I reckon it is. It's the impact point where it hit the rocky stream bed after being dropped by a bird.'

'Wow!' Rick breathed, clearly enthralled with the mystery. 'What did you do with the bone, Mal?'

'Left it in the stream.'

'What? You didn't bury it?' I exclaimed, and immediately felt stupid.

'What's the point? The poor bastard is probably all over the place by now.'

Rick stood up and walked over to the door. He peered out and then called back.

'Hey guys, it's really laying it down out here.'

We went over and watched the heavy snow flakes drifting down. Several inches had already piled up on the stone steps leading down from the door. People drifted back towards their tents leaving a brown trail in the muddy yard.

10

BLEAK HOUSE

The door of the hut opened and a blast of icy air rushed in, swirling the smoke in waves towards us. A white glare from the snowstorm formed haloes round the tall figure ducking through the low door. I sat with Mal in the smoky gloom. A candle flickered on the edge of the hearth and a glow of red light glimmered in the grate. Small oil lamps, jam jars with wicks, spluttered smokily on the window ledges creating a shimmering light. The man approached the Sherpani and talked urgently to her in a low whisper. She stopped smiling and looked suddenly serious and concerned, nodding her head vigorously and waving her hand to indicate that someone hovering outside the door should come in. I looked questioningly at Mal.

The man was dressed in unusual clothes, appearing for all the world as if he were part of the Jesse James gang. He wore a calf-length, belted, canvas drover's coat. His thin dark face, with a narrow band of black stubble along his jaw-line, had a cruel look. He wore stout boots laced high above his ankles. His heavy cotton trousers were tucked protectively into the top of his boots. The brown wide-brimmed Stetson-style hat gave him a roguish appearance. I wouldn't have been surprised if he had pulled back the folds of his coat to reveal a pair of holstered pistols and a set of cowboy-style leather chaps. It was difficult to tell whether he was European or Nepalese. He was a tall man, over six feet, and powerfully built.

'Wonder where he came from?' I whispered to Mal,

nodding towards the man as he looked over in our direction.

He seemed momentarily hesitant and then spoke rapidly to the Sherpani who shook her head. With that he seemed to have come to a decision and called out loudly to whoever was outside. After a long pause the door was pushed forward a few inches and a head appeared. It was of a young man, squinting into the dark and smoky room. Snow flakes blew in over his shoulders. The tall man removed his hat and hit it against his thigh, knocking the heavy wet circle of snow from its broad rim. He gestured to the young teenager at the door to enter. The boy stepped cautiously into the room, looking apprehensive and suspicious.

Another head popped round the door, peered in, and then disappeared out into the snow. There came the sound of animated conversation muffled by the thick walls and the falling snow. The boy crept stealthily into the room and squatted in the darkness to one side of the hearth. The Sherpani smiled at him but he didn't appear to acknowledge her. Abruptly, the tall man – who I took to be a guide of some sort – marched to the door and barked some peremptory orders. The noise of the discussion subsided. Another boy appeared in the doorway and made his way softly into the room, followed by another and another. When I had counted fifteen arrivals and the room was packed with quiet squatting figures, I turned to Mal.

'Who are these people?'

'Tibetans, I think,' Mal replied in a whisper. 'None of them looks much older than fourteen or fifteen.'

'How many more of them are there?'

Other heads peered into the room. We were now effectively trapped at the back of the room, with a sea of heads between us and the doorway. Another tall man, dressed in similar cowboy garb, appeared and spoke to the first guide. He kept glancing at us as he spoke, and was clearly uncomfortable with our presence.

'It's odd, isn't it?' Mal whispered when the door finally closed. 'They're all men, all young men. No women at all.'

'So? What's odd about that?'

'I don't know. It just doesn't seem right.'

'That guy's old.' I leant towards Mal, keeping my voice to a whisper and nodding towards a bald man with grey eyebrows and tired, wrinkled eyes.

'A monk, probably.'

'How do you know?' I asked, examining the old man's thick sheepskin coat that was belted at the waist. There was no sign of the traditional maroon robes of Tibetan monks. His head hadn't been shaved. He was naturally bald.

'His prayer beads.'

Mal nodded at the man's left hand protruding from the flared cuffs of his sleeves. His fingers were constantly fiddling with a necklace of beads, flicking one after the other between thumb and forefinger.

'Have you seen that?'

I pointed to a child being led through the ranks of squatting figures towards the fireplace. The Sherpani smiled at the boy and stroked his cheek. The old monk – if that was what he was – leaned forward and picked the child up under his arm pits and hoisted him into his lap. The child was no more than four years old.

'You don't think that kid has just crossed the Nangpa La, do you?'

'Looks like it.'

'But he's not much more than a baby,' I hissed.

The boy sat quietly in the old man's lap, looking remarkably relaxed and alert for a child that had just made an arduous crossing of a nineteen-thousand-foot Himalayan pass in a snow storm. He gazed around him with wide intelligent eyes, not in the manner of a child searching for something playful but with an adult appraisal of his surroundings. There was something eerie in his manner which I found unsettling.

'What's he doing here?'

'I don't know,' Mal muttered under his breath. 'And why are you whispering? I can hardly hear you . . .'

'Because you are,' I replied in a slightly louder voice. I still didn't wish to draw attention to ourselves. Most of the young men didn't seem to have noticed us in the shadows. The few that did averted their eyes and looked away, almost as if they didn't want us to see their faces. 'They look scared of something,' I said.

'Yeah, I noticed. Wouldn't you be?'

'Why?'

'Perhaps they think we might betray them,' Mal said rather melodramatically.

'Betray what?'

'Well, if they're illegal immigrants. If they've just fled across the pass - they shouldn't be here. They could be sent back, and then they would be in deep trouble with the Chinese authorities.'

'Oh, I see what you mean,' I said, suddenly connecting. We had been in the gloomy, smoky darkness for so long that I had lost touch with where we were, and what was happening outside. 'They're escaping Tibetan refugees,' I added hoarsely as Mal raised his eyes to the ceiling. The atmosphere in the small house seemed to be electric. All at once I felt a heightened sense of drama, of furtiveness, as if just by being here we were all part of a fiendish conspiracy. 'What could have happened to the toddler's mother, I wonder?' I said almost inaudibly, as if to myself.

A lad of fifteen or sixteen was kneeling close by us, rocking back and forwards on his knees, pressing the heels of his palms hard against his eyes.

'Snowblind?' I whispered, and Mal nodded.

'And those two.' He glanced to the left where two boys were braced against the rolled up mattresses. One was rubbing his eyes, the other peered through slitted lids. Both rocked back and forth in that unconscious way people have of dealing with pain. I winced at the thought of what the smoke must be doing to their inflamed eyes.

Snow blindness can be fiendishly painful, like ground glass thrown into the eyes, rasping against the lids, liquid hot tears like molten metal consuming the soft vulnerable gel. I knew the feeling. The insatiable desire to rub the torture away which continues even when the dazzling reflection from the snow has gone. The sudden burst of laser-like burns from exposure to the slightest light source are almost unendurable. The dark shadows of the hut must have been welcome relief from the bright glare of the snow but the acrid wood smoke would only renew the agony.

The boy kneeling close to me stopped rubbing and, pulling his hands away slowly, screwed up his face into wrinkled grimaces as he tried to open his tear-stained eyes. The door opened and a brilliant white light suddenly flooded in. Through the slight gaps between his wet eyelids I saw the hot redness of the whites of his eyes and the brimming tears building and then flowing down across his cheeks. He let out a low moan and pressed his hands back to his eyes. His neighbour placed a comforting hand on his rocking shoulder.

'Look, there's Chwang.' Mal nudged my elbow. I looked up, placing my hand on the floor as I did so. There was a high beeping sound and heads turned swiftly to stare at us and then down at the flashing red lights on the floor. There was a shuffling movement like swaying crops as Chwang moved through the crowded bodies. I turned the chess set off and closed the lid, suddenly ashamed of this piece of western luxury.

As Chwang crouched down beside us the door opened again and another group of young men crowded into the room. The two snow-blinded boys nearest me hissed with pain and jerked their heads down and away from the bright white light of the door as if they had been slapped sharply.

'Have we got any eye ointment?' I asked Mal, who was whispering to Chwang.

'Er, yes, somewhere in the first aid kit, but not very much.'

'Couldn't we offer them some?' I stared pointedly at the lad rocking back and forwards.

'Yeah, but it's in my tent. I'm just finding out who these guys are. Chwang says they are Khampas.'

'Khampas, eh?' I said, and turned to look again at the young men who had come in from the snows. Were these the fabled warriors of the high Tibetan plains? Were these the ferocious and proud fighters that Heinrich Harrer wrote about, the men who had helped the Dalai Lama escape into exile in India?

'And you know what?' Mal added.

'What?'

'I reckon they might be fighters.'

'Fighters! This lot? They're only kids.'

'Yes, but look at them,' Mal reasoned. 'They're all male. All young. They're all of a fighting age.'

'They don't look like soldiers to me.'

'Yes, maybe, but perhaps they're going to India to be trained.'

'What in the refugee camps in Dharamsala? I doubt it somehow. Anyway the Dalai Lama's against violent resistance, isn't he? In any case, I thought that sort of organised guerrilla campaign ended in Mustang twenty-five years ago. Don't you remember that bit Jeff Long wrote about the Khampas being betrayed by the C.I.A. and Nepal in Mustang when they were tricked into laying down their arms and most of their leaders killed themselves?'

'Yeah, but that's no reason for it not to have started again. What was that guy called, the leader who escaped and was then ambushed by the Nepalese army? Wang something.'

'Wangdu,' I said. 'You know that Long spent time in prison in Kathmandu with some of the survivors of that last stand, trying to piece together what happened to him.'

I remembered reading Audrey Salkeld's account of Wangdu's death in her book *People in High Places*. I had been surprised to learn that Nepal had sent 10,000 troops against the Khampa guerilla's holding out on the Mustang border in 1974. Washington and the C.I.A. had lost interest in the Tibetan cause by then and had re-opened diplomatic dialogue with the Chinese. Until that time the Nepalese had ignored the activities of the ageing guerilla force on its border with Tibet, but then China wanted revenge for the frequent humiliations that the rebels had inflicted upon their troops and pressured Nepal into finishing them off. After the rebels had rejected negotiations the Nepalese prepared to send in troops. The Dalai Lama, horrified at the thought of wasted Tibetan lives, sent a message urging the rebels to surrender.

Wangdu, the renowned and charismatic Khampa warrior, a near-mythic fighting leader, persuaded his men to obey. Bitterly disappointed but unable to disobey the Dalai Lama's orders, some of the rebels committed suicide by jumping into the river or slitting their own throats.

Despite the Khampas laying down their arms, Nepalese troops entered Mustang, reneging on their promise of amnesty, and arrested the rebels. Wangdu fled with forty men into the hills of Tibet and after a month of hide and seek with both Chinese and Nepalese forces headed west, hoping to find sanctuary in India. A massive Nepalese ambush on a high pass called Tinker trapped Wangdu and his small escort as he reconnoitred a way over the pass. He and four comrades were killed. The rest of his men, trapped by advancing Chinese soldiers, fought their way through the Nepalese ambush to seek sanctuary in India.

I peered at the contorted face of the young boy rocking on his knees beside me and wondered whether he could really be one of those legendary fighters that I had heard so much about. They all seemed so young, so passive, that I found it hard to believe they were even Khampas let alone potential guerrilla fighters.

'What does Chwang think?' I asked Mal.

'He's not sure,' Mal replied, 'but he knows that they are Khampas.'

'Could they be monks?' I asked. 'The old man is obviously their leader. Maybe they are on a pilgrimage to see the Dalai Lama?'

'Some pilgrimage,' Mal snorted. 'A one-way exile, more likely. Anyway, they don't look like monks. No shaved heads or purple robes.'

'Well, if they were fleeing in disguise maybe they wouldn't want to look like monks. See if Chwang can find out anything else. After all, he knows their lingo.'

I heard Mal muttering something to Chwang who slipped away to the other end of the smoky room. The tall guide was moving amongst his flock, and I saw small bundles of notes extracted from deep within their coats. The money was held tightly and counted slowly with great deliberation. There were a few bundles of possessions, but some carried nothing with them except the clothes they wore, and only the guides seemed to own rucksacks. The old man counted out notes for those who either had none or couldn't count. He spoke softly and encouragingly to the young exhausted travellers. The guides handed out packs of cigarettes in exchange for the notes. None of them bought food. The cigarettes were lit and passed around the room. I was amazed to see after what must have been a long and gruelling trek that so little attention was paid to sustenance. Perhaps they were used to such hardship.

Two large steaming bowls of stew were passed to the guides by the Sherpani while a few of the boys delved into their pockets and produced small plastic bags of tsampa, a flour made from roasted barley. They ate it dry, nibbling at their food. Some offered their meagre supplies to their neighbours. The Sherpani distributed glasses of tea. It was drunk hurriedly, with the insistent craving thirst of high altitude. When the thirst had been slaked some mixed their tsampa into the tea to form a sticky gruel which they dug from the glasses with their fingers. The snowblind victims seemed oblivious to what was happening. Friends pressed them to eat and drink. Only the boy beside me made an effort, taking the hot steaming glass and drinking the fluid quickly, his eyes streaming with tears in the steam. He tried a few sucks on a cigarette but shook his head with a low moan when the smoke burnt his eyes.

'I'm not sure I like those two,' I said at last, nodding towards the warmth of the hearth where the guides sat eating their stew. 'They don't seem very concerned do they?'

'I reckon they're paid just to get them across the pass,' Mal said. 'They don't look as if they have anything in common with the rest, do they? Different build, different clothes, even different faces.'

'How far do you think they'll go with them?'

'Not much farther. Chwang says they'll probably try to get past the police guard post at Thami tonight when it's dark.

This snowstorm should help them.'

'Won't it just show their tracks?'

'Oh they'll soon be covered, and anyway none of the guards will be out in this weather looking for them.'

'Even if they get past Thami, how will they get through all the check points on the trail to Kathmandu?'

'I haven't the foggiest.' Mal shrugged. 'But it's a regular thing apparently. Chwang says that more and more are coming across. Some go into the Rowaling, some into the Khumbu. He says they come over even in winter.'

'They cross the Nangpa La in winter?' I said incredulously, louder than I'd meant to speak. A few heads turned to stare at me. Two of the youngsters got up and moved away.

'They don't all make it either,' Mal whispered. 'Frostbite injuries. Chwang was just saying that there was trouble at Thami not so long ago. A group like this were rumbled and they tried charging past the post. A couple of them were shot and wounded, but most got through.'

'Bloody hell!' I muttered. 'Hey, maybe you're right. Perhaps they are fighters. They certainly look like a cohesive unit, don't they?'

'Yeah, like they're some sort of cadre. That's what struck me,' Mal said. 'Have you noticed the way they look up whenever we mention the Dalai Lama? It's immediate isn't it.'

I noticed how the young men seemed to be taking more and more of an interest in our conversation. 'They seem pretty nervous of us as well, sort of wary,' I added.

'I don't blame them. We're probably the last people they want to meet.'

I watched the Sherpani as she began lighting more small oil lamps with a flaming twig from the fire. She placed the lamps on the window ledges and by the side of the hearth, replacing the spent jars. The crude little lamps provided an extraordinary amount of light, or perhaps our eyes had adjusted to the stygian gloom. The flames flickered in the draught from the shuttered windows, lending an incongruous festive air to a bleak room packed with tired and frightened refugees.

In the soft yellow glow of their flames I could see how

poorly equipped the young Khampas were to make such an arduous journey. Only a few of them wore thick warm chubas, the traditional heavy Tibetan jackets. The rest were clad in a motley assortment of Chinese-made western-style clothing. There were a few with denim jackets, but most of them sported flimsy nylon wind-cheaters that would have been of little use in the storm that had swept over them on the pass. There were a couple of lads in red nylon track suit jackets with white go-faster stripes down the sleeves. These 1970's-style clothes looked out of place in the smoky old house that had remained unchanged probably for centuries. Thin cotton trousers were tucked into cheap white nylon sports socks and almost all of them wore baseball boots – the old white rubber-soled black canvas boots with the familiar white dimples on the ankles.

I couldn't imagine what it must be like to walk so far over such rugged terrain in this inadequate footwear. Trail-breaking in baseball boots through deep drifts in sub-zero temperatures at heights of up to nineteen thousand feet was a recipe for disaster. I wondered how many were nursing frost-bitten toes. The slightest storm could be dangerous and, in winter, fatal. A cold snap would inevitably lead to amputations of toes and fingers, and limbs, even for those who survived the crossing.

'Have they really come over the Nangpa La?' I asked Mal.

'So Chwang says,' he replied. 'It's hard to believe, isn't it?'

'What about the kid? He couldn't have walked all that way, surely?'

'They probably carried him most of the way. They don't have any yaks with them.'

I looked at the boy who sat on the old man's knee by the fire. There was something familiar about him – the direct intelligent gaze, the way he held himself stiff-backed, erect and formal, and the over-large sheepskin hat with its flapping ear pieces. With no hint of fear or anxiety, he seemed to me to be observing his colleagues from his lofty vantage point with a regal, confident air. I couldn't put my finger on what it was that seemed so familiar until he turned towards me and met my curious stare. At first I recalled a photograph I had seen of the Dalai Lama's infant brother, taken some years ago by Heinrich Harrer in Lhasa. Then in the soft lamplight, gold reflections glimmering on the boy's round baby-fat cheeks, I remembered a scene from the film *The Last Emperor*, set in the palace throne room in the forbidden city of Peking. In a wealth of soft wood colours and burnished gold, silk brocades and a wash of candlelight, the infant emperor was seated upon an oversize, ornately carved wooden throne, draped in luxurious silk robes and wearing an oversize fur hat. Fawned over by courtiers and advisors, he sat blank-faced, impassively surveying his surroundings just as this young boy in front of me did.

It wasn't only the semblance of light and colour and atmosphere but also the startling way in which the boy held himself as he slowly turned to observe me in a knowing and unquestioning manner. Whereas his companions had at first been wary of Mal and me, careful not to sit too close to us until the pressure of the numbers forced them against us, the child had walked directly towards us before being captured by the hands of the old man. When the Sherpani had stroked his cheek and smiled at him with motherly affection, he had paid no attention, almost as if it had not happened. Most children I know would have responded instantly to such tenderness. This boy's mannerisms were those of an adult. I sensed that he had never played, never really been a child. There was not the slightest hint of childish behaviour. I looked away, breaking eye contact with him. There was something odd about him, something unfathomable and disturbing.

'You don't think that kid has something to do with it, do you?'

'To do with what?' Mal asked as he waved his glass at the Sherpani who rose and nimbly stepped between the reclining bodies with the thermos of chang.

'I was wondering whether they were protecting him in some way. Perhaps he is important for some reason.'

'What do you mean, important?'

'Well, you know,' I said beginning to wish I hadn't brought it up, 'he's quite special, isn't he?'

'I still don't see what you're getting at.'

'There's something about him; something unusual.' I stumbled on. 'If you must know, he reminded me of the child in *The Last Emperor*, the way he is so adult and bright, and it just occurred to me that perhaps he was the same thing, a sort of living god, a reincarnate lama . . .'

'Living god?' Mal looked at me suspiciously.

'Well, you know, like the Dalai Lama.' I whispered, conscious of curious stares from all around the room.

'You think he's the Dalai Lama?'

'No, no, you pillock,' I snapped. 'Like him, like the way he was chosen. Don't they somehow know who the next one will be and go out and search for him? They have to find the child who was a previous Dalai Lama, a reincarnated consciousness – or something of the sort. God knows how they do that.'

'And you think this is the next one, do you? When the present one isn't yet dead?' Mal spoke with a sarcastic grin.

'No, no. I just wondered whether this kid was someone special, like an important lama of some sort. One they selected for special reasons, signs, portents, oracles, that sort of thing. It would explain why these guys are here. They are a sort of guard of honour – no, a protection force, to shield him and keep him safe.'

'Right,' Mal said slowly. 'And you've thought all this out because you saw a film, have you?'

'Well, yes,' I muttered. 'I suppose, put like that, it does sound a bit dumb. He just looks such a strange child, so self-possessed and grown up.'

'Probably traumatised by what he's been through,' Mal observed drily. 'God knows what these people are running away from, but I'll bet it wasn't pleasant.'

He was looking around him in an oddly furtive manner, keeping one hand down by his side.

'What's up with you?' I asked.

'I've got my camera here,' he whispered, opening his hand to show the small compact camera concealed by the fold of his fleece jacket. 'I've been wondering whether I should take a picture. What do you think?'

'Well, I don't know,' I said uncertainly. 'It might freak them out.'

'That was what I was thinking,' Mal said, looking tense. I could see he was working himself up to do it. 'It's just that they are so unusual. Chwang says a lot of the people coming over are mixed groups, families, often with enough money to bribe the police. Not like this lot. I'm still thinking they might be a fighting group, and if your incarnate lama theory is right, it would be a chance to document the escape. What do you reckon?'

'I guess it won't harm them,' I said in some confusion. 'We're not going to shop them to the police, are we?'

'Yeah, but they don't know that, do they?' Mal hissed. 'They could turn nasty . . .'

'What? Do you think they would attack us?'

'I'm not sure . . .'

'Well, why not let me get out of here and back to the tents and then you take the picture and see what happens. Make sure you get one of the kid.'

There was suddenly a tense conspiratorial atmosphere in the room, or at least in our minds. I was very conscious of how out-numbered we were.

'I bet they've got knives,' Mal whispered. 'Most Khampas carry them, and you can see how on edge they are.'

'Why not ask them? Ask the old guy. He seems to know who we are. The guides must have told him we're an expedition going in.'

'Yeah, why not? Chwang could ask him if he'd mind.' Mal slid the camera into his pocket and peered over the heads in search of our Sirdar. 'It would be a pity not to get some record of this.'

At that moment there was a stir in the room. The second guide ducked in through the door, brushing snow from his shoulders. He looked across at the old man and nodded gravely. The man spoke quietly and at once there came a scraping, shuffling noise as the group struggled wearily to their feet in the confined space of the lodge.

'What's happening?' I asked Mal in a normal voice as we found ourselves suddenly surrounded by milling legs.

'I think they're off.'

'But it's still light.'

'It'll be dark in an hour, maybe earlier with this snow. If they leave now they'll be in Thami around midnight.'

'What about the ones who were snowblind?' I said, standing up and looking round for the boy who had been rocking on his knees. He had gone. I saw the other two helped to their feet by their companions who steered them gently towards the door. They held their hands across their eyes and pulled woollen scarves up above their noses as they approached the white glare of the doorway.

'I was going to get them some ointment,' I said lamely as they stepped out into the snow.

'They'll be okay,' Mal said softly as he got to his feet in the now empty room. 'Come on, let's see them off.'

By the time we reached the door the group had faded to a thin, single file of distant black figures trudging through the snow. A black muddy track led back to where we stood.

'Damn! I never got that photo,' Mal said ruefully.

'I wish we could have helped them,' I said, watching the distant black line slowly being engulfed by the softly falling snow. 'They were really suffering.'

II

WHEN TERROR CAME

I sat in the contoured high-backed leather seat watching the optician fiddle with a bewildering battery of dials suspended above me. There was a buzz as the seat slowly reclined me into a supine position and I watched as the laser was lowered on its hydraulic arm towards my face. I shrank back into the seat and gripped the edges in a frightened spasm. There was a hum of electric motors and a green light sprang into view.

'Right. Now focus on the green light,' the man said. 'And whatever you do, don't move your head, don't look away, and keep staring at the light. Okay?'

'Hmm,' I said nervously.

'Okay, here we go. Nice and steady. Totally still for a twenty second burn please.'

I gritted my teeth and stared fixedly at the light. There was a sharp crack as the laser burst into life.

The bright sharp-edged Day-Glo green dot began to blur. The rat-a-tat-tat of the laser machine seemed unnaturally loud. I was aware of the optician leaning against the machine to my left. I watched the dot break up, spread out like an ink stain, and the surface of my eye burn, the soft gel bubbling. There was the sweet aroma of smoking flesh.

'That's it, that's it,' a disembodied voice wheedled in my ear. 'You're doing well. Keep focusing, keep focusing. Not long now, not long.'

And the death rattle of the laser went on and on while I observed my own eye melt as if I were looking through a goldfish bowl, watching through the thick base as the glass

146

turned fluid beneath an invisible heat. He had said the burn would take twenty seconds. No time at all, he'd said, but now the seconds stretched away into minutes while I tried to resist the urge to pull my head away and lurch out of the chair. *He could blind you. Don't move or he'll blind you. Trust him. You must keep trusting him.*

The green target dot had disappeared. I felt the panic building. There was nothing to focus on any more. If I couldn't focus, maybe my eye would wander? He would lose where to burn. Should I tell him I could no longer focus, could see nothing but bubbling opaque gel? There was an abrupt sharp click as the laser cut out and then a silence so sudden that I could hear the thump of my heart and the soft tattoo of the pulse in my temple.

I let out a whoosh of held air. Breathing deeply with a shuddering tremor, my nostrils were filled with the stench of burnt eyeball. There was no pain. He said there would be no pain but I hadn't been able to believe him.

I tried to blink. The lashes of my right eye scraped across the cotton wool eye patch that had been taped across it. Nothing happened to my left eyelids. They were clamped open with a steel clamp inserted above and below the eye ball. Two stainless steel lips curved up and down, spreading the lids apart, holding them wide so that the eye bulged from its gaping socket.

'Well done, that was good.' The voice broke the silence. 'How do you feel?'

'Uh!' I said absently, and I then came to with a start. 'God, that was scary. Christ! You never said it would be like that.'

'It's not so bad,' he said with the casual indifference of someone used to burning eyes on a daily basis.

'How do you know? Been through it yourself, have you?' I snapped, irritated by his arrogant manner. I felt embarrassed by my fear, by the tell-tale shake in my voice, by the fact that I was close to tears.

'Ah, come on,' he replied, 'strong tough man like you. I've treated pensioners, old ladies, who haven't let out a squeak.'

'Not much bloody imagination then.'

'It didn't hurt, did it?' He went on in his annoyingly mocking manner. 'Didn't last long, did it? What's all the fuss about, eh?'

'The fuss? The fuss is about watching my eye burn, smelling it bloody burn. The fuss is to do with thinking I'm being blinded, for God's sake.'

'Yes, the smell is strong, I must admit,' he conceded. 'I've heard that some of the patients report that they smell the same burning whenever they see a green light.'

'Oh, great!'

'It only lasts a couple of months, nothing to worry about. It's all in the mind. Psychosomatic, you see.'

'No. I don't see. That's what I said. I can't see a thing.' I was beginning to panic.

'Oh, don't worry about *that*,' he said airily, as I glared blindly at where I thought he was. 'You're not blind. It went well. You should have trusted me. The old women have no problem there,' he said with a hint of smugness.

'Well, I'm not an old woman,' I said testily, 'and I can't trust people when they're boiling my eye. And for that matter, I still can't see.'

'That'll be it, I suppose,' he droned on. 'You are used to being in control whereas these women are not.'

'What?'

'Women,' he said condescendingly. 'They make much better patients. They're used to being told what to do, you see. It's not hard for them to release control so they trust me. You on the other hand . . .'

'What is this?' I snapped. 'Some sort of group meeting for mysogynists? I still can't see.' I heard my voice rise sharply and wondered why the nurse hadn't poked him in the eye with a scalpel.

His face swam into view, looming in front of me as if I were seeing a reflection in a fairground distorting mirror.

'Soon fix that,' he said as his distorted face faded back into opaque greyness. 'Just scrape off the surface,' he added, and I flinched and pressed back into the chair. 'Don't worry. You won't feel a thing.'

'Heard that before,' I muttered as I watched the pink blur of his hand floating into view. There was a silvery glint of metal.

I felt drops of liquid splash on my cheek and the view through my gold-fish bowl suddenly flooded clear like a pail of water washing across a pane of glass. For a moment his hand and the steel surgical instrument were pin sharp and then the tip of the steel closed against the surface of my eye and I watched in a curiously detached way as it scraped across the lens. It reminded me of a surreal film I'd once seen with clouds cutting across a full moon and the shocking slice of a cut-throat razor across the surface of a staring eye. I squirmed in the seat.

'Not to worry,' he said in his patronising, calming tone. 'Soon be over.' I gritted my teeth and resisted the urge to grab his testicles and squeeze as hard as I could. At least it might give him a better conception of discomfort.

Vision smeared into a blur until another squirt of fluid cleared the view. It dabbed across my eye again but I could feel nothing. There was something oddly unsettling about being conscious during the operation, about being able to watch it all happen from the inside out. It made me feel nauseous.

'Okay, that's that.' The hand suddenly disappeared from view. The chair hummed and I felt myself being lifted into a sitting position. A nurse reached forward and held my upper arm reassuringly.

'Careful, you may feel a little dizzy,' she said with a smile.

I stared at the wall opposite me. There was a rack of shelving with various instruments and bottles stacked on it. I read the title of a framed print hanging on the wall above the shelves and studied the picture for a moment before it hit me. I could see it. I could read the letters.

'Good God!' I yelped. 'I can see . . .'

'I know,' the optician interrupted. 'I thought you'd be impressed.' He was smiling broadly.

'That's amazing.' I re-read the title and then looked around the room, seeing things that before the operation had been invisible. I had gone from a state of fuzzy, blurred, severely myopic vision to twenty twenty sight. The fear and nausea vanished in an instant as I gazed round in wonder.

I had waited years for this technique of laser operations to be perfected. Over eight diopters of short sight in both eyes had always worried me when I was climbing. If I lost my glasses or contact lenses in a storm on a mountain I would be virtually blind. My anxiety about experimenting with surgery seemed to have paid off. The machine was so precise that it could burn away a cell leaving my neighbouring cells undamaged and this precision meant that the shape of the distorted myopic eye could be altered far more accurately than with scalpel incisions. In my case they were taking a chance since usually they can only guarantee success with myopia of up to about five diopters. There was no pain during the operation but because of the greater area burnt I was soon paying the price for it.

Four hours later the pain started. He'd said I might suffer mild discomfort. He never mentioned agony. He didn't warn me that it might feel like sulphuric acid eating through my eye.

As the throbbing started behind my eye I began to suspect him of underplaying it. The building aching pulses began to form a hard solid rod stretching deep into my head burrowing like a hot worm through the sponge of my brain. It felt as if a thin white-hot skewer was pushing through to the back of my head. The sensation of tugging and pulling as the gluey flesh of the eyeball stuck to the dry glowing steel drove me to distraction. I clenched the bedclothes, trying to resist the urge to claw at my eye, to do anything that would stop the merciless fiery scratching at the inner walls of my skull.

I wasn't prepared for that dreadful burning that scalded my mind for the next fourteen hours, for the face-clawing agony of molten iron filings beneath my tear-flooded eyelid. I was scared that I might pluck the offending organ from its socket, gouge it from its red-hot seat and throw it across the darkened room. Sitting propped against plumped pillows, moaning, drumming my heels against the mattress, I took sharp, shallow, hissing breaths. Please stop it. *STOP!*

I jerked awake to find myself lying face down in my sleeping bag. Nylon brushed across my face and I rolled on to my side, searching for the drawcord and the cinched tight hood. It wasn't there. I twisted violently, feeling the claustrophobic panic rising up, scrabbling behind my head with my right hand. I felt the thin cord with its hard plastic toggle and pulled sharply. A wash of cold air hit the back of my neck. There was a glimmer of light inside the bag. Rolling on to my knees, I pulled the fabric of the bag round until I could get my head out of the hood and then slumped on to my side, breathing heavily.

I stared at the green walls of the tent illuminated by the early morning sun. The tinny sound of aluminium pans broke the silence and was followed by the roar of the primus stoves. I heard the cook boy's sudden laughter. *Why on earth had I dreamt about my eye operation?* It had been so vivid. I rubbed my eyes and peered blearily from between my fingers, surprised that there was no burning pain. I sat up and shivered as the icy cold burst a rash of goose-pimples across the bare skin of my back. As I reached for my pile jacket I remembered the Khampas, the boy rocking in tears, moaning, pressing the heels of his palms hard against his burning eyes. So that explained the dream; a subconscious recollection of that same agony only a few months before.

A stab of guilt hit me when I thought of the pain I'd suffered despite all the anaesthetic drops and ointments and remembered that I had offered those four lads nothing. I knew better than most what they were feeling and I had done nothing to help them; I had just sat there and discussed crazy theories about who they were and where they had come from and let them stumble off into the evening snowstorm blindly holding the shoulders of their companions for guidance.

I crawled out of the tent, feeling the sharp stones biting into my knees, and stood up slowly. The sun had barely lifted above the jagged black horizon of mountain ridges. A chill wind scurried up the rocky valley where we had camped raising puffs of grey dust. It was a bleak desolate scene. We were far above the vegetation line in a moonscape of barren grey scree and chaotic boulder falls – the shattered debris left behind by a retreating glacier. It was hard on the eye. On the surrounding valley walls snow dusted the jumble of rocks, black shadows sharply etched by morning light and pristine white. Blue-grey cliffs of granite streaked with frozen meltwater rose above the valley floor behind which a shapely sweep of blue ice led the eye up to a high corniced summit.

The harshness of the landscape lent the peaks a radiant contrasting beauty. I took a long, deep breath and stared at the mountains, feeling the familiar rush of excitement coursing through me. Despite misgivings, I was still captivated, enchanted by their dominance, by all the potential they held so silently. There was about them a sense of menace thinly veiled by beauty; an intoxicating blend of threat and arousal. I was an intruder standing within their shadows, overwhelmed by the aura of their power, glad to be living there again – scared, excited and spell-bound.

The dark blue shade of retreating night lay in a band low on the horizon. Above it a pale sun was washing the sky clean in layers of graduated colour. I watched the dark shadow line cast by the intervening mountain ridge in front of me. It would be a good hour before it had crept past the tents and the rising sun spilled its heat into the valley.

I looked around the campsite as the tents were dismantled and the loads packed. There were several dome-shaped circular stone shelters. A few had open roofs where the key stones had fallen in. I went over to the largest shelter and crawled into the small doorway. It was markedly colder in the dark shadows. Dappled sunlight filtered through cracks in the stone. I lay on my back and gazed at the pattern of stones forming the arched roof. The heavy flags of granite pressed coldly through my thin t-shirt. It was like being in a stone igloo. There was an aroma of damp musty earth and dung and the wet charcoal smell of scattered fires.

I wondered whether the Khampas had stayed in these shelters on their way through. I imagined them huddled in steaming groups, chattering through the night, talking of the journey to come and how long in exile they might be, voicing fears in quiet murmurs lest an enemy should hear, or sitting silently in dumb misery, waiting for the dark hours to end. I doubted whether laughter would have echoed from the rocky chambers unless it was tinged with a manic sadness; the brief voluble excitement of crossing the pass and leaving Tibet erased all too quickly with the knowledge of what they have lost. It would have been a bitterly cold night of shivering sleeplessness.

I sat up and was surprised to find how low the roof hung. My head grazed the keystone. I heard the sound of yak bells and men's voices coming from the sunshine beyond the walls. There came the clicking sound of hooves on rock and the snorting heavy breath of the beasts as they lumbered past. The sounds seemed to echo from another distant world.

There was an aura of past lives held within the shadows. I fancied I could see dark figures from ages past huddling round the walls, travellers and exiles leaving a faint trace of their passing. I read the patterns of old fires on the smoke-blackened roof stones. The wash of a sudden breeze fanned the open doorway. There was an eerie spectral feeling in the old shelter, as if I had broken into an ancient tomb, invaded the sacred hallowed centre of some prehistoric barrow and awakened long dead souls.

I shivered involuntarily and chided myself for being so fanciful. There was nothing there, I assured myself, and looked around warily, unable to disbelieve my senses. Something was listening. I could hear its presence, smell the ancient fetid dampness of its passing, feel the quiet sadness in the stones.

The central stone in the roof was a thick slab of granite about four feet square. I couldn't work out how the builders of the shelter had managed to set it in place without bringing down the whole structure. Its massive weight obviously served to press down and outwards on the curving stone walls keeping them solidly upright. I tried to imagine what would happen if it came loose. I lay back again and stared at the cold stone which seemed to press down upon me. A ticking sound seemed to be coming from the stones. *Had they moved?* I looked around in alarm. Suddenly the dark cold shadows and the crushing claustrophobic atmosphere of the shelter rushed over me. The centre stone hung directly above where I lay on my back. It was poised in uncertain stillness, waiting to fall. If it came down I would have no chance to move in time. Anyway there was nowhere to go. Once the centre fell, the walls would cave in on top of it.

I sat up hurriedly and crawled towards the entrance, feeling the tingle of pins and needles running up my spine. The moment I had acknowledged my fear and turned my back on the dark shadows behind me I was consumed with the urgent need to escape from the shelter. I emerged blinking into a bright spray of sunlight and stood up, glancing back to check that no ghouls had rushed out after me. The shelter looked harmless enough. Crouching down and peering inside, I wondered why I had been so spooked. A gust of wind passed the entrance, creating the sort of whooming sound you get when you blow across milk bottle tops. I straightened up and chuckled at my over-active imagination.

'Hey Joe. How're you doing?'

'Eh?' I looked round to see Geoff Pierce standing close by. 'Oh, just having a look inside.'

'Did you see the grave?'

'Grave? What grave?'

'There's a grave further down the trail. We passed it yesterday.'

'I didn't see a grave,' I said, trying to remember the walk up from Ari.

'It wasn't very obvious,' Geoff added, 'just a mound of stones really.'

'It wasn't one of these that have collapsed then?' I asked, and Geoff shook his head. 'So how did you know it was a grave?'

'Chwang told Mal about it. It's quite recent apparently. Some woman died crossing the pass.'

'How?'

'I don't know,' Geoff shrugged. 'She got sick I suppose. Probably the altitude.'

'Was she Tibetan?'

'I'm not sure. Could have been, I guess. Why?'

'Oh, nothing,' I replied. 'It just struck me as odd. There were no women in that group yesterday, that's all.'

'So?'

'It's just odd, that's all, especially with that kid being there.'

'I suppose so. I hadn't thought about it really.' He looked perplexed for a moment and then said brightly. 'The grave. It's not far away. Do you want to see it?'

'Er . . . no,' I hesitated. 'I don't think so. Not now – I'll see it on the way down.'

As I set off after the others I couldn't get the woman's grave out of my mind. *Who was she? Who buried her? Why did she die?* I wondered why she hadn't been brought down for cremation or given a traditional Tibetan air burial. *Maybe they don't do that round here.* I turned the volume up on my personal stereo and tried to forget her but she kept coming back to me. It was troubling to be hexed by the memory of a grave that I hadn't seen and a woman who, for me, might never have existed. I thought of the wind-whispered voices in the shelter and remembered the sense of past souls calling to me from the shadows.

The bleak emptiness of the stony valley where she had died unsettled me. I hoped that she had died in the company of others, even the arms of strangers, rather than face that ultimate loneliness by herself. The barren mound of rocks she had become was something to warn passing travellers and quicken their steps; a grim lonely site, unmarked, almost indistinguishable from the surrounding rubble. I turned my back to the valley and strode towards the sunbathed mountains astride the Tibetan border.

I wondered whether she had been with a group or if passing traders had stumbled across her body as it was released by the melting winter snows. Perhaps she had been separated from her party in a storm, slowed down by her weakness until at last she succumbed to the insidious grip of winter's frost. Maybe she simply got lost in a blizzard and passed the group of shelters never knowing how close she was to protection from the storm.

Who was to say that it was a storm or altitude sickness that had killed her? Her frailty may have already been created long before she attempted to cross the pass. She could have been a nun escaping imprisonment and torture, half-starved, staggering down from the mountain, abandoning her beloved homeland and carrying away with her the scars of rifle butts and electric batons, broken bones and battered organs. I remembered Ama Adhe's story that gave me disturbed nights for weeks after I had read it in David Patt's harrowing book, *A Strange Liberation*.

The mountain was rocky and snowcapped, reaching high into the thin, cold, blue sky. She said it was called Nyate Khalori. It was surrounded by lakes and thick forests teeming with wildlife. There were meadows carpeted in wild flowers, so many you couldn't name them, so numerous that they collected in your toes as you walked.

Nomadic people tended their herds of goats, and sheep and cattle on the passes and the plains. In the winter her family tended their crops in the lowlands and in the summer they drove their livestock up to the highland regions where they joined the nomads and their herds of yaks. People went up into the highlands and pitched their tents, and there was music and dancing, horse races and chang drinking, sharp-shooting competitions, games and picnics.

In the early mornings all the cattle would be sent up into the hills. The yak and dri, the dzo and dzomo spent the day grazing while the people boiled the dri milk, churned the butter and made yogurt. After that the day was free for games and fun and times of inner peace for everyone. There was respect for each other and freedom for all to do as they wished. Monks were living among them, performing pujas in their tents, and there were many temples and monasteries and hermitages. Life was very good. This was how Ama remembered it.

There was little violence in her world. Killing and brutality were considered dirty. The Buddhist doctrines of Karma and rebirth were an inextricable part of life, giving it meaning, and everyone had a sense of right and wrong. Present and future lives were dictated by one's behaviour. Generosity, kindness and patience in life would be rewarded with health, and happiness and security, while evil, stealing and cheating would bring poverty and unhappiness. It was not a perfect world, but to Ama it was idyllic, full of happiness and peace. That was her memory of four decades ago. Today that idyll has gone forever.

When the Chinese soldiers came to Ama Adhe's tent she knew that they had come for her. Her role in helping the resistance to the Chinese had been discovered. It was very early in the morning. Her infant daughter was gurgling peacefully in her sleep. She was dressing her four-year-old son, putting on his yellow chuba. She heard the dogs barking and, looking up, she saw the group of armed policemen and civilian officers walking towards the tent.

While they tied her with ropes her daughter remained sleeping but her son became hysterical and clung to her when she was dragged outside. She pleaded for mercy, begging to be left with her children. A man hit her hard in the ear, permanently damaging her hearing and the others began hitting her with rifle butts and kicking her, and her son became even more distraught. As the men hauled Ama away, the boy ran after her, screaming incoherently, and she saw her infant daughter laughing happily as if it were all a game. The little boy fought desperately to cling to his mother but the men were too big and strong, kicking him hard and high into the air. He got up and came for her and they kept hitting him and kicking him until he could no longer keep up. She glimpsed her son in the far distance as she was marched to the nearby Dri Tse Monastery, which had been converted into a prison – a tiny, hysterical figure in a yellow chuba, running and running and crying for his mother. She never saw him again.

Ama spent the next twenty years in nine Chinese prisons and camps. Tortured, starved and worked nearly to death, she survived. Most of her fellow Tibetan prisoners did not. Two years after her arrest, in the autumn of 1960, at about the time of my birth, she was transferred to a lead mine at a place called Gothang Gyalpo on the border between Tibet and

China. Most of the women she had been with in Dartsedo Prison had died of starvation. She joined a hundred other women in the lead mine. Over the next three years all but four of the women died. In that short time Ama learned that 12,109 prisoners were starved to death in that hellish camp.

Throughout her suffering she clung to the hope that her children had been looked after and were still alive. After sixteen years she learned from her brother, Nyima, that her son was dead. Hysterical with shock and grief, the toddler had been inconsolable, refusing comfort and food from friends and neighbours, biting their hands to get away from their care, until he escaped and ran away, a tiny yellow figure lost in a sadness he could never have imagined. They found his body in the river where he had fallen and drowned.

She came back to a destroyed, denuded, unrecognisable homeland. Almost all the monasteries had been sacked and destroyed. Only nine out of 1,500 survived. Hardly any people remained. Her mother had starved to death, her husband had been killed, probably by poison. Her brother-in-law, who had been imprisoned with her, had been executed, his brains blown out as he stood in front of her. Ama also lost her 'elder' mother, brothers and sisters, and three close relatives to the Chinese. Only her infant daughter had survived.

Nothing whatever remained of her former life. There was no place in which to practise her religion. The monks, lamas, and nuns and the entire educated class of their community had been exterminated. What remained was fear and deprivation and a police state.

Ama Adhe's story is only exceptional in that she survived the holocaust visited on her land and the Tibetan people by the Chinese. Holocaust is exactly what it was. There is no other word for the systematic destruction of a people and its culture. The Chinese claimed that they came into Tibet to liberate the serfs from their feudal slavery. In attempting to transform Tibet into Mao Tse-tung's insane ideological notion of a workers' paradise, they virtually annihilated it. His dictum had been: 'Destroy first and construction will look after itself.'

In the first thirty years of Chinese occupation one fifth of the population – one million two hundred thousand Tibetans – were killed either by execution, slow torture or starvation. More than six thousand monasteries, convents and temples were destroyed and their precious statues and contents melted down or sold for foreign currency. Sixty per cent of Tibet's literary and cultural heritage was burnt. The region of Amdo has become the world's biggest gulag, believed to be capable of holding ten million prisoners. One in every ten Tibetans were imprisoned, one hundred thousand in labour camps. Tibet was now China's largest Inter-Continental Ballistic Missile base.

On 7th October 1950, 30,000 battle-hardened troops of the Chinese People's Liberation Army invaded Tibet from six different directions and there was little effective resistance. Tibet's forces were outnumbered ten to one, as well as being disorganised, inexperienced and poorly armed. Ancient flintlock rifles, swords and horsemen were no match for modern automatic weaponry in the hand of a veteran army that had recently fought and defeated Chiang Kaishek's Nationalist army. Only six months before invading Tibet the Communists had declared China a People's Republic. In defeating the Nationalists the People's Liberation Army (PLA) had taken the Tibetan province of Amdo and entered the formerly Nationalist controlled province of Kham. Tired of war, they hoped to achieve a peaceful 'liberalisation' of Tibet.

Resistance from the Tibetan army collapsed almost immediately, encouraged by the Governor of Kham, Ngabo Ngawang Jigme, who at first news of the advancing Chinese abandoned his forces and fled. The mountainous territory of Tibet's eastern provinces bordering China would have been an ideal place in which to fight a guerrilla campaign. Supply lines for the Chinese were tenuous and there were no roads for tanks, artillery and armoured cars. Many thought it would have been impossible to sustain the invasion if there had been resistance in the east. Some even believed that the Chinese could have been defeated. On his flight westwards, Ngabo met an armed Tibetan relief column sent from Lhasa to support the struggle for Kham. On 20th October he ordered his troops to throw away their weapons and flee with him. He was not the bravest of men at a time when Tibet sorely needed heroes. If only he had been Wangdu. After that, Tibetan military resistance came to an end. It is questionable whether they could have driven back the Chinese but at very least they could have seized the chance to show an indifferent world that they did not wish to be returned to 'the great motherland' and would fight to the death to preserve their independence.

Amdo, the north-east region of Tibet, and Kham, the eastern region, had long been disputed territory. Most of these areas were ruled by fierce independent kings and chieftains who owed no allegiance to the Dalai Lama's rule. He governed the territory between the border with Ladakh in the west and the border with Sichuan on the Yangste river in the east. This area, called U-Tsang and part of Western Kham is all that is left of Tibet today. The huge kingdoms and tribal lands of Amdo and Kham have been absorbed into the Chinese provinces of Qinghai and Gansu, Yunnan and Sichuan, and it is these regions which contained the vast bulk of Tibet's mineral wealth.

The fiercely independent Khampa warrior-chiefs had no liking for the rule of what they saw as an arrogant, aristocratic government in Lhasa. Although devout Buddhists and loyal to the Dalai Lama they hated the Lhasa officials and resented the appointed governors of the Khampa regions who made them pay high taxes. At the time of the Chinese invasion some of the tribal chiefs were actually planning to seize power from the government in Lhasa. With the collapse of Tibetan military resistance, the Chinese were only too pleased to play upon these existing tensions, but the softly softly approach did not last long. There had been frequent Chinese incursions into the region before the Communists arrived and Khampa hopes that this new invasion would soon end were quickly dashed. This time the Chinese were here to stay.

Crude political indoctrination was soon followed by mass deportations of Tibetan children, even babies, to China to learn about the wonders of communism and free their parents to work harder. Feeding the Chinese invaders became a terrible burden as food prices escalated and the villagers could no longer afford to feed themselves. Less than a year after the invasion Tibet's economy was in tatters, inflation rose to 500 per cent and the capital, Lhasa, was on the verge of famine, its granaries exhausted by the demands of the Chinese.

A massive road building programme which sought to connect Chengdu in the east and Xining in the north with Lhasa was undertaken. The road from Chengdu to Lhasa crossed fourteen mountain ranges and seven major rivers at an average height of 13,000 feet. As they worked the road builders died from starvation and exhaustion. The roads were vital if China was to subdue the mountain regions. Although they claimed to have built them with the interests of the Tibetans in mind, the truth was far more prosaic. By the end of 1954 China was able to flood the country with the masses of troops, supplies, tanks and artillery that were needed to overwhelm Tibet completely. With the army came the Chinese settlers. Mao Tse-tung wanted to outnumber the Tibetans in their own land by four to one. Tibet's ancient trading links with Nepal, India, Sikkim and Bhutan ceased almost overnight and the nomadic tribes were forced to trade exclusively with China.

The stranglehold on the country was now complete. It was time to re-educate the people. Atrocities became commonplace. Mass public executions, sometimes involving two to three hundred victims at a time, took place in Amdo and Kham. The liberators were seen for what they were, colonial oppressors of unspeakable barbarity.

Mao's policy of 'divide and rule' separated the landowners and chiefs from the serfs and set one against the other. Those loyal to their employers were arrested, tortured, and executed. When there was no longer any support for the chiefs and landowners, the 'bloodsucking exploiters' as the Chinese regarded them, the authorities felt strong enough to move openly against them. Thousands were denounced simply for being prominent members of society. Before long the Chinese were confident enough of their power to take on what they knew had to be eradicated, the monasteries, and the religion that was the glue holding together the fabric of Tibetan lives. The horror, not yet visited on Lhasa, came first to Amdo and Kham with unimaginable ferocity.

By 1956 open revolt had broken out in both provinces. The flash point in Kham was probably the destruction of the Lithang monastery, one of Kham's largest. The Chinese surrounded the building after the monks refused to carry out an inventory of their possessions and urged the people to fight back. Threatened with air bombardments that the monks could scarcely imagine, they resisted the siege for sixty-four days. Four thousand men, women and children, sheltering within the monastery, were slaughtered by Chinese jets strafing and bombing the building. Lhasa was not to know of Kham's despair until the refugees trickled into the city three months later. By then a savage scorched earth policy had been started which was to unite the people against the Chinese and create a legacy of genocide and terror that still remains today.

In 1957 twenty-three Khampa chieftains finally abandoned their historic feuds and agreed to fight together against the Chinese. They formed a guerrilla force named the Chushi Gangdruk and with arms and training supplied by the C.I.A. they began a war from the impregnable fastness of their native mountains, though they could never hope to defeat the Chinese. Thousands of monks, driven from their monasteries, abandoned their vows of non-violence and joined the rebels. This desperate struggle was to continue for seventeen years until the final murderous betrayal of General Wangdu in August 1974 in an ambush on a high pass leading into Nepal. To all intents and purposes the resistance of the Chushi Gangdruk, weakened by in-fighting and old age, died with him.

Amdo and Kham suffered the brunt of Chinese atrocities. When, after many months, the Dalai Lama heard of what had happened in Kham he could scarcely believe it. He was faced with the nightmare of perpetual confrontation and endless retribution meted out to the Tibetan people.

By 1959 Tibet's once self-sufficient society was in tatters, and famine and starvation rampant. Mao's Great Leap Forward policy had been a disastrous blow to China's economy. Poor harvests and a rift with the Soviet Union, which cut off imports of grain, meant that the country turned to Tibet for its grain. Harvests were seized and what was not consumed by the army in Tibet was sent to the motherland. Rice was grown instead of the traditional barley which flourished at such harsh altitudes. Tens of thousands of Tibetans died of starvation while China sang the glories of the socialist workers' paradise of Tibet to the world. Parents fed their children tsampa mixed with their own blood, people ate dogs, cats, rats, insects, and the refuse thrown out by the Chinese. Even the undigested grain found in the soldiers' horses' manure was scavenged. In Lhasa cart-loads of corpses were taken from the prisons daily for burial in huge pits or to be used as fertiliser in the fields. Production increased enormously but for the people it meant virtual slave labour and mass starvation. They saw nothing of the fruits of their toil.

This was Mao's road to happiness. It was a road of blood and a descent into a dark age of medieval tortures and insane depredations. How could any sane human being reconcile such behaviour – scalding alive, burying alive, dismemberment, crucifixion, mass execution and starvation – with the ideology of the socialist cause? The methods employed to strike terror into the hearts of the people and crush any further resistance were so sadistically cruel as to make it easy to believe that they couldn't possibly have happened.

Monks were publicly tortured and executed, whole villages wiped out, monasteries razed to the ground. Refugee camps and nomad settlements were machine-gunned. Abbots and lamas were forced to copulate with prostitutes, monks made to copulate with nuns in public and desecrate their holiest sacred images and destroy their precious libraries. In some places entire communities, lamas, monks, nuns and novices, were slaughtered and the buildings systematically levelled.

Yet there are numerous eye-witness accounts from

survivors fortunate enough to escape the slaughter. Their stories present mind-numbing reading and indict China for a reign of unspeakable terror and perhaps unprecedented brutality, more cruel than the worst excesses of this violent century. It is hard for us to imagine such depths of depravity to which human beings can sink.

Alexander Solzhenitsyn said, 'The Holocaust that happened in Tibet revealed Communist China as a cruel and inhumane executioner – more brutal than any other communist regime in the world.' Stalin, Pol Pot, and Mao – the communist seems to have an aptitude for genocide.

Government policy or not, it was individuals who committed these atrocities, individuals who cannot wipe their hands clean of the stains of their inhumanity, cannot say they were simply carrying out orders. To do such things requires far more than obedience.

How could it have happened? Tibet's remoteness must have contributed. There is a tendency to think of Tibet as a mysterious, fabulous kingdom set amidst the great mountains of the world, a land that is both physically and spiritually aloof, an enigma, not existing in the real world. This isolation, and the preconceptions people in the industrialised world have about the country perhaps helped imprison it behind indifferent walls of silence. In her disturbing account of Tibet's forty-year nightmare in *Tears of Blood* Mary Craig suggests as much. 'Tibet is no fantasy land of mist and magic . . . behind those majestic peaks which isolate it so effectively from an indifferent world, it endures the kind of lonely martyrdom which ranks in this, our bloodiest of centuries, with Stalin's persecutions and purges, the destruction of Europe's Jews by Hitler, and the blood-lust of Pol Pot in the killing fields of Cambodia.'

An ancient peace-loving non-violent civilisation was driven to the point of extinction. Even as the dark horrors descended upon Kham, the people of Lhasa had no inkling of what was about to befall them. The Dalai Lama was still desperately trying to save his country, trapped by his own compassion, his innate pacifism and distaste for violence. Mary Craig describes him as both a political king and a pope, the spiritual leader of the Tibetan Buddhists. 'The Dalai Lama, the present incarnation of Chenresig, the Buddha of compassion, the patron deity of Tibet, is not so much a god in the shape of a man as "a divine idea that has been realised in a human being to such an extent that it has become its living embodiment."' What hope did he ever have of dealing with the insanity of Mao's China?

To shatter all loyalties and destroy any shred of social patterns, the Chinese introduced *Thamzing* struggle sessions in which the victims were accused of being 'counter revolutionaries' or 'exploiters' before being tortured, humiliated, and often killed. The people were forced to attend these sessions and take part, to applaud as their loved ones had every shred of dignity stripped from them, suffered execrable tortures and were then publicly executed. Any of those horrified onlookers who wept or failed to show sufficient enthusiasm were subject to beatings and their own 'struggle sessions'. Even children were forced to attend the *Thamzing*. If a man survived a *Thamzing* he was no longer a man. He lost everything. His own people destroyed him and in their guilt and shame they tried to forget him; he ceased to exist.

The purpose was to destroy and rebuild; to create a population without individuality or independence, slavishly under the iron rule of the state, efficient, organised and dehumanised.

Tibet's name in China is Xizang, meaning the treasure house. The Chinese, however, underestimated the extraordinary faith the Tibetans have in their religion. They found a people who could not be broken to their will. Instead of freeing them, they had no option but to annihilate them and everything that gave them meaning.

Since Mao's death it has been a common Chinese defence to claim that the destruction of the monasteries, the worst excesses in Tibet, occurred during Mao's Great Proletarian Cultural Revolution. In fact the majority of the monasteries were destroyed between 1959 and 1961, six years before the

Cultural Revolution. This time of national insanity, beginning in 1966, was inflicted by brigades of Red Guards on the entire Chinese population but it was as nothing compared to the terror meted out in Tibet. The assault on the remaining religious heritage was ruthless. These repositories of the nation's culture, centres of learning, great libraries and universities, guardians of the soul of Tibet, were systematically torn down and looted. Anything of value was carted off to China, the rest was destroyed.

The entire population of Dzokchen monastery, over a thousand monks, was forced to marry and destroy their community. When made to torture their lamas and abbots they refused. They had heard of the fate of other monasteries and turned on the Chinese soldiers, killing them all, setting fire to their monastery and escaping to join the growing band of Khampa guerrillas in the mountains. The last straw came when they were ordered to surrender their weapons.

To a Khampa, the rifle was an essential part of his identity. As a warrior people they had defended themselves and their land from the bandits that had infested it. Although devoutly Buddhist, they had always been prepared to fight to defend themselves. To surrender their weapons was to denounce themselves, almost akin to committing suicide. With this final humiliation and the destruction of the Lithang monastery they were set on the inevitable course of rebellion and all that that would bring down on them.

12

GUILTY AS CHARGED

I could not get the young boy who had looked at me with such old and appraising eyes in the lodge at Ari, out of my mind. *Where was his mother? Was she dead too? Could that have been her heaped under the cold hard stones? Had she been with him? Is that why his eyes were so old?* The questions kept returning and there were no answers, only a sense of discomfort.

Eventually the slow hard grind up the lateral moraines leading to base camp pushed the thoughts to the back of my mind. The camp was situated on a bleak desolate plateau of broken boulders. Snow lay in small drifts between the rocks. Looking back, I saw a horizon ringed with spectacular ice mountains which seemed to rear up abruptly from the barren wastes of rock rubble. The low afternoon sun cast a soft golden glow across the summit ridges of two pyramid-shaped mountains. In the foreground, almost lost amid the endless grey boulder fields, I could just make out the squat dark shapes of the Austrian tents which belonged to the only other team on the Nepalese side of the mountain.

We camped in the lee of a vast rock wall sheathed in ice that gleamed a hard blue light down on us. The sun faded behind the jagged ridges, setting them momentarily alight with dancing flames.

The temperature dropped rapidly as we cleared spaces among the boulders in which to pitch our tents. A knifing icy wind scythed across the plateau. I found the remains of an old yak shelter, a three-sided wall some six feet high with flat slabs of rock paving the floor. My tent fitted neatly inside, giving me shelter from the wind and peace from the eternal flapping and shaking of nylon.

I lay in the doorway watching flurries of snow swirling across the ice cliffs at the foot of the mountain which loomed above us. I traced a possible route up its right flank, a great sweep of wind-hardened ice capped with a serac band. The seracs hung out over the icefield ready to plunge down at any moment. I studied them warily. If a sizeable section of those blocks of ice collapsed it would obliterate our camp site in seconds. There was nowhere to run, no place in which to hide.

'It's not bad, is it?' Mal said as he appeared framed between the stone walls of the doorway.

'Do you think they're safe?' I asked, and he followed my gaze.

'Oh aye,' he said after a moment's pause. 'They look pretty stable to me. Nothing to worry about there.'

'Let's hope not,' I said fervently. 'Listen, which one's Cho Oyo?'

'Up there.' Mal pointed towards a sea of rubble-strewn glacier. 'You can't actually see it from here. It's round the corner to the right, but that's the Nangpa La, there. That notch between those two peaks.'

'What do you suppose they're up to?' I nodded in the direction of the distant cluster of tents.

'That's the Austrian-Brazilian Cho Oyo Expedition,' Mal replied. 'Three blokes and a lass. A model, I think, or was she a stewardess?'

'Really?' I said brightly.

'She's getting married to one of them in Kathmandu after the trip,' Mal said, laughing at my sudden interest. 'They've already made one attempt,' he went on. 'Reached eight thousand metres, but they were forced back by wind. Said they'd have one last go. They look pretty wasted to me.'

'Are they doing the same route as us?'

'Yeah. Apparently it is the fortieth anniversary of Herbert Tichy's first ascent by the route we're trying,' Mal said. 'He was Austrian. Do you want some coffee?' I took the small steaming mug of fresh percolated coffee. 'Brilliant. I didn't know we had such luxury with us.'

'We don't,' Mal said with a grin. 'Just Rick and I have got it. Secret stash, so keep the noise down.'

I sipped the strong black liquid and looked up the valley. Beyond a sea of moraines the glacier spilled down from a high bowl hemmed in by mountains. On the right there was an obvious corridor of smooth uncrevassed snow leading up to where a small icecap was just visible. To the left of this corridor, through the jumbled icefall, I could see a chaotic mass of tottering cliffs and crevasses with blue fins of ice poking through the grey moraines at its foot.

'It looks like quite a slog to get up there,' I said. 'We could easily get lost in that lot!'

'Should be fun,' Mal said with gusto. 'There must be a well-marked trail through it. The Tibetans come across all the time.'

'How far do you think it is to the Nangpa La then?'

'We'll put an intermediate camp on it because Chwang reckons it'll take six to eight hours, and then Camp I is way round the corner, another three hours more.'

'Eight hours of staggering up scree – my legs will love that,' I moaned.

'Don't worry about it. You'll soon get used to it. How are you feeling?'

'Oh, pretty good, but I haven't managed to shake off that cold. I've been coughing a lot today. Still I don't think it's a chest infection.'

'Ah well, we're taking it easy for a couple of days so it should give you a chance to recover. By the way, Chwang says he's got some monk to perform the puja tomorrow. He's a cousin of one of the Sherpas. It should be a good one.'

'Why? Will it be more than the usual rice throwing and offerings?'

'Yeah. There's a serious amount of prayers and blessings, and endless mantras. It'll be the full works if the monk does it, and that's good for the lads. Good omens.'

'Do you believe that?' I asked in surprise. 'I didn't think you went for all this spiritual stuff.'

'I'll take every bit of help I can get, and actually, yes, I think it does help. It has a bonding effect on us as well as the Sherpas. I can tell you that when they have bad pujas, it's no joke.'

'What do you mean by bad?'

'Oh, if the prayer flags catch fire or the pole falls down. I don't know what they do exactly, but there's a lot of driving away of demons and evil spirits, and calling on the sacred mountain gods for protection and help. It really freaks the Sherpas out when it goes badly. Me too,' Mal added ruefully.

'Didn't that happen to that West ridge of Everest trip a while back?'

'What? The pole falling down? Aye, and I think the flags caught fire as well.' He laughed at the thought. 'There was some heavy trouble after that. The Sherpas wouldn't go on the hill until they got a new pole and had another puja.'

'Do you blame them?'

'It's all very well – where do you find a damn great pole in the middle of nowhere? It must have taken days to send someone down to fetch one. I just hope our puja goes smoothly. I know it sounds superstitious but I've been to so many now that I would feel uncomfortable without one. I can do without demons on the hill.'

'I know what you mean. It gets inside you after a while, doesn't it? All the prayer flags, and ceremonies. It's impossible to ignore it. It becomes part of our lives when we're here, like we've been dyed by it.'

'Aye, it's a sight more real than all that lip-service religion we have at home. Here they live it all the time.'

The wind tugged at the long stream of prayer flags that Jetta was struggling to fasten to a pile of heavy rocks. They arched out in a brightly fluttering curve, flying at a man's height above the ground. The altar to which they had been attached was only partly built. Chwang and Gompu were attending to the final details. They planted the central pole in the flat stone top of the altar and wedged it in place. Jetta seemed to be doing his best to pull it down. As he battled with loops of loose string and fluttering coloured cotton Gompu strung another ninety-foot length of flags away into the distance, fixing it firmly to a raised spike of rock. He jammed heavy slabs on top of the taut string to keep the flags in place. Jetta could now stretch his line in the opposite direction so that opposing forces held the pole upright. Two more strings of flags were attached and drawn off to distant moorings.

The pole had a sprig of juniper tied to its top and a white ceremonial scarf (*khata*) streamed out beneath it. A rush mat had been laid on the ground in front of the altar facing a small hole built into the front of the waist high plinth of layered stones. By its side lay a supply of fragrant juniper branches for burning on the altar. This practice of burning incense (*sang*) is a pre-Buddhist ritual. A circular woven straw platter laden with offerings had been placed in front of the rush mat. After the puja juniper would be burnt when climbers were on the mountain as a prayer for good weather and fortune. The flags flapping in the wind would send their prayers to all corners of the world. Offerings usually include five types of grain, butter lamps, and chang, but they are not restricted to these items and I have seen anything from Mars bars to half bottles of Polish vodka on offer. Rice is thrown and water sprinkled in all directions. Water plays a purification role in the Buddhist religion. Unlike the Hindus, who indulge in ritual bathing in what are regarded as sacred waters, Tibetan Buddhists have abstracted the ritual to such an extent that they simply dab some on their heads and sprinkle droplets in all directions. There is an old Tibetan saying: 'Hindus clean outside, Tibetans clean inside.'

The puja ceremony was explained to me as an act of giving on the road towards fulfilment, knowledge, enlightenment, and peace, a benefit to mankind. It is also intended to cleanse sins accumulated in the past and expand the devotee's spiritual consciousness. On a personal level, this offers the chance of a better re-birth, an opportunity to escape the privations of the present life and exchange it for a better future. The casual pilgrim may briefly copy the actions of the dedicated *sannyasi* (one who has formally renounced all earthly ties and taken the vows of abandonment) and by so doing receive a taste of true insight.

The aim of the serious pilgrim, I was told, is to achieve spiritual merit. By enduring a series of mental and physical trials a state of awareness is reached which enables the pilgrim to follow in the footsteps of the great masters to where all existence is unified in a state of pure love. Admission to the state of Sukhavati is forever; it can never be left for it is impossible to discover the return route.

The goal, it seems, is entry to the Buddhist 'paradise' where one is finally liberated from the repeating cycle of re-birth and suffering. There are various ideals of paradise and, according to Tibetan scripts, several paradisiacal sites have been identified in Tibet as 'opened' by former masters. These opened sites, or hidden valleys called *'beyuls'*, are believed by the Buddhists to be special places where followers can take refuge when disaster threatens the survival of mankind. They include Khembalung in Nepal, the Pemako valley in south-east Tibet, Lapchi and Rongshar on the Nepal-Tibet border and Dremojong and Chorten Nyima on the Tibet-Sikkim border.

Perhaps the most famous *beyul* is Sukhavati, the fabulous 'western paradise' of the Buddha Amitabha which Victor Chan described in his comprehensive pilgrimage guide, *Tibet Handbook*.

> . . . this fabulous retreat is full of wish-fulfilling trees, where no wish is denied. There is no suffering or sorrow; the finest silk, food, and precious stones are there for the taking. Caves have springs where milk flows perpetually, lakes bestow clarity of mind, and certain caves promote full enlightenment. While here the *budhicitta* ('Buddha mind') of a pilgrim increases and ignorance is wiped out.

It is hard to comprehend the terrible suffering endured by the Tibetan people at the hands of the Chinese and how they managed to reconcile such a dreadful nightmare with the teachings of their religion. Perhaps the holiest and most devout are able to be philosophic about their fate. How many of the lamas and abbots and monks who were humiliated, tortured and slaughtered managed to take comfort in their faith at that final defining moment of their existence? Was the unspeakable violence inflicted on them just another manifestation of the cycle of re-birth and suffering? Or was it so depraved, so abjectly inhuman, that it became impossible for them to believe that this was the life accorded to them for the sins of their past? How many of those select few, I wonder, reached the embracing sanctuary of those elusive paradisiacal *beyuls*? To the majority of the people, all those except the holiest, most precious lamas and the dedicated *sannyasi* pilgrims and *yogins*, that holocaust must have been inexplicable.

To be allowed to enter an opened *beyul* the pilgrim must have not only absolute faith in its existence but also much accumulated merit, abandoning all worldly goods and desires. Only the most devout and practiced *yogins* can enter such a place. Even then the disciple wishing to enter a *beyul* must learn the way and know the exact timing needed for entry. This knowledge is usually passed down orally by a teacher (*guru*). A lifetime of meditations and spiritual transformation is needed to get past the many psychological obstacles set in the path.

I watched as the monk sat cross-legged on the mat before the altar, chanting a continuous stream of prayers as he performed the puja. Another man sat beside him, turning the yellowed pages of holy script that lay in the monk's lap. The long narrow pages flapped in the cold wind which threatened to rip them from the silk-bound book. The monk's voice rose and fell on the wind as the prayers resonated in what sounded to me rather like the rhythms of Gregorian chant. I knew that they were distinct prayers, not to be mistaken for the ubiquitous *mantras*. The mantras are repeated by pilgrims as a way to reach a meditative state on their journey. They are believed to have magical qualities and supernatural effects, such as curing sickness or misfortune, or blessing a barren woman with children.

What stage of enlightenment, I wondered, had the young monk achieved? I wasn't even sure that monks followed the same path. It seemed sacrilegious to think he might just be doing his job. He certainly didn't look very impressive. He was a small man with a shaven head, dressed in simple clothes. There was nothing about his appearance to suggest great spirituality and deep inner calm.

We stood in respectful silence in a semi-circle behind the chanting monk. His head nodded with the murmured rhythms of his prayers. Every now and then Gompu would step forward and take an offering from the platter and place it reverentially upon the altar. The cold wind made the juniper flare up in bursts of sparks and the smoke streamed horizontally away from the altar. More twigs would be fed into the flames. Occasionally the sweet-scented smoke blew into my face reminding me of past pujas I had witnessed; the beginnings of so many other adventures. I remembered with a pang of regret that the only time I had climbed in Nepal without a puja I had suffered severe injuries in a terrifying fall. I looked intently at the monk's bowed head and hoped he was having a good one.

When at last he had finished chanting the prayers, and we were shivering in the icy wind that swept across the rocky plateau, rice was handed to each of us and we were encouraged to scatter handfuls in all directions. There were broad smiles all round as the gifts on the platter were handed out and bottles of fiery spirits were opened to toast our safety and success. I looked up at the flanks of the mountain above our camp with its forbidding black cliffs and the gleam of hard blue ice surging down from the summit headwall and wondered if anyone or anything had heard us. I hoped so.

A year before Reinhold Messner climbed Everest alone in 1980 Tibet was just beginning to feel the influence of a new Chinese policy of liberalisation instigated by Hu Yao-bang, Deng Xiao-ping's successor. Horrified by what he had seen on a fact-finding visit, he sacked local Party leaders and introduced a six-point plan designed to improve the economic and social conditions of the Tibetans. Most of the Chinese cadres were to leave Tibet within three years and be replaced by Tibetans. Private enterprise would be encouraged, taxes abolished for two years, and efforts would be made to develop Tibetan culture, education and science.

For the first time in twenty years people could move up to ten miles outside their villages without a permit. People were allowed to wear their traditional clothes, the chuba, learn the Tibetan language in schools and sing Tibetan songs. The hated daily political meetings became weekly. Monasteries and nunneries were reopened, some partially rebuilt. Some holy statues and relics were restored to Tibet from China. There was even talk of the Dalai Lama returning. It all sounded too good to be true – and it was.

For the first time China encouraged foreign tourists to visit Tibet in large numbers. These visitors saw, despite supervision by the Chinese, the destruction of Tibetan culture and the ruins that littered the land. The truth was all too obvious. By 1983 the Tibetans had given up believing that anything would really change. Independence groups roused themselves to action and the authorities responded even to a show of passive resistance with enthusiastic violence. Hundreds were arrested, beaten and tortured. Public executions increased in number and the Chinese rediscovered their old practice of cutting a prisoner's vocal chords to prevent them crying 'Free Tibet'.

Tibet was flooded with Han Chinese. This method of overcoming opposition in minority ethnic regions was one that China had tried successfully in Manchuria and Inner Mongolia. Induced by offers of high wages, interest free loans, guaranteed housing, and paid home leave, the Han came in their tens of thousands. In some areas, such as Amdo, they already outnumbered the Tibetans three to one. The Tibetan people were becoming strangers in their own land.

Despite the vast amount of land space per person, harsh birth control measures had been imposed on Tibet in the 1970s, and although they were only loosely applied at first, now strict control was introduced and enforcement teams established throughout the country. Many forced abortions took place as late as three, four and even five months into the pregnancy. Refugees gave harrowing accounts of foetuses being aborted at a very late stage in pregnancy and some witnessed the slaughter of tiny babies born to mothers of two-child families. Lethal injections and drowning were often used to dispose of babies on delivery. The killing of unborn children is all the more horrifyingly traumatic for a Tibetan Buddhist who believes the taking of any life is a terrible sin.

Seven years after I had attended Messner's lecture about his solo Everest climb, violence once again erupted in Tibet. Riots broke out in Lhasa. A new generation of Tibetans, born after the horrors of the Cultural Revolution, had never known a Tibet without the Chinese presence, yet they fervently wanted independence and freedom. The old communist orders of eastern Europe were beginning to crumble; it was time for a change, time to demand freedom. Intensive re-education classes all over Tibet could not erase the growing sense of unity among the people. They wanted the return of the Dalai Lama and an end to the Chinese occupation.

On the 24th April 1988 five young nuns were arrested for shouting 'FREE TIBET' and calling for the release of political prisoners as they circled the Jokhang temple in Lhasa. For this heinous crime they suffered unimaginable humiliation. As Mary Craig recounted in her book, *Tears of Blood*, one of the nuns, twenty-three-year-old Gyaltsen Chodon, described how they were beaten, stripped and chained to a wall, how electric cattle prods were applied all over their bodies by several men at a time pressing them into their eyes, their mouths and their vaginas. Killer dogs were set upon them and heavy iron rods were dropped on to their spines as they lay face down on the ground. Their hands were stamped and crushed, urine and excrement was poured over them and even their food was dipped in this filth. They were strung up by their thumbs, made to stand for twelve hours at a time in freezing ankle-deep water in the middle of winter, and as a matter of routine kicked and beaten with sticks while they were interrogated.

This happened, and I knew about it, and still I wanted to climb in Tibet.

After March 1990, after the Tiananmen Square massacre in the Chinese capital itself, there was a sense that, perhaps for the first time in forty years, they might no longer be alone. The international community was starting to take notice. China's ludicrously extravagant attempt to celebrate the fortieth anniversary of Tibet's liberation was boycotted by Britain, the United States and several European countries. Few went to China's party. For the first time governments, including those of Britain and the United States, talked openly of Tibetan independence. In April 1991 President Bush declared his support of Tibet's freedom, and then strangely went on to renew China's most favoured nation status, in the hope that trade would be a powerful enough incentive for the Chinese to improve their human rights record. The US Senate accepted that the true leaders of Tibet were the Dalai Lama and the Tibetan government in exile in India. It was a major shift in attitude – yet the regime of Chinese terror goes on apace.

The Tibetan people are still dying, and their land and culture are dying with them. There have been many conflicts in the world throughout this century that were conducted with all the savagery that man's ingenuity could devise. The Holocaust that Nazi Germany inflicted upon the Jews, Stalin's maniacal slaughter of so many millions of his own people, Pol Pot and the Khmer Rouge's excesses in Cambodia – these three horrors stand out clearly above the miasma of other crimes against humanity. They are widely known about. The tragedy of Tibet should be added to this catalogue of depravity. It is Mao Tse-tung's enduring legacy, the fruit of his tyrannical rule. His Great Leap Forward, his Cultural Revolution, his megalomania, evidence of his insane lust for power, were imposed upon his own people with appalling consequences, but what was meted out in Tibet is both China's enduring shame and our own. For we in the West simply turned a blind eye and allowed it to happen.

I knew a little of Tibet's history, and for my own convenience I chose to ignore it, or at best I made excuses for myself. I wanted to play expensive, dangerous games on big mountains. It was about adventure and excitement, vicarious thrills, toying with the idea of being an explorer. There are no explorers any more. Most of us on mountaineering trips are simply credit card adventurers.

13

THE CROWING OF THE COCK

It was a beautiful mountain, probably unclimbed, and yet, set in the panorama of peaks surrounding us, it was of little significance. At about six thousand metres, it was not much higher than the proposed site for our first camp on Cho Oyo. The sheer scale of these, the world's highest mountains, was breathtaking and humbling. They induced in me a delight and a passion I could scarcely believe I possessed, and at the same time they would intimidate and humiliate me and quash any vain hopes I had of climbing them. There was a precarious balance between confident ambition and fearful insecurity about venturing up these soaring peaks. I had always been aware that success lay in the mind. So many factors beyond technical ability and fitness determine whether one will succeed in getting to the summit. More often than not it seems to be a matter of desire – how much I really want to do it – rather than being there and thinking I'll have a go, give it my best shot. Eighty per cent of it is a mind game. Passionately wanting it, and with some conceit, knowing it is mine for the taking – that's what tends to win. The slightest doubt, the merest suggestion that I might prefer to be somewhere else, and the game is lost.

Already the first doubts had begun to creep insidiously into my mind. The cough that had plagued me since Namche was steadily getting worse, and with it came worries about high altitude sickness. I have always been a coward when faced with the threat of pulmonary and cerebral oedemas. The lonely deaths of abandoned friends in the past have been

178

bleak warnings that I have never been able to shrug off. I can get my head around the idea of being killed by storms, or avalanches or falls, but I have never come to terms with being killed by the invisible effects of altitude. It is the idea that my body can betray me which I find so difficult to accept.

The very nature of the illness is also deeply disturbing. The blindness, incoherence and loss of co-ordination that indicate the onset of cerebral oedema, or the frightening, bubbling, breathlessness of pulmonary oedemas, are the stuff of nightmares to me. To make the end more horrible, there is a period before loss of consciousness and the final coma when you are fully aware of what is happening to you. It makes me think of the rabies victim who surfaces from intermittent bouts of madness to discover that his disease-ravaged brain is still functioning, allowing him awful moments of lucidity. Then he knows what is happening to him, that what he has is an incurable descent towards disintegration and death, relieved only by the blessed oblivion of insanity. The worst of it is not the manner of execution but the prior knowledge that you are going to die after prolonged hanging on to life when seconds become hours and hours became days and your mind wriggles like a tortured insect with the knowing of it.

I have talked to friends who have survived both types of oedemas and their descriptions of the panicky feelings that threaten to overwhelm them have sent shivers up my spine. The arduous attempts to descend as fast as possible, to lose precious height, despite the suddenly enfeebled state they found themselves in, made harrowing listening. There was always a feeling of horror at the speed with which the condition deteriorated from seemingly mild symptoms to unmistakable signs that disaster was close at hand. These were stories from highly experienced mountaineers who had been to high altitudes many times without the slightest evidence of trouble. They were shocked to find that, despite their proven ability at height, the sickness had struck them down as well. I could see how it had changed them. There was a serious worried look in their eyes. I have no doubt that it irrevocably changed their approach to the mountains, making them feel vulnerable, more wary, but as a result probably better mountaineers.

It is true that previous experience at altitude does help you to acclimatise quicker and better, but it certainly does not make you immune to the dangers. In fact there is a risk of creating a false sense of security, an immortal confidence founded on the notion that, if it didn't happen before, it won't now. Unfortunately oedemas like surprising people. They are poor respecters of ability or prior experience.

There is always the temptation, of course, for the climber to ignore the symptoms, to think that a combination of tough-it-out, grin-and-bare-it machismo and the huge amount of hard work and ambition that has driven him so far will see him through. It is easy to persuade yourself that you are just having a bad day, that it is always hard and tough, that illness will never strike you – until that scary, lonely realisation that your sight is fading or your lungs are bubbling with the drowning fluids of incipient oedema.

For me the dangers are all too real, the price of ignorance so very high. I've had too many close calls in my past to be able to dismiss lightly such a threat. Although I realise and accept the dangers in climbing, and understand the speed with which things can go disastrously wrong, there are some fires I will not play with. Dying of oedemas is one thing I wish to avoid. It is the manner of the dying that disturbs me so much. I know that it is all the same in the end, that death is no better in a thunderous avalanche, or a heart-freezing plunge into space, but somehow they seem an infinitely preferable way to go. At least there is minimal time to think about it. The pathetic gurgling asphyxiation or the helpless treason of a brain crushed into silence are my archetypal fears. They hold for me all the horrors of terminal illness, malign invading diseases eating you up from the inside, shades of pitiable failure, an enfeebled dribbling away of life. The irony of course is that such ends unavoidably come to us all. I simply can't equate it with the vigour and life and passion to be experienced on mountains.

Often it is difficult to assess what is happening either to a partner or to yourself on high mountains. Even doctors profess to know only a relatively small amount about the highly complex physiology of acclimatising and altitude sickness. There are general guidelines to follow, but since people acclimatise differently – some fast, some slow – it is hard to judge anyone's real condition. Keeping a careful eye on each other, checking up all the time, can help to reveal hidden symptoms or unmask the despondent climber who is hoping to conceal the awful truth from others as well as himself. I have often seen people behaving in just this sort of delusive manner.

It is almost as frightening to witness it happen to others and have to help them down, frantically hoping that it will not be too late, that they won't suddenly collapse on you and sink into that final coma. The very thought of sitting helplessly by a friend as he inexorably fades away into the dim twilight region from which there is no return is too awful to contemplate. Even worse is to be forced to abandon your comatose partner in a last ditch attempt to escape from whatever has trapped you on the mountain. Accidents in the past, combined with an innate revulsion for such a grisly end, have conspired to make me a wary and sometimes cowardly mountaineer. I'm quite proud of the fact. Being bold and pushy is fine, admirable even; being bold and pushy and dead is pointless, not to say plain stupid.

I turned away from the smoking altar and pushed such pessimistic thoughts from my head. *Listen to your body*, I told myself, *that's the key. Listen carefully and then there's nothing to worry about.* I half-believed it.

I watched as Gompu strode confidently past carrying a huge rucksack casually over one shoulder. Four years earlier he had been with me on Ama Dablam, although not as a climber, and even then he had looked strong and powerful. I have always known the Sherpa's reputation for awesome strength and stamina in the mountains but, even so, Gompu was an exception. He seemed now to have doubled in size and strength.

He was a friendly, helpful man, always smiling and with a

keen ambitious glint in his eye. He noticed me looking at him, grinned broadly and waved. He was heading up to the Nangpa La to establish a temporary mid-way camp, carrying not only his own personal equipment but a huge load of tents, food, fuel and stoves. He and three others would make the carry, establish a cook tent and the cache of food and fuel, and all but Gompu and Jetta would return to base that night. The following morning, and over the next few days, it would be our turn to ferry our own gear up to this intermediate camp while Jetta and Gompu stayed up on the pass to guard the gear from inquisitive passing travellers who might be tempted into a little opportunist thievery.

It was a long slog up the moraines to reach the start of the glacier flowing down from the pass. Despite its frequent use and age-old reputation as a trade route, it was very easy to get lost among the towering piles of loose scree and labyrinths of ice cliffs. It was safe from any danger of avalanches or crevasses, and this merely added to the tedium of struggling for hours up shifting dusty rock slopes.

This early in the season few yak trains had come through, so the path was not clearly marked. Where it could be detected, it was usually marked by a few inconspicuous cairns that blended effortlessly with the background of similar-coloured rocks. Oddly enough, it was easier to follow on the way up than on the return. Everyone bar the Sherpas managed to get thoroughly lost while descending back to base camp until it became a standing joke and bets were laid as to who was going to spend the most hours in the maze.

It was a cruelly frustrating experience since you usually became lost when you were within about half an hour's walk from the comforts of camp and just salivating at the thought of steaming kettles of tea and the chance to sit and rest after a gruelling ten-hour day. Distances were confusingly deceptive, not least because it was impossible to walk in a straight line. The terrain continually forced you to contour round obstacles, often almost looping back on yourself in landscapes that seemed to look always the same, so that it was hard to fix your bearings on any one point. For someone who has the sense of direction of a dead warthog, as well as a fragile understanding of patience, I found the whole business both infuriating and exhausting, especially on loose treacherous ground that battered my legs.

On the final approach to base camp I devised any number of schemes by which I hoped to outwit the mystifying terrain, none of which worked. I would line up particular volcanic cones of rubble with distant summits only to find that the clouds had rolled in and obscured the higher peaks. I would look back every hundred yards or so on the way up to familiarise myself with how it appeared going the other way. This proved fruitless: the moment you strayed slightly off trail you realised that the landscape wasn't at all the same.

Probably the most irritating aspect of getting lost was that it so often happened within shouting distance of base camp and in full daylight. You knew it was there, just over that hill, or beyond that ice lake, and yet once you had staggered to where you felt sure you would find the final brutal climb up to the tents, there was only another tottering pile of boulders.

We had erected a small sentry-box toilet tent which stood out clearly, framed against the back-drop of ice mountains looming above base camp, pointing like a finger at where the hidden tents sat huddled among the boulders. I can remember cursing and swearing at R.J. Secor as we stumbled up and down endless loose slopes only to find the nylon finger pointing mockingly from a completely different direction. Tempers became frayed as we each insisted on the merits of different routes.

'We've just bloody well been there!' I yelled in exasperation at the silhouetted figure of R.J. atop yet another slag heap.

'I can see some ducks,' he yelled back insistently.

'What?' I shouted, wondering what he was talking about.

'Ducks!' he hollered. 'I can see ducks from here.'

'Oh, for God's sake,' I muttered. 'What's wrong with him?'

'I'm sure it's this way,' came a distant shout.

'No, hang on,' I called, suddenly flooded with confidence. 'There's a cairn over here.'

'What?'

'Cairns!' I screamed, feeling my parched throat beginning to crack under the strain. I scrambled up an incline of loose pebbles until I could clamber on to some larger boulders and hop towards the elusive cairn.

It turned out to be a pile of rocks, just like all the rest, just like a cairn in fact. In the distance the black obelisk of the toilet tent seemed to be shaking with mirth. I knew that everyone at camp could hear our high volume arguments and were probably laying bets at that very moment.

'Bugger this.'

I sat down despondently on a convenient rock. Looking back, I saw R.J. traversing a knife-edge rim of scree overhanging a circular frozen lake hundreds of feet below him. He seemed to be coming my way.

'Well, at least he's still following me,' I mumbled to myself. 'He must think I know where I'm going.' I laughed at the idea.

'Ducks, more ducks.' I looked up to see R.J. hopping from foot to foot in excitement and pointing in the opposite direction. 'DUCKS!' he screamed at me as if I were some sort of imbecile.

'Are you mad?'

'What?'

'Mad, you're barking mad.' He didn't seem to hear. 'What are you blathering about? Ducks! What have ducks got to do with it, you gibbering idiot. I don't care about goddamn ducks . . .'

'Ducks.' R.J. yelled confidently.

'I know he's Californian,' I moaned, 'but does he have to be bonkers as well?'

'Bollocks to your ducks,' I screamed in his direction and gave him the finger. He waved back in a friendly manner as I grimly set off down the slope below me, determined to get away from this crazed man.

An hour later we both staggered into the camp from diametrically opposite directions. I slumped down in the cook tent and drank as much lemon tea as I could get my hands on, glowering furiously at R.J. He seemed blithely unaware of my annoyance.

'Gee, that was real confusing down there,' he said, breaking the sullen silence.

'You and your flaming ducks didn't help,' I snapped.

'But there were ducks everywhere,' he said, hurt by my angry tone. 'That was the trouble. There were these ducks that just turned out to be rocks.' He looked sincerely confused.

'Ducks, eh?' A thought struck me. 'What exactly do you mean by ducks?'

'Well piles of stones, of course,' he said in surprise. 'You know the sort of thing, markers on the trail.'

'Cairns! You mean cairns?'

'What are they? Never heard of them.'

'Cairns,' I said wearily, 'are piles of stones. Markers on the trail, as you put it.' And I buried my head in my hands and cursed the communication cock-ups of international teams.

'No kidding?' R.J. said with a grin. 'You call ducks cairns. Hey, that's weird. I mean, what does cairn mean, man. Weird word.'

'It means ducks apparently,' I said. 'Why the hell do you call them ducks, eh? I mean, why not call them piglets or rottweilers or . . .'

'Cos they look like ducks, man. Big rock, little rock on top. It looks like a duck. We call them ducks, okay. So why do you guys call them cairns?'

I stared at him, dumbstruck for a moment. Why did we call them cairns? I hadn't the first idea. Do they really look like ducks? Is 'cairn' a Scottish word?

'Um, we just do. They've always been cairns. You must know that?'

'They're ducks where I come from,' R.J. said as he walked triumphantly out of the cook tent, clearly feeling the logic of calling them ducks was irrefutable. I smacked my forehead with my palm, stumped for words. He had a point though. Why did we call them cairns?

Far below, a frozen circular lake lay in the early morning shadows. I shifted the straps of my rucksack and shrugged my shoulders to get the pack to sit more comfortably. I was carrying all my personal gear through to Camp I in preparation for load-carrying higher on the mountain. So far I had done precious little work on the hill and was painfully aware that the rest of the team were forging further and further ahead. It was depressing to find oneself lagging so far behind.

Turning the volume up on my Sony Walkman, I began to trudge wearily along the knife edge until it reared up into a wall of rubble. The path zig-zagged steeply. I followed the trail of yak dung and occasional pieces of litter that indicated the best line up the wall. My leg muscles burnt with the hot ache of lactic acid building up. I slowed down, determined not to stop altogether. Stopping simply made things worse. I would start coughing again, and then trying to get going would seem even harder. The constant loose, slipping steps made it impossible to develop an easy mile-consuming rhythm.

Above the sound of music in my ears I heard a shout in the distance. Looking up, I saw a crowd of young men coming towards me in single file. I had reached the top of the rubble heap and was examining a distinctive fin of blue ice rising up to the crest of yet another volcanic heap of moraines. There was a grey dusty path up the edge of this fin and on top I could see where a large boulder was balanced precariously on a slender pillar of sun-melting ice.

The men came slowly towards me. I kept walking, now and then stepping aside to let individuals pass. They stared curiously at me. With my bright yellow glacier glasses and stereo head phones I must have looked outlandish to them. I stared back, hidden behind the dark shadows of my glasses and nodded curtly in acknowledgement. They were Tibetans, Khampas by the look of it; all male, and all young. Some smiled at me, most looked scared and quickly glanced away.

Again I heard a vague distant shout above the music. I didn't want to know. I simply wanted to get my head down and trudge up on the endless screes. I wanted to blank out any distractions and get the next four hours out of the way.

Holy man on the steps of a Hindu temple in
Durbar Square, Kathmandu. (Photo: Simpson)

Previous page: The Monkey Temple, Kathmandu. (Photo: Simpson)

The burning funeral ghats on the holy Bagmati river
at Pashupatinath. (Photo: Simpson)

Two Nepalese children playing with a Chinese
liquor bottle in the streets of Lukla. (Photo: Simpson)

Left: Children of the Khumbu, near Monzo. (Photo: Simpson)

Below: First campsite on the walk-in to Cho Oyo, Thami with the mountain Kwangde in the background. (Photo: Simpson)

Right: Gompa surrounded by sacred trees between Jiri and Namche Bazar. (Photo: Simpson)

Below right: A stupa near Thami. (Photo: Mike Shrimpton)

Building the altar for the puja at Cho Oyo base camp. The mountain Nangpai Gotaya forms a background to the prayer flags which are to carry the puja offerings to the four quarters of the earth. (Photos: Simpson)

The approach to Camp I situated above a steep gully cutting through the rock walls on the right, Cho Oyo looming above. (Photo: Simpson)

Spirit masks in Namche Bazar, Nepal. (Photo: Simpson)

A boy stumbled as he came towards me. I stepped round him as he wearily pushed himself up from the loose ground at my feet. I noticed he was squinting and that he was not wearing sunglasses. Snowblindness was already beginning to burn his eyes. He held a small white cotton bag, more like a parcel, that had been secured with twine. His baseball boots looked old, worn and wet from crossing the snows on the pass. He smiled wanly as he straightened up in front of me. I looked blankly back at him. I wanted to get on. Another young man came up and pressing his hand to the boy's shoulder, gently urged him on. The boy stumbled almost immediately.

The shout came again, insistent and familiar. I switched off my stereo.

'Joe!' the voice called. I looked around but could see no sign of anyone.

'Joe! Up here.' I looked up to see Rick holding his arm aloft. He stood out from a group of people huddled near the top of the ice fin.

I walked slowly up the path placing my boots carefully in the icy footsteps.

'What's up?' I asked as I approached the group.

'This guy looks sick,' Rick said, nodding at a young man slumped on the ice.

'Has he just collapsed?'

'No, he's capable of walking,' Rick said. 'He just sat down like that, sort of resting, but his friend here is asking for medicines or something. What shall we do?'

'What do you mean, we?' I snapped, irritated that we were going to have to waste time.

'Well, he just asked me, man. I mean, we gotta help him, eh?'

'Yeah.' I hung my head and peered at the man on the ground. 'What's wrong with him?' I asked as he looked at me and smiled weakly. I took off my glacier glasses and stared into his face.

'This guy says he is sick,' Rick said, and I turned to see a concerned lad of no more than fifteen gazing intently at me with unnerving directness. He tapped his temple and squeezed his eyes tight.

'Headache,' I said, mimicking the action. He nodded and then mimed someone sleeping. 'Tired, eh? I know how he feels.'

'What do we do, Joe?' Rick asked again.

'Well, what can we do?' I snapped.

The man slumped on the ground wore thin cotton trousers, and it must have been cold sitting on the wet ice of the glacier. His eyes were clear and the pupils appeared normal. I noticed the cheap sunglasses tied around his neck with string. There was a hint of puffiness in his cheeks but it was hard to tell whether it was the first swelling signs of oedema or simply youthful puppy fat.

'He must go down,' I said. I pointed vigorously downward, miming the action of walking downhill with two fingers. The young boy nodded. 'And drink.' I poured imaginary drinks down my throat. 'Chai, paani, dherai paani, drink much water,' I said, and the boy nodded at me despite looking confused.

'Can we give them anything?' Rick asked.

'Like what? Have you got a first aid kit on you?'

'No, but . . .'

'Nor have I, and anyway it wouldn't make much difference. The guy's knackered that's all.'

'Well, should we help him?'

'How, for God's sake?' I glared at Rick angry that we were getting involved. 'He's dehydrated and obviously suffering from the altitude. He must keep going down. Base camp's only an hour away.'

'Are you sure he can make it?'

'If he's got this far he'll make it. Look, he has all his mates with him. There must be twenty of them. They're staying together, so he will be okay. When he gets to camp the lads will help out with food and water.'

'But what if he doesn't make it?' Rick persisted.

'He will, I'm telling you.' I turned back to the boy and made sure he understood about the need for water and above

188

all to keep losing height. He nodded and then held up his fingers as if putting a pill in his mouth.

'No. I have none,' I said, holding my palms out and shaking my head. 'No ha.' He looked perplexed. I shrugged. 'Down,' I said again, pointing to base camp. 'Chai, paani, water, yes?' The young lad bent down with a resigned expression to help his friend to his feet. He swayed unsteadily.

'Are you sure . . .'

'No, Rick, I'm not sure, but I can't see what we can do. If twenty of them can't get him down, what difference can we make?'

'We could help.'

'We can turn round, go all the way back down to camp. We could go all the way to Namche if need be, but it would make no difference.'

'I guess you're right.' Rick looked unconvinced.

'Look, either we climb this mountain or we escort Tibetans but we cannot do both.'

'Yeah, okay.' Rick shrugged and refused to meet my angry stare.

'I don't feel good about it either, you know. We're here now. We're climbers, okay, not baby sitters. This is the third group through this week. What about their guides? Why don't they help? We can't rescue the whole world you know.'

'I didn't say we could, Joe. I just want to help, okay?' He reached into his rucksack and pulled out his water bottle. 'Here man, take it.' He proffered the metal bottle to the two Tibetans. They looked incomprehendingly at the shiny water bottle. Rick unscrewed the top and handed it to them. They drank thirstily as I watched, feeling guilty and helpless. I'd forgotten to offer them my water.

'Hell!' I said angrily and turned away. I flicked the music on, cranked up the volume and stomped towards the Nangpa La, thrusting my ski-sticks down in a furious rhythm.

An hour later Rick caught up with me as I sat on the edge of the snowslope leading up out of the chaos of the moraines. I had sat down in the sun and was thinking about the refugees and what I was doing here. It seemed that whatever clever excuses I devised to justify what I was doing, they all sounded hollow and contrived. At home the excitement of the climb, the chance to visit Tibet, the adventure, everything in my past had conspired to make it easy to believe my excuses. Now, feeling sick and frustrated and out of love with the mountain, I felt shallow and hypocritical.

It was almost as if these people were not real. Until then Tibet's tragedy had been no more than words on a page to me; now seeing it stumble blindly past me, it was hard to comprehend.

It made me angry that I should be made to appear so heartless. They were an indictment of my selfishness. They made me feel uncomfortable in the one arena where I felt most at home. *At least I was there to witness it.* I repeated my most frequent justification. It didn't seem a good enough reason.

Climbing Cho Oyo appeared suddenly to be an absurdly pointless and selfish thing to do. Faced with the Tibetan boy's obvious distress and poverty, I couldn't help wondering at the immense extravagance we were exhibiting in our attempt to scale this huge lump of rock and ice. My glacier glasses alone were probably worth more than they had ever earned in their lives. There we were, with warm double boots, expensive rucksacks, luxurious hi-tech clothing systems, sleeping bags worth a small fortune and all manner of fancy gadgets to help us climb the mountain and they had pathetic clothbound bundles, baseball boots and thin cheap western-style Chinese-produced clothes for their attempt to escape from their mother country. That was all that they could possibly take on their journey into exile in India or Nepal.

For us, crossing the Nangpa La was one small event in a great adventure. To them, it was a once in a lifetime's commitment – a poorly equipped arduous struggle into exile, fraught with the potential of death or worse, capture, imprisonment and torture. I had thought climbing one of the world's highest mountains was a significant achievement. Set against this tide of sad and weary people leaving their homeland forever, it was a shallow waste.

I wondered how much they had sacrificed to pay the guides

to take them across the pass. I had heard that some of these so-called guides were making thousands of dollars. An American team witnessed three guides dividing up between themselves roughly £25,000 in rupees after one mass crossing. Knowing how impoverished most Tibetans were, and how the best jobs and wages were reserved for Chinese settlers, it made me wonder how many years they would have saved to attempt the difficult night crossing of the Nangpa La with no certainty of making it to freedom, if exile in a refugee camp can be called freedom.

I knew that there was nothing we could have done; that they would safely reach base camp and escape down to Thami and beyond. Yet the logic didn't help my sense of betrayal. I had always thought that, faced with such circumstances, I would willingly help and yet twice in a few days I had failed to do so. Once more and I'd start feeling like St Peter at the Garden of Gethsemene with his three betrayals before the cock crows.

'Hey, Joe. How you doing?' Rick squeezed my shoulder and sat down on his rucksack.

'Better than them,' I muttered and looked out over the sea of barren rocks. I liked Rick. He was a genuinely nice guy. There was nothing hidden about him. I felt embarrassed to have vented my angry petulance on him.

'Yeah, that's for sure,' Rick said. 'Hey, you were right man, he was okay once he got going again. I mean, he was slow, but they helped him, and he was making it. I gave him some headache pills in the end,' he added, and I winced, remembering that I had pain killers in the top pocket of my rucksack. *Strike three*, I thought, *and the cockerel crows!*

'Look, I'm sorry I was so abrupt,' I said. 'They just made me angry, you know. It's like . . . well, I wish they weren't there, spoiling it all.'

'Yeah, but it's not their fault.'

'Oh, I know that. It's just that there really isn't anything we can do for them, and that makes me feel bad, and so I resent them, get angry with them being here. I shouldn't have taken it out on you.'

'That's real cool,' Rick beamed cheerfully. 'Hell, it's not easy to watch. So don't feel guilty. I'll help if I can but I don't feel guilty. Not seeing them come by don't mean they're not there.'

'It's my old Catholic guilt, I suppose,' I said ruefully. 'I had thought that because we're not paying the Chinese authorities, not supporting the regime, we wouldn't be harming anyone.'

'Hey, this is too heavy, Joe. Lighten up. What more can you do? We're just going to climb a mountain and go back home. It's no big deal.'

'Maybe, but I don't think it's as simple as that. They're still running away from some serious shit and we're just walking past them, just playing games.'

'Listen, those guys will be okay. They'll be on the way to Ari by now.' Rick stood up and shouldered his rucksack. 'It's getting cold. I'm heading on.'

I watched him stride off up the stony ground protruding from the ice and join the wet sludgy trail through the snow. I knew he was right. My guilt feelings were about me, not about the plight of the Tibetans. I was using their pain as an excuse for my own poor performance, my own weakness. The thought only made me feel worse.

I had always held a candle out for the idea of the freedom of the hills, the notion that the travelling climber knew no boundaries of politics or religion, there were no borders constraining his world. Now I felt a chill wind beginning to gutter that weakened candle flame. There were no borders for us because we wanted it that way. It was a convenient ideal that allowed us to continue playing egotistical games in distant countries. If there were no political or religious borders then there were no moral ones either.

14

THE NANGPA LA

I set the pressure cooker back on top of the burner after screwing down the release valve.

'One minute from now, right?' I said to Mal who was lying in his sleeping bag.

'Aye, okay. What's it like out there?'

I poked my head through the tent flap and saw the summit of Cho Oyo bathed in a soft golden light. The surrounding peaks had already turned pink in the alpenglow of the setting sun. High above the summit thin streamers of cloud marbled the blue evening sky.

'Looks good. Though I'm not so sure about the clouds. Probably a front passing over.'

'What does your barometer say?'

'Five nine fifty. Height has gone up a bit, but not much.'

'Probably just a weak front then. Should be okay tomorrow. Here, grab that, will you?' He passed me his mug. I reached over and felt the familiar tickle in my throat as I moved. I suppressed the cough.

'Don't think I'm ready for going up tomorrow. I'm not right.'

'It's just an altitude cough,' Mal reassured me after I had voiced my anxiety.

'I don't think so, mate.' I wished he had agreed with me. It would have made the decision easier. 'There's something wrong. It's not just a tickly dry cough. I'm gobbing up all sorts of muck.'

'It'll be all right,' Mal answered airily. 'Why not have a few rest days, take some antibiotics.'

'I've had rest days and the pills don't work at base camp. It's too high,' I said morosely. 'It's not just the chest I'm worried about. I'm not firing on all cylinders.'

'You seem fit enough to me.'

'Yeah, but I'm not getting any fitter and I should be. I could hardly keep up with Rick today,' I protested. 'Something's not there. My legs are not recovering. It's as if I'm not acclimatising.'

'You haven't had any headaches or anything, have you? You should be acclimatised by now.'

'I know,' I said. 'And I think I have, but there's something . . . scaring me.'

'Well, what are you going to do?' Mal looked at me, knowing the answer.

'Haven't much choice really.' I stared at the ground to avoid Mal's eyes. 'I mean, the only chance of shaking off the chest infection is to lose height; go all the way down to Namche and come back when I've got rid of it.'

'Why not do that then?'

'Because by the time I get back it will all be over. At our present rate you lot will be making a summit attempt in the next few days.'

'Aye, but there'll be more than one summit team. You could go up with Neil, R.J. and Rick.'

'No, I'll be too far behind, and if I'm honest, I don't want to try. I don't want to risk going to eight thousand metres with a dodgy chest.'

'Fair enough.'

'I'm packing it in,' I said, voicing a decision I had made twenty-four hours before but hadn't wanted to reveal. 'Call it what you like, wimping out, chest infection, whatever. It's pointless to go on if I feel like this. I don't want to screw up your chances.'

'So, are you going to wait at base camp?'

'No, I'll pack my main gear and leave it with the lads. Then I'll walk out alone. Chwang can write me a note to sort out the flights from Lukla. I'll see you when you get back to Kathmandu.'

'Okay, if that's what you want.'

Mal shrugged, and I felt a pang of remorse for being weak in front of him. Then I pushed the idea away. It would be ridiculous to get all macho and competitive about carrying on regardless.

'Jesus wept!' Mal cursed. 'How long has that pressure cooker been on?'

'Oh my God!' I lurched towards the pot on the roaring gas stove, grabbed it and flung it out into the snow, expecting it to explode as I did so. We both stared intently at the aluminium pot melting into the snow outside the tent door.

'It's all right, I think,' I said, giving the pot a suspicious poke with my ice axe. 'I don't think it'll blow.'

It was a light-weight pressure cooker I bought from Doug Scott who had got a job lot from Russia. The trouble with it was the lack of a pressure release safety valve. Once steam issued from the valve at the top, you were supposed to screw down the valve, closing it completely, and then leave the cooker on the flame for no longer than one minute. After that you turned the heat off and waited three or four minutes whilst the rice, lentils, or pulses cooked quickly inside. If you fell asleep, or forgot about it while it was sealed and on heat, there was a very real chance it would explode. Judging by its light weight, I guessed it would be no more than a matter of minutes before pressure built up to a critical stage. I didn't want to think of the consequences of that happening. If it had been black, it would have looked exactly like the sort of bomb thrown at Tsars and Archdukes by deranged anarchists at the turn of the century.

The following morning I set off for base camp with Neil who had decided to take a rest day. He too was having an amusing personality clash with R.J. and wanted to get away for a break. California and Yorkshire didn't seem to mix at all well.

We swung down the fixed rope hanging in the bed of a steep couloir of dangerously loose rocks and then trudged a meandering path alongside serried ranks of blue ice fins that led towards a junction with the Nangpa glacier. Neil soon outstripped me as I continued to be plagued with paroxysms of coughing. I watched him dwindle into a small dot among the snow-covered boulders with the broad white swath of the Nangpa La behind him. To my right the land opened up as I approached the pass. There was a hint of distant brown and purple hills. That was Tibet – the fabled land. In fact, I was actually in Tibet at that moment, although it didn't feel like it. The mountains displayed no distinctive borders once you were on them. I was on the same snow as lay a mile away. What was the difference?

I glanced back at the summit of Cho Oyo, looming thousands of feet above me. The vast bulk of the mountain was intimidating. Camp I, at just under twenty thousand feet, was really the start of the climb, and all the hours of flogging up moraines and glacial debris was simply the approach to the base of the mountain. I realised with a pang of regret that I had failed before even starting. I stared wistfully at the summit, wondering whether I had made the right decision. Plumes of powder snow were being whipped off the summit ridges into huge swirling streamers that twisted frantically like white dust devils. There was an opalescent halo around the sun, caused by the veils of ice particles violently blasted from the summit snowfields. The wind must have been terrifying. I had seen plumes like that on Pachermo and heard the deep roaring boom of the wind, like a living force battering against the mountain. It was strange to watch the muted, silent violence of the wind storm and realise that, in spite of the clear blue sky and warm sunshine, conditions on the higher slopes were lethal.

I was unaware at the time that it was destroying all the camp sites above Camp II. Tents were being shredded, sleeping bags and personal gear blasted all over the mountainside. Fortunately our team had yet to establish the next camp, and so were spared the setback which had ruined the summit hopes of several other expeditions operating from the Tibetan side.

I watched Neil's tiny figure begin to step out across the broad open white sweep of the Nangpa La. There were no crevasses large enough to be a danger and he moved, unroped, across the expanse of ice as a slow-moving black speck. The scale made him appear to be creeping, hunched against some invisible menace, along a white throat cutting through the mountain ramparts. On each side mountains rose up from the col. I wiped the spit from my lips, cleared my throat, and stepped off the rocky path marked by a red-flagged cane and walked out on to the glacier.

The prayer flags on the centre of the pass were tiny black specks in the distant white haze. I saw Neil take off his rucksack and sit close by them. I trudged along his steps, feeling stronger and lighter with each step I took. It wasn't simply because I was losing height; I felt suddenly free from a dark cloud that had been lowering over me for weeks. Perhaps I had always known I would give up. It didn't seem to matter any more. I had finally made my choice and whether it was right or wrong didn't seem to be worth agonising about.

It has always been hard to admit to failure, always a tussle between conflicting emotions. It is said that you learn much more when you fail than when you succeed. Maybe so, but recognising this never got any easier, and the result was no less humbling. It always felt like a double bind. Having agreed to go on the expedition, I had set in stone my intention of climbing an eight thousand metre peak. It had been announced to my world. All the exhortations to take care and be strong now seemed to have been for nothing. *It'll be a doddle. You'll be fine. It's not technically difficult. Have a good one.* I had believed them. The reality was disappointingly different. *I've given up cigarettes for eleven months to climb this bugger, and now I am giving up because of a chest infection.* I could scarcely believe it. *The first thing I'm going to do when I get to Namche is buy twenty Bensons',* I assured myself as I strode across the ice.

The prayer flags crackled in the wind that was seething across the ice. Knee-deep veils of spindrift rushed towards me as I approached Neil where he sat fiddling with his camera. It looked as if the glacier had become liquid, like a black-and-white photo of a waterfall frozen by the shutter in a smooth rush of white. It tugged insistently at my legs, threatening to unbalance me. I leant forward into the wind feeling it pushing me upright.

The flags formed a thicket of rattling canes and the sound of flapping cotton contrasted with the clacking noises of the canes whipping against each other. In the distance beyond the curve of the glacier horizon, a fearsome tooth-shaped peak reared up above the rim of the pass. Steep rock walls plunged down to the glacier from an apron of ice cliffs that guarded access to the summit pyramid, a sharp incisor of ice-streaked grey granite. Ice particles blasted across my face as I leant on my ski-sticks, trying to quell the bout of coughing that had ambushed me the moment I stopped.

I looked at the white *khatas* tied to the top of the canes, lashing furiously in the wind, and wondered why they hadn't been swept away. The shrine of flags was constantly renewed by each passing band of travellers. Part of the structure had collapsed in on itself in a tangle of knotted string, coloured squares of cloth adorned with prayers and mantras, and banked up with drifted snow.

The prayer flags were there to mark the top of the pass and show the way but they were also an example of the practice of making offerings to express thanks and obeisance to the gods. Such offerings imply giving, or *jinpa*, and the giving plays an important role in Tibetan Buddhism since it offers a way towards self-knowledge, peace and fulfilment. It must be done voluntarily, with no expectation of reward, and to this end giving one's life must be the supreme sacrifice. The traveller adding a stone to a cairn on a mountain pass, or fixing another string of flags to those already there, performs a simple act of giving. It helps others to find the way and enhances all the blessings of previous travellers who added their gifts. It is known as *chezing*, or the 'eye viewed' offering.

I was surprised to see a brown felt hat swinging from the top of the highest cane. It swirled in the wind like a plate spun on a pole by a circus performer. Beneath it a sun-yellowed scarf threatened to flick it off and send it spinning and bouncing across the ice into Tibet. It was a fine, if somewhat battered, trilby and must have been a valued article of clothing for whoever had been crossing the pass. It would have provided protection from the fierce sun and insulating warmth in a storm. I reached up and grabbed the spinning rim, expecting it to be tied to its pole, but it came away freely.

'That's odd,' I said to Neil. 'Leaving a hat up here.'

'I'm amazed it hasn't blown away. It was here two days ago when I came up.'

'You'd think someone would have nicked it.'

'No, that would be bad karma, surely . . .'

I turned the hat in my hand and then impulsively put it on my head. It fitted perfectly.

'What do you think?' I asked, giving Neil a twirl.

'Very nice,' he remarked sarcastically.

'I quite fancy a hat like this.' I looked at the stand of clattering poles. 'It'll just get blown away if it's left here.'

'It hasn't so far.'

'It's okay, I wasn't really going to take it.'

'No?'

'Well, it crossed my mind, but I don't fancy upsetting the mountain gods and getting myself haunted.' I placed the hat back atop its pole, looping the scarf around it to tie it securely in place.

We headed off towards the neck of ice leading down from the pass and into the sea of rubble-strewn glacier, hurrying our steps as we passed beneath the ice cliffs that hung from the flanks of the tooth mountain. Only a few days before, an avalanche had come sweeping down from these cliffs and sprayed across the wide expanse of the pass. Mal had heard the whoomphing roar as the cliffs collapsed but in the stormy white-out conditions had been unable to tell where it was coming from. He had instinctively started running before realising he could just as well be running towards it. José, bringing up the rear some two hundred metres back, had been blissfully unaware of the avalanche as the noise from his personal stereo drowned out the low menacing thunder of the collapsing cliffs.

The debris had swept between Mal and José, momentarily pushing the clouds aside. Five minutes later, or earlier, and one of them would undoubtedly have been hit by the blast. I was glad I had replaced the hat as I forced myself to keep up with Neil's fast pace. It was no place in which to offend the mountain gods.

As I made the last awkward steps down from the ice and on to the moraines I came upon the mummified remains of an unfortunate yak. The carcass was partially frozen, twisted back on itself in a grotesque manner. Its teeth were bared in an anguished grin as if it had died laughing. Black vulcanised lips, stretched tautly in the sun, pulled back over the upper teeth. The eye-socket was dark and blank. The hide on its head was perfectly preserved but the body had been partly stripped to reveal wizened pink sinews and an exposed chain of brown vertebrae. The naked rack of exposed ribs protruded obscenely above the gaping empty stomach cavity. Tufts of brown fur clung to the yellowed bones. The body was dry and free of snow but the icy night-time temperatures had glued it firmly to the straw and dung that covered the stones. The vicious sweep of horns curled up and back, pointing towards a distant rocky peak.

It was impossible to tell how long ago the yak had died. There was no evidence of worms or insects feeding on the carcass and no sweet putrid smell to indicate that maggots or bacteria were hard at work digesting their enormous feast. It was too cold for the normal processes of decomposition to take place.

Looking around, I couldn't believe that foxes or wolves might venture this far out into the middle of the barren rubble of the glacier. Large birds – such as eagles, lammergeiers or Himalayan griffons – could account for the partially-consumed body, but the yak might have lain there for years in the freezing temperatures, rotting only by slow degrees.

'Another one?' Neil Lyndsey asked as he saw me stop.

'Yeah,' I said. 'They're everywhere.'

I had counted nineteen dead yaks between base camp and the Nangpa La. Some looked perfectly preserved, others half-eaten; one was visible as through water beneath the ice of the upper glacier – an ominous lurking warning to those who passed by.

Another body lay in scattered pieces, torn apart on its slow surge down the valley from the icy chamber that had buried it for so many years. The crevasse, which had long since fused around its prey, now reluctantly released its catch in broken pieces, sheared off bit by bit, as the glacial ice melted and the grind of tons of moraines cracked it from its icy kernel. A hoof protruded from beneath a boulder, some hairy hide in a lake, and a lone head sticking surreally from a grey grit-covered ice wall, one horn still buried in the ice, while the other poked out at an odd angle, as if from some eccentric's trophy room. Several days earlier I had stood on the knife-edge of loose rocks that overhung this black ice wall like an ill-kempt moustache and peered down at the yak's head.

An hour later as we descended a steep cone of shattered rocks I noticed a small hollow and the tell-tale red dung-strewn straw where two yaks had been abandoned.

'Shall we take a break?' I called to Neil and pointed towards the hollow. 'I want to get a photo of these two.'

We sat on our packs in the warm mid-day sun, sheltered in the hollow from the bite of the wind. The bulky black-haired corpses were huddled against some boulders opposite us. The yaks lay in composed solitude, resting against one another, as if they were merely sleeping. When I had first seen them, I was taken aback, wondering what the two stray yaks were doing in the middle of nowhere. I looked around the hollow for some clue as to what had happened. There was a scattering of earth and soil mixed with dung. It looked as if many animals had sheltered in the hollow. I imagined them packed together, black mounds of steaming hair, gradually whitening as the storm enveloped them. In the morning, roused by the cries of their handlers and the impact of accurately thrown stones, they would have struggled stiffly to their feet, shaking off the thick layers of snow and ice matting their hides. The hollow would have echoed to the sounds of jostling hooves, men struggling to saddle cumbersome loads, bells clanging as yaks shook their shaggy heads and uttered deep lowing protests.

Two had remained silently on the ground, one resting its shaggy head on the other's flank. No amount of kicks and cries could stir them. No life-betraying steam rose from their heavy bodies. Perhaps the urgent need to escape from the ferocity of the early monsoon storm meant that there had been no time to butcher the beasts, and so they were left there to be covered by the encroaching snow, silent witnesses of the dangers of the crossing.

Neil took a photograph of me cuddling the head of one of the animals in my lap. When I twisted the horns to turn the huge head to camera, there was a crunching sound and the air reeked of rotting liquefied brains suddenly released from the skull. Retching and gagging, I hung on to the head while Neil took delight in a slow and painstaking line-up of the shot.

The following morning I waved goodbye to Neil as he headed back up the moraines to Camp I. It had been kind of him to accompany me down to base, and although he said he had needed the break from the rest of the team, I also suspected he knew how despondent I was at having to give up. I wished him well on his summit attempt and hoped he would manage to tolerate R.J. for a few more days. He grunted and shrugged his shoulders at the suggestion. His summit bid was eventually to fail because of a logistical cock-up at Camp III, where he spent a night without a stove at 7,400 metres. This in turn fuelled more fractious acrimony between him and R.J., and would have led to fisticuffs had they not both been too tired and emotional at the time. Conflict between the gruff no-nonsense of a Yorkshireman and the political correctness of a Californian provided great hilarity for the rest of us.

15

FOOLS RUSH IN

I stood by the long low mound of stones and thought about the woman frozen beneath them. A flurry of snow flakes whipped against my bare legs. The sky had darkened and heavy-bellied clouds were jostling for space on the ridge-tops. I shivered, feeling the goose bumps rising. I thought of changing out of my shorts, and then looked at the grave again. It seemed rude to change in front of her.

I tried to imagine what it would be like to lie there in such a cold and barren place. For a brief moment I felt a strong urge to get down on my knees and remove the covering stones. There was no one around, no one to see me. I wasn't sure why I wanted to do it. I wanted to see her, to see that there was actually someone under those rocks. *Was she Tibetan? Would I learn anything?* The grave seemed so unreal, not a grave at all, just another mound of shattered cold rocks in a stony landscape. It wouldn't take long to uncover her.

I pulled back in alarm, feeling furtive and dirty. It was as if some perverse shameful secret about myself had just been revealed. *Why would I want to do that? Why even think it?* It had been just a thought, a stupid idea, but the temptation to carry it out was frightening. It was like that familiar pulling, mesmerising effect of looking over great drops, the feeling that, however horrible the outcome, however much I didn't want to do it, the hypnotic sense of looking down was urging me to let go, to accept the swooping fall.

'Bloody hell,' I said aloud to the windswept hills. 'I'm going

203

mad.' I turned and walked swiftly away from the grave. It disturbed me to have even contemplated such a thing, despite knowing that I would find only the remains of a corpse beneath the stones. Yet I couldn't stop wondering about her under that cold crushing weight, all alone in nowhere. Maybe seeing her would have been a way of acknowledging that she had existed; a greeting and a farewell. It seemed callous just to walk by.

Earlier I had thought to make some offering at her grave when I returned from the mountain, to leave something there, a salute of some sort; maybe just to think of her, as if thought itself were a gift, like a prayer. I wasn't sure. I hadn't reasoned it out properly, and then the grave was there, unexpectedly appearing from the ground as I walked down the track. It caught me out, and instead of offering her something I had stood dumbly staring at the pile of stones, lost in thoughts.

'Sorry,' I said quietly as I walked away. Maybe it was she who had suggested that I should uncover her. Perhaps she was unhappy, or her spirit was lost. I felt a chill of superstition run up my spine. It was ridiculous. She was not there now, only her bones, so what was the use of apologising to her? I was suddenly aware of how small and alone I was in such a vast, glowering land. It was easy to believe in demons and mountain gods, spirits and spectral shadows haunting the hills. I glanced back at the grave and shivered, remembering the clammy sense of fear I had experienced in the dome shelters earlier in the expedition. Could there be any connection?

As soon as my back was turned a panicky dread urged me to run. It was like it had been as a child when passing darkened open doorways, expecting something horrible to rush out at me. I stumbled on the path in my haste to get away.

'Get a grip,' I muttered to myself as I forced my legs hard and fast down the rough track, feeling absurdly melodramatic as the distance increased between myself and the lonely grave. 'It's all in your head. You don't believe in ghosts.' I said it aloud and didn't look back.

I had left base camp that morning hoping to reach the small hut at Ari by nightfall, but I had made such fast progress that I was now aiming to get as far as Thami that night. It would be a long day, covering nearly seven thousand feet of descent. The same distance had taken three days on the way up. Now acclimatised and feeling fit, I reckoned I could make it back in ten hours' hard slog. By midday the clouds had covered the sky and a storm was threatening.

I kept heading towards the Matterhorn mountain, the familiar landmark of the walk-in, sure that the route was quite straightforward. When the mountain disappeared behind a wall of grey cloud, my confidence began to fade. I kept glancing to my right, checking that I was in the same glacier valley and had not by mistake forked off to the left. Now, in the misty gloom, everything looked exactly the same. I had neither map nor compass, only a three-week-old memory of the valley.

I pulled on my pile jacket and zipped it up under my chin. The snow was coming in short bursts, after which there would be a brief clearing. I waited for a clearance, hoping to see down into the valley below me. I felt sure that I was too high. A huge square-cut monolith of golden granite had appeared suddenly from a bank of cloud. I couldn't recall seeing it before. It stood on the edge of the high lateral moraines, pointing up into the clouds like some melancholy tombstone. *Surely I couldn't have missed it on the way up?* It was far too distinctive. I was lost.

For the past hour I had seen no trace of a path, no yak dung or litter. Either I had entered a side valley or had simply strayed too high up the hillside. The wind gusted against my hunched back, and for a moment I could see what lay below. There was a glimpse of dry stone walls and flat fields where I had expected only the terminal moraines of the old glacier.

I thought I could see the shadow of a house on the other side of the river. *Could it be Ari?* No, *that would be hours away*. Whatever it was, I had to find out. Squatting in the shadow of a hundred-foot tombstone wasn't getting me anywhere.

I scrambled down the steep boulder-strewn hillside until I reached an area of spongy grass and stunted shrubs. I had ducked below the cloud ceiling and the whole valley was laid out beneath me. I did not recognise any of it.

When I reached the river I got up on to a high boulder and peered across to the other side. A wall ran along the raised bank of the river and merged with what looked like a shingled roof. I felt certain that we hadn't crossed on the way up and was confused by what appeared to be a small farming settlement.

The river rushed past the rock on which I was teetering with alarming power. I had made a series of committing leaps from rock to rock in a foolhardy attempt to cross the torrent. The jumps took me by a torturous zig-zagging route into midstream, and the last rock from which I'd leapt toppled over as I left it and sank into the freezing water. I watched it go with dismay.

The ski-stick I poked into the surging flow nearly pulled me off balance. I wavered, flapping the sticks around wildly, trying to regain my balance. There was no way back. Even if the rock hadn't disappeared, I doubt if I could have made the return jump. I looked grimly at the far bank. It was about twelve feet away, separated from me by a flood of deep water issuing from between two large rounded boulders. I dismissed the idea of making a lurching jump at them and I tried again with both sticks, managing to force them down through the current into the rocky bed. As I did so, I found myself leaning out far over the water pressing down as hard as I could and unable to push myself upright again. I remained fixed in the position of a downhill skier with planted sticks, staring manically at the rush of water and feeling foolishly trapped. I was going to get seriously wet.

I craned my head to the left in an attempt to see whether there was anything I could grab hold of once I was swept away. There was nothing. I remembered how the river had thundered through the gorge below Thami at the point where Chwang had undergone extreme dental surgery. It had not been wide, but it was ferociously powerful. I couldn't remember whether there were any similar gorges further up. *I could die in this,* I thought, and began to giggle.

I heard a shout above the noise and looked up between my outstretched arms. Two Sherpanis were peering over the wall above the river bank in front of me. They were laughing and waving with delight. I couldn't see what was so funny, and my arms had begun to shake with the effort of holding myself up. At that moment my rucksack chose to slip to the side. As a precaution I had unfastened the belt buckle when starting to cross the river. If I fell in, I wanted to be able to rid myself of the sack which would otherwise pull me under. Now the damn thing had swung to the side and was dragging me in anyway. I gave a howl of fright and launched myself out over the water, swinging between the sticks in pole vault fashion and landing up to my waist in the freezing water.

Immediately the current tore my legs from under me as I thrashed out and down with my left stick and it jammed against something on the bottom, momentarily halting the fall. I made a desperate forward lunge as my legs cleared the river bed and my hand plunged between two large rocks just beneath the surface. I heard shrieks of laughter from the wall above me.

'Ari?' I said, staggering from the clutches of the icy river. I was shaking with the cold and the adrenalin surge of fear. The girls laughed louder at my question and pointed at one another, and then shrieked some more. They disappeared behind the wall. Looking over, I found them sitting by a pile of potatoes, laughing happily.

'Ari?' I repeated, pointing to the nearby house. The elder girl stood up and shook her head. She held the palm of her hand up, covering her nose and mouth, but I could see from her eyes that she was trying not to laugh.

'Not Ari?' I shook my head. She pointed down river.

'Ari down there, yes?' I interpreted. 'On this side.' I pointed vigorously at the river bank. She shook her head again and pointed at the other side, and then she sat down abruptly and erupted into laughter. Her companion, who was cutting up the seed potatoes ready for planting, had her head on her knees. Her shoulders were shaking.

'Not this side,' I mumbled, 'well, that's just great.'

Half a mile downstream I found a place where I could squelch across to the opposite bank and sat down on a boulder to squeeze out my socks. At least I knew now where I was.

An hour later I found myself walking across the flat alluvial gravel leading to the hut at Ari. I kept looking over my shoulder. I was being followed by some peculiar creature. I had spotted it shortly after leaving the river. It had been a small dot moving among the rocks. At first I had thought it might be a stray yak but quickly realised it was too small. Whatever it was, it was steadily gaining on me. I quickened my pace, checking behind me from time to time to see whether I had shaken it off. To my dismay, it was drawing closer. It looked vaguely like a small black haystack. I couldn't see any legs, just this odd spiky dark shape moving rapidly across the gravel pan.

I was almost running by the time I reached the hut. The door was padlocked. There was no one there. I wanted some tea and a few minutes rest, but more I wanted to be inside the hut in case whatever was following me had less than friendly intentions.

'Hello,' I shouted hopefully at the silent door. There was a rustling sound behind me and I leapt round to face it. A huge stack of what appeared to be juniper branches was waving in the wind. A tiny pair of feet poked out from beneath the foliage. To my amazement, the branches were suddenly thrown to the ground to reveal the small figure of the Sherpani who lived in the hut. I stared at her – all four-feet-eight of her – and then at the massive pile of juniper branches she had been carrying. So I had been followed by a haystack.

She unlocked the door and motioned me to enter. She quickly produced a thermos of tea and some boiled eggs and then went out to rearrange her load of juniper, stacking it neatly against the wall. Obviously she had spotted me ahead of her on the path and had tried to overtake me so as to be at the hut when I arrived. It was a peculiar feeling to be stalked

by a high speed haystack and to lose the race. It was also hard
to believe that she could walk so fast under such a heavy and
awkward load.

I reached Thami in darkness, cautiously feeling my way along
the path that followed the contours of the hillside above the
loud roar of the river. My legs ached from ten hours of rough
descent. The head cold that had been plaguing me for weeks
began to release itself and I was suddenly awash with fluids.
The cough had eased but I had to blow my nose almost
continuously. Was it an indication of pulmonary oedema? I
felt healthy and strong and knew that if I had been really ill I
could not have made such a long arduous descent so quickly.

When I reached the door of the lodge I stopped outside for
five minutes, spitting great quantities of what seemed to be
water from my lungs. I took it as a sign of improvement but
at the same time was quite shaken by the thin watery white
phlegm. I stood in the darkness trying to listen for the tell-tale
bubbling sound in my chest. There was none. I felt cheerful
for the first time that day.

The ladies of the house welcomed me with broad smiles.
The old gold-toothed grandmother ushered me solicitously to
a table and brought me a steaming bowl of stew and piping
hot tea. The stew was a mixture of rice and egg and potatoes
with the odd gristly lump of yak meat hidden in the thick
broth. I watched as the old woman's daughter came in
carrying her infant child and laid it on a bench opposite my
table. The grandmother lit a kerosene lamp and laughed when
I called her *didi* and asked for a beer. They returned to their
places by the hearth in the next room, leaving the baby
sleeping contentedly in the golden glow of the Tilley lamp.
The infant was swaddled so tightly that the only part of it I
could see was a little pink nose poking out from the taut
cocoon of blankets.

I remembered being in the same lodge with Mal two years
earlier and seeing a similarly swaddled infant sleeping on one
of the tables nearby. We were silently playing chess,
concentrating on the moves, when I noticed a movement in

the shadows at the back of the long rectangular room. I looked across and was astounded to see what looked like a stoat walking across one of the tables. It was heading directly for the sleeping baby. I nudged Mal with my foot to tell him silently to look at the stoat. He glanced suspiciously at the animal, which was no more than twenty feet from us. It froze momentarily in mid-stride, keeping its long sinuous body close to the wood and sniffing warily. It appeared not to have noticed us.

At that moment there was an hysterical scream and then bedlam broke out. The young mother came rushing across the room, screaming in fury, and hurled something in the direction of the stoat. It simply vanished. I was looking at the creature but didn't see it move. It just disappeared. The Sherpani rushed to the spot where she thought it had gone and began kicking and stamping, screaming all the while. The older woman came running into the room wielding a large stick and repeatedly shouting the same word. The mother grabbed her swaddled baby and held it protectively in her arms while the grandmother began a ferocious counter-attack. The stoat must have been in Namche by then.

I heard later that there had been incidents in the past when helpless babies had been severely savaged, blinded, and even killed by these animals, which look like a large ferret or a small stoat. The baby, tightly bound with its arms trapped beneath the blanket, had no defence against such an attack. If the mother had been outside in the fields at the time, she might never have heard its cries, and from what I knew of ferrets, I guessed it would have begun to eat the baby alive. I had once hunted rabbits with ferrets in my youth and clearly remembered listening to the high-pitched squeals of agony coming from deep inside the warren. When we dug it out, I was horrified to see an adult rabbit among its slaughtered litter with its eyes gnawed away. It was still alive. I was overwhelmed with revulsion and never went ferreting again.

When the Tilley lamp began to fade, the grandmother returned and vigorously pumped up the pressure. She hung the lamp on a soot-blackened hook in the ceiling, picked up the sleeping baby and rocked it gently in her arms. Her daughter handed me the key for the bunkhouse adjoining the lodge, and soon I lay in my sleeping bag, gazing through the wire grill on the window at a full moon rising over the dark fields of Thami. If all had gone to plan, Mal and the first summit team would be moving up to a high camp in readiness for an attempt on the summit. The sky was clear and the weather looked set fair. The light of the moon was astonishingly bright, filling the small room with a silvery grey light that was almost strong enough to read by, but I was tired and soon slept.

I awoke with a start in the cold dark of approaching dawn. The moon had gone and the stars flooded back across the sky. I was shivering violently. My sleeping bag had slipped down exposing my naked chest to the icy night air. A light breeze came through the window with the low thunder of the nearby river. I heard heavy animals rustling in the straw-filled byre behind the wall and the heavy metallic clink of something swinging against the shutters. Pulling the hood over my shoulders, I snuggled into the downy warmth of my pit and wondered what had wakened me so abruptly.

I had faint uneasy memories of a dream of a round hairless head with piercing black eyes and a woman walking through snow alone. There was something vaguely familiar about the bald staring head which at first I could not recognise. Then I remembered the boy with the adult gaze in the hut at Ari. Why had I dreamed of him? I tensed, wondering if someone was in the room with me. I peered cautiously out from the rim of my sleeping bag, pulling it down with one finger and eyeing the starlit shadows nervously. A figure stood at the foot of my bed, hooded and black. My heart jumped and I shrank back against the soft down until I recognised the outline of my jacket hanging from a hook on the ceiling beam and felt childishly foolish at my fear.

The walk down to Namche next morning was a delight. Leaving the lodge at Thami in shorts and a T-shirt, I had come upon a small herd of Himalayan Tahr, a species of wild goat, feeding on the hillside no more than twenty yards from where

I stood on the path. Usually these animals confine themselves to steep inaccessible, craggy hillsides, moving surefootedly in family groups across almost vertical rockfaces, feeding on the sparse patches of lichens and tufty grasses. In the spring they are lured down to the lower valleys by the temptations of abundant fresh growth. I was surprised to see them so close to a relatively busy trail.

As far as I could tell they were all female. They were powerful, agile-looking animals standing about waist high and sporting distinctive curling horns. I guessed that most of them were pregnant after the winter rut, and that probably explained their uncharacteristic bravery in coming down so low. They needed to fatten up in preparation for the birth of their young in little more than a month's time. Winter at such altitudes must be a harsh test for such animals.

I watched them feeding nervously, huddled in a tight protective group, ready to flee at the slightest hint of danger. I reached slowly for my camera, trying to be as quiet as possible, but when I lifted it to my eye I was disappointed to see them bounding skittishly away into the trees. The reflected sun had flashed an alarm signal to them as I raised the lens and they were gone; a golden amber memory lost amidst the stunted trees.

The sides of the path were edged with flowers blooming in the warmth of early spring. The contrast between the cold rocky base camp that I had left the day before and the lush colourful hills below Thami could not have been more marked. The air seemed thicker and fresher and the colours had an added vibrant intensity. The smell of wet dew-soaked foliage and rich damp earth seemed wonderfully fragrant. After the sparse Alpine scrub hillsides above Thami the land swiftly became forested and verdant. Even higher up I had noticed the early blooms of dwarf rhododendrons and tiny flowers like primulas and primroses sheltering from the wind in the lee of boulders and earth banks. Here and there strange hairy plants with spiky leaves hugged the ground to escape the extremes of temperature.

Here in the valley the vibrance of spring was breathtaking.

Masses of rhododendrons in full bloom mixed with stands of birch and silver fir. There was an urgent sense of growth wherever I looked. The sunlight filtered through the branches as I walked down packed mud paths like tunnels through the trees. In places light green lichen hung from the branches of the birch trees, backlit by the morning sun and revealing strips of red and amber through papery peeling bark.

I reached Namche before noon and had a celebratory beer and a cigarette that made my head spin until I was forced to sit down and fight the urge to vomit. I have never understood why I start smoking again after long periods of abstention. The first couple of packets always make me feel dizzy and nauseous and I find the taste repulsive, yet every time I persist despite my disgust, reassuring myself that they will taste better eventually. I have heard that nicotine addiction is as powerful as heroin, and although not convinced, I do sometimes wonder how it is that I can force myself to persevere when every sense in my body is crying out for me to stop.

It was still sunny and warm when I set off down the steep red dusty switchbacks of the Namche hill, intent on reaching Phakding that afternoon. From there it was a leisurely two-hour stroll up to the airport at Lukla. By the time I had left the National Park and reached Monjo, the weather had completely changed.

I looked back up the valley at the notch in the blue pine-covered hillsides where the Sherpas' sacred mountain, Khumbi-yul-lha, dominated the view. Only the very tip of the summit rocks was visible. Heavy dark clouds were swelling up on either side and soon it was engulfed. The air was warm, almost muggy despite the cooling rush of wind dragged down by the river. I glanced at my watch and tried to work out how quickly the weather was deteriorating. It was less than two hours' walk to Phakding, and even if it began to rain within the hour, I decided that I could dry out in front of the fire in the lodge easily enough.

Before setting off down the steep cleft in the rock which led to a crossing of the Monjo Khola, a tributary of the Dudh Kosi river, I checked to make sure that the contents of my rucksack were waterproofed by a large plastic bag. At the small village of Chumowa I turned down towards the main river until I reached a rickety log bridge, reinforced with slabs of rock, which spanned the Dudh Kosi. I had barely stepped down from the bridge when a deep ominous vibration echoed through the steep-sided canyon.

The music blaring through my headphones made it seem as if it was coming towards me from high above the canyon walls. I flinched in alarm and quickly looked up at the mass of trees searching for signs of the landslide. A porter, bowed down under the massive weight of his load, smiled at me as he trudged slowly past. The top of his load which was crammed into a traditional conical wicker basket was covered in plastic. The first heavy rain drops spattered down. There was another long rumbling peel of thunder which reverberated down from the heavy cloud cover as I hurried on up a steep track leading to a path that contoured the canyon walls above the river.

The river careered down through rocky rapids in a flood of boiling icy green water and surging piles of white foam where whirlpools and waves fought for space among the largest boulders. The trail wound through pine forests, clinging to the steep walls of the canyon. Occasionally rockfaces loomed through the drifting clouds and small waterfalls spewed out across the path, cutting deep clefts in the eroded mud.

My guess that it would be a short-lived shower was wildly wrong. In minutes I was as soaked as if I had fallen in a river. The rain fell in torrents of huge fat drops, but it was fairly warm, so I continued to walk in my shorts and light shower-proof jacket, hoping to keep my main clothes dry.

On the opposite bank I could see great cone-shaped brown scars cutting through the trees where landslides had swept down into the river. An impressive cascade, swollen by the flood of storm waters, burst out from a red-streaked cliff and free fell for hundreds of feet. The wind tore at the falling curtains of spray, blasting it into smoky clouds of vapour across the swaying trees.

Another thunderous bellow, closer this time, echoed round the valley and I stopped abruptly and stared suspiciously up into the trees above me, half expecting to see boulders and a deluge of red mud to come crashing down. The ferocity of the storm was beginning to worry me. An enormous quantity of water had already been dumped on the surrounding hills, and I could sense the pressure of all that retaining moisture. It had to come down to the river and I began to wonder how safe it was to be walking on the trail at this time.

I became aware that the stream of porters usually to be seen on this main route had vanished. I had passed only the one heavily laden porter by the bridge, hurrying to cross to the other side. Another rumble and then a loud cracking report made me look up fearfully again. It sounded like breaking timber. I began to slow down, conscious that in many places I was walking on no more than loose, unstable mud, often undercut by landslides that had swept into the river hundreds of feet below. More and more frequently I was crossing torrents of mud spewing down culverts through the trees. I had walked this trail seven or eight times in the past and it had never been anything more than a pleasant relaxing stroll through the forests. It now felt distinctly dangerous and menacing.

My question about the porters was soon resolved as I came round a corner to find a huddle of about twenty sheltering beneath the dry overhang of a massive boulder, almost a cliff, that was set into the side of the path. They had stacked their baskets in a semi-circle around themselves and a few small fires had been coaxed into life. A blackened pot, balanced on rounded stones, was bubbling and steaming. The porters were passing round cigarettes and chatting cheerfully among themselves when I arrived. They all looked up in surprise and then burst into laughter at the sight of me. I was bedraggled, wet through, and looked quite idiotic in shorts during a downpour. One of the men waved me towards him, indicating that I should take shelter.

I glanced around hesitantly, trying to remember how far was the next village. Thinking that the most precipitous part of the trail was behind me, I declined the invitation and began to walk on. Two more men waved at me and others shook their heads. They were no longer smiling. I thanked them, turned away and hurried down the track.

The muddy path was almost washed away in places where natural gullies fed the storm waters down through the forests. I held on to scrappy pieces of vegetation as I teetered across, glancing down between my legs at the mud and rocks slithering off the remnants of the path beneath my feet and plunging vertically into the river below. The whole side of the valley seemed to have become a potential landslip. The scars in the hillsides that on sunny days I had paid little attention to now seemed to be loaded with menace. Some of them were huge, extending in narrowing cones for nearly a thousand feet up into the trees, and at the river's edge spreading out to cover a width of three or four hundred feet. These were no small slides but huge collapses, which showed where great areas of the hillsides had slumped in a sudden titanic surge towards the river.

I edged along the track keeping tight up against the valley side, wary of what was holding the path up. In places I could see rock walls and steep screes stretching down to the thundering chaos of the river, but frequently there was nothing to indicate that it had been undercut. I began to regret my impatient desire to get on, ignoring the advice of the porters, whose generations of experience should have warned me that something was seriously amiss.

By the time I reached Benkar, about an hour from Phakding, I had decided to abandon any further attempt to reach my goal and instead looked for a lodge in the village. Unfortunately the whole place seemed to be closed. All the doors were locked and shutters on many of the windows were barred. I felt distinctly unwelcome, although the villagers were probably quite naturally taking precautions against the storm.

I squelched through a river of ankle-deep muddy water that had once been the main street. There was no one around. I saw a sodden miserable yak calf tied to a post. The creature stared accusingly at me with huge wet eyes but nothing else moved. The muddy stream that had been the path swirled around a corner and then cascaded down some high steps and flooded into a courtyard formed between the enclosing wall of terraced fields and an L-shaped lodge. A three-feet high wall of dressed stone ran round the side of the lodge pooling the floodwater into a deep brown rectangular basin. I stopped at the top of the rock steps wondering how I was going to get to the other side where a similar flight of steps emerged from the swirling water.

The lodge appeared to be closed. I felt reluctant to go round banging on doors and disturbing the occupants even though I felt sure that they would welcome my custom. The rain was teeming down with increasing savagery. It had been pouring from the skies for the last hour and showed no signs of abating. I couldn't begin to guess at the millions of gallons of water that must be flooding down from the surrounding hills. I reassured myself that storms like this must happen every day during the monsoon season, or at least, I hoped they did. It would explain the heavily eroded nature of the path along which I had just come.

I had heard accounts of floods in the past that had caused devastation in the valley. Nearly ten years before, on 5th August 1985, an ice lake hemmed in by moraines above Thami had burst through the retaining walls of loose mud and rocks after a period of heavy rain. August is the wettest month at the height of the monsoon. The ensuing flood had created a huge wall of water that rushed down into the Bhote Kosi, destroying the recently-built hydroelectric power plant below Thami, devastating the tree nurseries, and washing away most of the bridges between Thami and Phakding. Some of these were strong, well-engineered structures built by Sir Edmund Hillary's aid programme. Ancient trails and sacred carved mani-boulders had also vanished in the flood waters. Fortunately no one was killed, although some of the mani-boulders had been carved to commemorate the deaths of Sherpa families in a similar flood when a moraine lake burst beneath Ama Dablam years before.

The empty silence of the village suggested to me that the inhabitants might know something I didn't and had long since left their precariously sited village to seek temporary shelter in a safer place. I sat down on the edge of the steps and watched the debris of litter and grey foam swirling round the courtyard. I was so wet that there seemed little point in seeking shelter beneath the porch in front of the lodge – and anyway I couldn't work out how to reach it without wading. The traverse across the intervening wall looked to be too difficult in the wet muddy conditions.

I lit a cigarette, cupping it in my hand to protect it from the rain, and sat on the rocks feeling dizzy. A peal of thunder resounded from the surrounding forests followed by some abrupt sharp cracks like gunfire. I ducked instinctively, looking out from the hood of my coat for signs of lightning. I raised the cigarette to my lips and inhaled deeply until a particularly heavy raindrop snapped it at the filter and it dropped with a hiss into the pool.

There was a sudden banging noise and the door of the lodge flew open as two girls stumbled, laughing, on to the wooden boardwalk. A young man came to the door and leant with studied casualness against the frame. The girls were young, in their mid-teens, and dressed to the nines. Their brightly-coloured silk blouses contrasted with the dark cloth of their long body-hugging *ingis*. White bob-socks flashed from beneath the hems of their long dresses and they wore startlingly white baseball boots. They looked as if they had just been freshly dyed that morning. Their waist-length hair hung down their backs in silky black plaits. Both had black aprons with red stripes, held in place by the traditional broad silver clasps. The elder of the two girls wore a long necklace of blue turquoise and pink coral. I noticed that her waist clasp was bigger and more ornate than her companion's. It had distinct patterns of scrolls worked into the silver and a single pale blue turquoise set in its centre. She also wore a small charm box around her neck.

The young man and his friend, whom I noticed looking out over his shoulder, were in western-style clothes – jeans, white shirts and black leather jackets. The girls chatted and giggled with the men for a while before an older Sherpani emerged from the house and presented them each with a square of clear plastic about three feet by three which they held above their tightly plaited and braided heads with arms outstretched.

Without hesitation they stepped into the brown flood waters of the courtyard and waded daintily towards the far steps. Their white bob-socks instantly turned brown and there was a wash of white on the surface of the water from their baseball boots.

I stood up and lifted my rucksack on to my shoulders. If they were happy to travel, then I would follow. I had been surprised to see that the water was only ankle deep. Jumping confidently down from the last rock step, I sank into murky water that reached my lower thighs. The two boys laughed and the girls turned and giggled as I floundered towards a tall prayer flag which stood in the centre of the courtyard.

Switching off my Walkman, I began to follow the two girls, barely able to keep up with them as they skipped and jumped along the track leading out of the village and up towards the main trail which climbed through the forests that clung to the steep hillside. Occasionally I saw them glance back and then laugh delightedly at one another as they saw me thrashing along in their wake, ski-sticks clacking and jets of water squirting out from my boots.

When we entered the woods I noticed that the path seemed to be even more heavily eroded than it had been earlier. We jumped and ran across patches where flood-water and debris washed across the path. Thunder crashed in almost continuous cacophony above, resonating like some immense drum roll. I began to enjoy myself. It was no less dangerous than before but I was encouraged by the carefree happiness of the girls running ahead of me.

They were probably sisters out courting, the younger girl acting as chaperone to her older companion whose more elaborate jewellery and the young man's obvious interest in her made clear enough. The value of her jewellery was a symbol both of the wealth and the status of her family on display to her suitor's family.

I tried to remember the complicated system of marriage that the Sherpas adhered to as the girls ran laughing and giggling ahead of me, looking back every now and then to be sure that I was keeping up. Like a skeletal structure of bones, the clan forms the essential framework of the Sherpa social system; to be a member of one of the twenty-one clans is to be a Sherpa. All Sherpas must marry outside of their own clans; sexual relationships between clan members are regarded as taboo, much as we think of incest. It also has the effect of unifying the various communities of clans. Clan membership is passed down through the male line since the Sherpas believe that the child is given blood (*tahk*) by its mother and *rhu*, the all-important bone, by its father. Children inherit the clan of their father until such time as a daughter marries into the clan of her husband.

Marriage is usually arranged by the parents but the Sherpas are remarkably tolerant and will respect the wishes of their children if they are unhappy with a particular arrangement. Courtships and eventual marriage can be a long drawn out business taking several years and three separate ceremonies. This prevents couples rushing into things and gives them a chance to consider what they are doing, as well as providing the time for them to establish their own household and family.

Betrothal usually takes place in adolescence, but sometimes happens after the couple have become lovers. The second ceremony, the *dem-chang*, or 'beer tying', is arranged when they are in a marital state although still living apart in their family homes. Children can be born at any time, but after the 'beer tying' they are regarded as legitimate, and from then on some form of payment is due if the marriage is called off. The last ceremony is when the husband takes his wife to his own family home. The wife provides a dowry of cattle, jewellery, clothing or land depending on her wealth. The husband's family usually provides the family land for the new household.

There was a time when the Sherpas were traditionally polygamous (two women married to one man), and occasionally polyandrous (two or three brothers married to one woman) but this has largely died out since the practice was outlawed by the government. In any case, it usually happened only in childless marriages or where there might be an unwanted division of family property.

The relaxed nature of the marriage system creates a warm

secure informal family relationship in which the children can develop happily. Unfortunately there is a higher proportion of unmarried women in the Khumbu than men, partly due in recent decades to the high level of male fatalities in mountaineering accidents. This places a considerable social and economic burden on the society.

I guessed that the older girl had either already been betrothed (the first ceremony) or was on the point of the 'beer tying' stage and about to enter the semi-marital relationship. Clearly they were returning to their own households and their own clan in the neighbouring village of Phakding.

The girls soon grew bored with allowing for my slow pace and took off, running through the tunnel of interlocked pine trees, their baseball boots slapping on the muddy path and the plastic shields flapping wildly above their heads. I felt oddly dismayed at the loss of their smiles and tinkling laughter and quickly reverted to my gloomily pessimistic mood about the dangers of the track. I turned my stereo back on and the sounds of Billy Idol erupted in my ears, momentarily drowning out yet another crash of thunder.

It came as some surprise, then, to round a spur overlooking the river far below and find them huddled on the track deep in earnest conversation. They looked up as I came along the path but they were no longer smiling. I had a feeling that they had been waiting for me. It was then that I saw why they had stopped. A massive landslide had completely destroyed the path. A swath of rocks, mud and water had cut across the path and plunged down the almost vertical bank to the river below. I noticed how the green and white surge of the river was stained a bloody reddish brown colour downstream of the slide.

There was the faintest line across the slippage where the old track had not been totally ripped away. It presented a vague flattening in the steep slope of debris that was still pouring down the hillside. I stared despondently at the hundred yards of slippage and knew that there was no choice but to retrace our steps to Benkar.

I was sure we were no more than fifteen minutes walk from

Phakding and began to feel cold now that I had stopped. My legs quivered from tired muscles.

Just as I was about to turn wearily away I noticed that the girls seemed to have come to some decision. They stared at one another intently with half-smiles of excitement on their faces and then both looked deliberately at me. It felt as if some sort of challenge was being laid down which I couldn't quite understand. Suddenly, without warning, the girls crouched down, pressed their fingers to their lips, uttered a banshee scream of high-pitched hysteria and launched themselves across the landslide.

I couldn't believe it. The damn thing was still moving. I glanced fearfully at the plunging drop into the river. If they lost their footing in their slippery baseball boots, or if the surge increased at all, they would have no chance. Even if they survived the tumbling, lacerating fall the river would swiftly have ripped them away to instant death.

For a frozen moment I stood paralysed in the rain, staring at their crazy howling dash across the treacherous slopes – and then I was hollering and yelling and charging after them with Billy Idol screaming 'Nice day for a white wedding . . .' in my ears. The younger girl looked back, nearly losing her footing, and screamed with delight at the sight of me bounding after her, and then ran on with her *ingi* flapping dangerously at her ankles and the strip of plastic held buoyantly aloft.

My initial spurt of deranged madness abruptly evaporated. It was like trying to run sideways across crunchy toffee with my feet threatening to slither away from me and my lungs bursting with the effort of staying upright. It was quite impossible to think of stopping, let alone turning back. I would have been winging towards the river the moment I hesitated.

Right in the middle of the cone of moving sludge a stream of fast-flowing clearer water rushed down a deep culvert. I hurdled the gap, thumping heavily into the crumbling bank of the far wall, and for an instant almost toppled into the flood of water. With a squeak of fear and a hard shove with a ski-stick I somehow managed to regain my momentum and gallop on after the girls.

On the point of tears from the pain of running so strenuously at nine thousand feet, I stumbled to my knees with exhaustion on the far side of the landslide. I heard the girls laughing hysterically as I hung my head and gasped for breath. When at last I looked up I saw that they were standing a few yards away, supporting one another in their arms and staring at me as they laughed.

'Very funny,' I said, and then I felt the panic subside and laughed with them. They clapped their hands together in a rapid excited applause at our success and then took off down the track, clear plastic flapping defiantly in the wind.

I staggered wearily after them, praying that there would be no more surprises ahead. The track wound round the hillside contouring over the spurs that reached down to the river. There was a final steep climb up a muddy hillock before the track led down to the village of Phakding. As I rounded the bend and saw the hillock rising into the grey clouds I was dismayed to find another landslide blocking my path. It was not nearly as wide as the earlier one but somehow it seemed more threatening. It also looked suspiciously as if it had only just happened. I could see where some of the exposed earth was still dry. I stopped to examine the geography of the path and realised what had happened.

At the point of collapse the track had curved round an intervening spur which protruded out over the river. I remembered it from the walk-in. It was close to where the stampeding yak had plunged off the path and broken its back. From the look of it the wildly undercut path had simply fallen into the river below. There were tell-tale grooves in the sheered-off wall of conglomerate mud and stones where seeping water had undermined the trail. As I stared grimly at this impasse, wondering how I was going to get past it, my eye was caught by some movement far below by the edge of the river.

It was a large piece of clear plastic flapping in the wind. One corner was partially buried in the earth holding it in place.

'Oh God, no!' I stared fixedly at the pathetic flapping plastic and wiped the rainwater from my face. 'No. It couldn't have taken them?'

I looked around for signs of footsteps in the freshly cut landslide scar showing that they might have crossed after the collapse. There was nothing to be seen.

I sank to my knees and stared hopelessly down at the raging river. Nothing could have survived down there. It was only chance that the flimsy piece of plastic had been trapped by the falling rocks. I searched the debris, praying that I was wrong, and hoping I would see no more evidence of what had happened – a baseball boot sticking from the wet compacted earth, a torn apron – but I saw nothing. They were gone.

Half an hour later, after gingerly creeping across the crumbling scar, I stepped on to the dilapidated cantilever bridge that spanned the river between the two halves of Phakding village. Prayer flags and sodden white *khata* scarves tied along the wire handrail blew out in ragged streamers. I walked carefully out to the middle of the dipping, swinging bridge, gripping the cold steel cable for support and placing my feet carefully. In places the wooden planking was split and there were a few large holes revealing the torrential spate of the river beneath me. Halfway across I stopped and, grasping the handrail, faced upstream and searched the west bank for any signs of the girls. Through the gusting grey sheets of rain I could just make out the shadowed prow of the spur where the path had collapsed. I found it hard to believe that they had been killed and yet the evidence seemed so irrefutable.

I wondered if I should tell someone what had happened. I didn't know whom to approach and felt numb and very weary.

The lodge where I had stayed so many times before was open. The young Sherpani recognised me at once and, laughing at my sodden state, hurried to light the fire in the deserted lounge room and bring me a welcome bowl of steaming potato soup.

'Do you know two girls from the village coming here from Benkar?' I asked, but she didn't understand.

'Land falling.' I mimed the movement of a slide and pointed in the direction of the bridge. Her eyes lit up, and she smiled.

'Yes, very bad.' She nodded.

'Two girls falling,' I said, trying to show figures falling with two fingers. Her face clouded over and she pointed at me.

'No, not me,' I said hurriedly. 'My friends. Two Sherpanis.' I repeated and made a toppling action with my hand. 'Into river.'

The Sherpani looked confused and worried. She turned to the top of the wooden stairs and called out. A man appeared and she spoke urgently to him. His face was tanned a dark leathery brown and was deeply wrinkled. I couldn't begin to guess at his age. He looked at me as he listened. He held up two fingers and made a questioning shrugging gesture.

'Yes, Dui bahini (two younger sisters),' I said and shrugged. He made a falling gesture. 'I think so,' I murmured, not sure now what I had seen. He said something sharply to the woman and I heard his heavy thumping steps on the stairs.

At that moment there was a peal of excited laughter from outside. It was very familiar. I felt a surge of happiness rush through me as I went to the window and looked down. The two girls stood in bare feet washing their bob-socks under a stand-pipe, flicking droplets of water at one another in the pouring rain and laughing. One held a sheet of plastic across her shoulders while the other hunched against the rain without protection. I recognised the charm box and the swinging red and blue necklace. I laughed as I saw the cotton bobble on the heel of her short sock. I'd never seen anyone wearing such socks in Nepal before.

'It is okay, didi,' I said, turning to the worried Sherpani. 'It is them. No falling.' I shook my head vigorously. She looked out of the window and smiled, pointing to the girls for affirmation. I nodded. She leant out and called to the wrinkled old man who had just emerged into the yard pulling a coat on to his shoulders. The girls looked up, recognised me, and hid their giggling faces behind their hands.

I sat in front of my bowl of soup listening to the Sherpani shout down my mistaken idea that they were dead and heard in reply their cackles of delighted laughter.

16

THE OLD SOLDIER

I spent seven fruitless days in Kathmandu before boredom with my own company urged me to have a go at white water rafting. I found a cheap trip, leaving the next day, which needed one more person to fill the crew, and I grabbed the chance of fighting a roaring torrent for $20, travel and food included. I soon realised two things: one, taking your boredom somewhere else doesn't get rid of it, and, two, cheap trips are not necessarily good ones.

There were four Japanese men and one woman, two Nepali crew and myself. The Japanese spoke nothing but Japanese. Pemba had a few words of English. The other Nepali crew member left the raft after an hour on the first day to visit his family and we never saw him again. I sat in the bow wondering how much longer the river could be.

Although the Japanese were friendly and painfully polite, smiles and encouraging nods were soon wearing thin and to all intents and purposes I had become an unpaid white water rafting employee. Unfortunately the others seemed under the impression that all they were required to do was sit in the back and watch the scenery go by. Frantic sign language and paddling demonstrations by Pemba had elicited no more than a few polite bows and a lot of laughter.

When we surged towards the first large rapid, aptly named Killer Choke, Pemba's panic-stricken exhortations finally drew an alarmed response. I was already paddling for all I was worth since Pemba had made it absolutely clear that hard forward strokes on his commands were the only thing that

226

would get us through the foaming standing waves that loomed ahead of us. The four men grabbed their paddles at the last moment and thrashed hopelessly at the water. The young woman sat primly in the middle of the raft, keeping one delicate hand on her designer sunglasses and trying not to look totally baffled at what was happening.

Despite enthusiastic efforts it was immediately apparent that the crew was hopelessly ineffectual. One man lost his paddle at first strike. Another tumbled over the side, having forgotten to hook his foot securely under a restraining rope, but fortunately managed to cling on to one of his friends' paddles. The remaining man clung to his friend to prevent him from being dragged over the side. The woman started screaming. Pemba and I paddled like lunatics but we could not generate enough forward motion, and with the drag from the overboard crew member we spun helplessly in circles into the first rapid of the day.

Thirty-six hours later not much had improved as far as team efficiency was concerned, and Pemba and I were exhausted. The water may have been white in places but it had become obvious very quickly that the rapids were not what I had anticipated. I had hoped for huge standing waves, surging green stoppers, and titanic battles to stay on the raft. At the end of the first day I was convinced that if Pemba and I had taken a handful of Mogadons and fallen asleep we would still have found ourselves drifting gently on to the sand spit where we spent the first night.

Pemba assured me that the seven day trips, particularly on the Karnali river, were far more serious, with grade four and five rapids and the very real possibility of death if anything went wrong. He also explained that the Trisuli was very low because of the time of year and that after the monsoon, when it was in full flood, it would be a much more alarming experience. He pointed out marks on the high granite walls of the canyons we floated through that were thirty feet above us. That was the normal post-monsoon levels. I was suitably impressed and quite glad the river wasn't in that state of flood.

After two days of rapids and a lot of hard work on the part of two out of the seven, we disembarked at a bend in the river where the roar of passing traffic on the main road to Pokhara was audible above the surge of the water. I thanked Pemba and clambered up the steep path leading to the road. A dilapidated shack sheltered in the shade of some dusty trees. In the cool shadows I found the Japanese team smiling and sipping Coca Cola. They were waiting for the next bus to take them on to Pokhara.

I sat on a wobbly wooden bench and ordered a cold beer from the young lad waiting on the tables. I wasn't entirely certain how I was supposed to know which bus was heading for Kathmandu, nor for that matter how to stop it. Pemba had suggested waving them down. I watched the trucks and buses careering past the shack at terrifying speed in clouds of dust and exhaust fumes. I didn't fancy standing at the side of the road with them bearing down upon me, let alone trying to wave one to a halt.

I had heard that the road had recently been improved and was now metalled all the way from Kathmandu to Pokhara. As far as I could gather, this had done absolutely nothing for the road safety statistics. It simply meant that there were no pot-holes, landslips or rockfalls to slow down the drivers who were now free to hurtle, grand-prix-style, to their destinations.

While on a bus at the start of the Gangchempo expedition, on a less than smooth road to Dhunche, we heard that forty-seven people had died when one vehicle, on the way to Pokhara, had lost control and flew off into the Trisuli river.

I was halfway through my second beer when there was a gruff command in my ear. I looked up to find a short stout man with an angry face pointing aggressively at my head.

'Why do you wear that?' he demanded. I looked around in confusion to see whether he was addressing someone else.

'Why?' he repeated.

'Why what?' I stared at him. He was about five feet tall with close cropped salt-and-pepper hair. He wore a towel that looked distinctly dirty, sarong-style around his waist, and nothing else. His large and spherical beer belly sat proudly above the towel. He was still staring angrily at my head, so I removed the baseball cap I was wearing. He promptly snatched it from me and, pointing to the cap badge pinned to it, angrily demanded an answer.

'Oh, *that*,' I said, reaching for the hat. 'It is a Gurkha regiment cap badge.'

'I know this, sir. I am a Gurkha soldier.' He said it proudly and squared his shoulders, thrusting out his chest.

'Right. That explains why your English is so good.'

'Yes. I have fought in the British Army, sir. But why do you wear this badge? You are not a soldier.'

'No, you're right there, but my father was . . .'

'Your father was a soldier?' he interrupted, looking considerably less aggrieved.

'My father was a Gurkha soldier,' I said with some pride.

'A Gurkha, eh?'

'Yes, and this was the cap badge of his regiment, which doesn't exist any more. It was disbanded after the war. Look,' I said, offering him the cap. 'Prince of Wales Fourth Gurkha Rifles. You can see the fleur-de-lis and the IV and the crossed kukris underneath. See here.'

He grabbed the cap and examined it with a dazzling white smile that transformed his previously fierce appearance. I remembered how my father had often commented on his war experiences with the Gurkhas. He thought the Gurkhas were the only troops that the Japanese soldiers genuinely feared in battle and had talked about the extraordinary contrast between their friendly smiling appearance and their ability to become ferocious in battle. The most cheerful soldiers ever to cut your throat, he used to say.

'I am very happy to meet you, sir,' the man said very formally as he handed back the cap.

He turned and clapped his hands together and spoke rapidly to the young boy. A bottle of beer appeared at my elbow. For the next hour we talked about his life in the army, his nights on the booze in Aldershot, and his service during the Second World War with the British in Burma, and then with the Indian army when his regiment had been taken over after partition. I tried to find out if he had been involved in any of the campaigns in which my father had fought, but we ended up in confusion. By the time the fifth beer appeared I was beginning to realise I might not see Kathmandu again and told him that I needed to catch a bus.

'That is not a problem, sir,' the Gurkha soldier said, waving his son over and barking a few peremptory orders at him. 'No good people,' he added, glaring at my Japanese raft companions who looked apprehensively at me. I was glad they couldn't understand English.

The lad ran straight into the middle of the road and stood his ground as vehicles thundered past on either side of him. At one moment two over-loaded and swaying buses passed each other and when the dust cleared I felt sure he would be seen lying mangled in the road. To my surprise, I saw him running barefoot down the almost melting tarmac after one of the buses. It careered off in a cloud of blue smoke.

The old Gurkha shouted a few impatient commands and the boy looked back with a crestfallen expression. After what sounded like a stream of oaths in Gurkhali that seemed oddly familiar, the old soldier himself marched out into the road without once looking to see if anything was coming. He stood solidly in the centre, as if to attention, and then held his arm straight out palm raised. A bus screeched to a halt in a spray of gravel. It was the most astounding piece of traffic control I have ever witnessed. After a brief conversation with the driver, the man waved me over to him.

I hesitated on the edge of the road, unwilling to make the seemingly suicidal error of attempting to cross to the other side, and painfully aware of the man's critical gaze. Then I made an unseemly dash.

'This is a luxury bus,' the Gurkha in his towel announced gravely. 'Very good and very fast.'

'Ah well, that's great,' I said with a forced smile. A slow bus would have been fine.

'Come with me, sir,' he said brusquely as he led me into the bus.

'No, it's okay. I can do it myself,' I protested vainly as he strode to the rear of the vehicle, ejected a young man from his seat and indicated that I should sit there.

'But . . .'

'This is the finest position,' he said. 'No bumping here.'

'Thanks,' I said with a smile. 'Look, I haven't paid you for the beers,' I added, but he shook his head in a rolling manner.

'It is no problem. And do not pay the driver,' he added quietly. 'I have talked with him.'

'Oh, right. Well, thank you very much.'

'It is a great pleasure,' he said, shaking my hand in a firm grip. 'I like the British people very much.'

'Yes, of course.'

'Good bye and safe travelling.'

He turned and strode imperiously down the aisle. I watched him whisper to the driver before he stepped out into the road. As the bus pulled away with a loud and throaty roar, which suggested we were about to go very fast indeed, I smiled at the man and his son as they stood by the roadside and waved farewell. I laughed as I saw the man give his son a cuff round the head for what was obviously cowardice in the face of the traffic. He was about the same age as my father, same height and build, even the same sunken chest, as my father called his stomach. I remembered the string of Gurkhali swear words and recalled how I'd heard my Da utter similar oaths when I was a child and he had banged his thumb with a hammer.

The smooth ride was deceptively safe. I noticed the occasional blare of horns and the wind buffeting of passing trucks, but since I couldn't see the drop into the gorge of the Trisuli river on the left, I wasn't particularly alarmed.

As it grew dark I stared out at the sky. There was another huge build-up of black storm clouds and the first drops of rain spattered against the window. I wondered how the lads were faring on the mountain. Down in the Kathmandu valley the weather had been unsettled with regular afternoon rain storms. If they had experienced the same conditions, I doubted that they could have reached the summit.

The storm broke just as darkness enveloped the land. A

spectacular flash of lightning lit the interior of the bus with a white electric glare. The bus driver kept his foot pinned to the floor and we charged on regardless. I looked out of the window at the wet black tarmac speeding by and felt the first tremors of unease build up inside. I had been sufficiently terrified in the past by a lunatic Punjabi driver on the Karakoram Highway not to need another demonstration of demonic bus driving. After the baking heat of the day and the sudden downpour I guessed the road surface had about as much friction as an oiled marble floor.

I tried to close my eyes and concentrate on the music in my head phones, but the lightning flashes kept glowing blood red through my eyelids, and I would look up to see what was happening. Occasionally I leant into the aisle to watch the driver happily fighting the huge steering wheel as he swung the coach around a series of sharp s-bends. It was while doing this that I realised he was driving without headlights. I didn't know how long we had been without lights, or indeed if we had ever had any in the first place. Peering out at the rainy darkness, illuminated from time to time by flashes of lightning and the sudden wash of on-coming headlights rushing by, I tried not to think about how the driver was managing to keep on the road.

The long day's hard work on the river and the Gurkha's generosity with his beer took their toll and – despite my fear – I felt myself nodding off to sleep. The lightning exploding across the huge water-streaked front window and the crazed flashes of headlights and blaring horns seemed oddly unreal, as if I were watching an exciting road movie on a glass screen with sensorama and 3-D special effects. I was too tired to connect it to reality.

I awoke with a start as I was thrown forward into the headrest in front of me. We had stopped. There was a hubbub of voices at the front of the bus. I looked down the aisle to see passengers leaning to the left and staring out of the window. Others were hurriedly pushing their way forward towards the door. We didn't appear to have crashed. I stood up and made my way to the front of the bus.

As I reached the driver's seat I saw a huge axle and a double tyre, still spinning, filling the view through the side window. Ducking down, I saw the rest of the capsized bus stretched half over the edge of a steep dark drop. I got off for a closer look.

A crowd of about thirty passengers sat and stood in a patient huddle in the teeming rain beside the overturned vehicle. They all appeared to have sheepish expressions on their faces, as if they had just been caught doing something naughty. Vehicles swept past the two buses, swerving to avoid the crash with blasts on their horns and the high speed swishing noise as their tyres skidded past on the wet tarmac. The driver of our bus was talking to a man who I took to be the other driver. There was much waving of arms and gesticulating. Three men crouched by one of the rear windows of the crashed bus, peering at the gap between the cut away bank and the shattered glass of the window. A bare arm stretched forlornly out from under the bus, fingers clenching and groping.

I turned away, sickened by the sight, not wishing to see more of the crushed passenger. One of the men stood up and carried a bag to the sodden huddle of passengers at the front. I glanced back at the arm and ducked down to see into the bus. Two men were crawling around the upturned interior retrieving bags, sacks and various items of personal property. Another lay on his side, poking his arm out through the broken window to pass the baggage to those outside.

No one appeared to have been killed or injured. Perhaps that's why they looked so sheepish. As I passed the group sitting on the verge a heavily loaded truck ground slowly by and for a moment the wet faces of the passengers were illuminated by its headlights. I caught sight of a young boy, round faced, sitting on an old man's lap looking around him with studied indifference. Just as the light washed over him our eyes met and I was unnerved to find myself staring at a pair of familiar adult appraising eyes. It was the boy from the hut at Ari! We were plunged back into darkness. I stepped towards the group, searching for the boy. A man shouted and the passengers from the crashed bus began to rise to their feet and shuffle towards our bus with their possessions. As they brushed past me I tried to look over their shoulders for the old man and the boy. Another set of lights flashed by. He wasn't there.

I went to the door of our bus, noticing as I did so that we did actually have lights working – sidelights with the candle power of a couple of trapped, exhausted fireflies. I moved slowly up the aisle, searching the now packed bus. There was no sign of the old man or the boy and I began to question what I had seen. *It must have been a trick of the light,* I told myself.

After a short, silent tussle with the three sodden passengers in my seat, I fought my way down beside the window and sat cramped between the glass and a passenger who smelt like a soggy sheep dog. Every now and then, as we rumbled on towards Kathmandu at a more sedate pace, I squeezed myself into a standing position and scanned the passengers crammed into the bus. When we stopped in the city I examined all those disembarking and drifting away into the wet night. The boy had vanished – or perhaps had never existed.

I waved down a black and yellow auto-rickshaw and bounced off towards the Thamel district. As I walked wearily towards the Blue Note bar I met Geoff Pierce on the main street outside the Kathmandu Guest House. He and Dave Hall had left the expedition even earlier than I had due to altitude sickness.

'Hi, Joe,' he yelled above the noise of the departing auto-rickshaw. 'How was the river rafting?'

'Riveting. Like watching paint dry,' I said sarcastically.

'Hey, I've heard from the team. They made it.'

'Made what?'

'They topped out. Mal, Gompu, Clive, José and Dave Horrox summited last week.'

'How do you know?'

'There was a fax from Mal at the agency office when I went to look for mail. They're in Lukla now. Should be here tomorrow morning.'

Namche Bazar, '*place shaded by trees*'. (Photo: Simpson)

The two saddhus, one with a monkey on his shoulder, the other holding a begging bowl on a chain. (Photo: Simpson)

Blue ice on the west ridge of Gangchempo. (Photo: Richard Haszko)

(From left) Ian Tattersall (Tat), Kate Phillips, Brendan Murphy, John Stevenson, Richard Haszko, Ray Delaney in the yak shelter before the avalanche. (Photo: Joe Simpson)

Heidi Sinz treating Joe's ankle and knee on the walk in to Langtang. (Photo: Haszko)

Right: Tents buried after the storm on Gangchempo. (Photo: Haszko)

Heinrich Harrer's portrait of the infant brother of the Dalai Lama.

Refugees below Ari, heading towards Thami. (Photo: Mike Shrimpton)

Joe at the prayer flags on the Nangpa La. (Photo: Neil Lyndsey)

Joe with dead yak. (Photo: Lyndsey)

Cho Oyo from the Nangpa La. (Photo: Simpson)

Tibetan traders returning with unladen yaks to Tibet. (Photo: Simpson)

Chwang Rinsi and Mal Duff, trusted friends. (Photos: Duff and Simpson)

Joe with a lethal pressure cooker at Camp I. (Photo: Mal Duff)

'Are they all safe?'

'Yeah, as far as I know. Clive has frost-bitten feet apparently, otherwise they're fine.'

'That's brilliant news. Come on, let's have a beer.'

I was delighted for Mal. He deserved the success after the years of hard work he had put into his guiding business. It also meant that I could stop worrying about them and look forward to getting home at the end of the week.

Later, drinking a beer on the balcony of the Blue Note, I watched the throng of tourists and Nepalese in the streets below as a light evening rain began to fall. A legless beggar pushed himself along the street below on a homemade trolley – a square of wood with castors at each corner. One arm was withered and twisted. The beggar wore a red Nepali hat and had draped a yellow plastic binliner across his shoulders to ward off the rain. He held a block of wood covered in the rubber of a tyre inner tube in his withered left arm so that he could reach the ground. His right fist had bandages wrapped around it to protect it against the rough road surface. He stopped besides three statuesque young women who were asking a policeman for directions. The beggar's scraggy beard and matted hair were covered in dust. The girls hadn't noticed him looking up hopefully, hand outstretched for alms.

The policeman puffed out his chest and tried to impress the girls with his macho appearance. His uniform was immaculate – a navy blue tunic and a maroon beret setting off the startling white puttees and belt with its brass buckle. A holstered pistol was fixed to a gleaming black lanyard, and he gave a sharp blast on his silver whistle before waving imperiously at an unimpressed *tuc-tuc* driver.

The taller girl, blonde and curvy, smiled brightly at the policeman who twisted the corner of his Saddam Hussein moustache with practised panache. Her short red skirt billowed in the draught of a passing rickshaw. I could see through the thin white cotton of her blouse. Her friends in hippy style dress stood to one side. At that moment I saw the beggar drop his hand resignedly and shuffle forward on his trolley. He stopped and looked straight up the tall girl's dress.

I burst out laughing. He was determined to get something for his efforts.

Four days later I let myself in through the back door of my house in Sheffield. A set of keys lay on the doormat with a note from my girlfriend explaining why she had left. It came as a shock. Tom, who had collected me from the airport, looked uncomfortable and embarrassed.

'Ah well, that's seven years down the drain,' I said with feigned bravado.

'Look, I'm sorry it was like this, Joe. I really didn't know. I . . .'

'It's okay. It's not your fault, mate.' I re-read the letter and then crumpled it up. I tried to be angry but only succeeded in feeling sad and ashamed of myself. 'I can't blame her really. I was pretty stupid, I suppose.'

'Yeah, well maybe if . . .'

'No, it's okay, don't worry about it.' I stopped Tom from getting himself into an embarrassing analysis. 'I thought this might happen. I mean, not like this, but it was going that way. Just wish I could have been more honest about it and not hurt her so badly. I never wanted that to happen.'

'That's what they . . .'

'. . . all say.' I completed his sentence. 'Yeah, I know.'

'Are you okay?' Tom looked concerned.

I reached for the crumpled ball of paper on the floor. 'Yes, I'm okay. I'm off to Peru in three and a half weeks. Running away as usual.'

'You might be able to work it out,' Tom suggested hopefully.

'I don't think so,' I said, flattening out the crumpled pages of the letter.

PART TWO

17

FIT FOR NOTHING

The mirrors are everywhere. In every gym and fitness club in the country the mirrors shine back at you. There's no getting round them. They begin to play insidious games with your mind. At first you avoid them, alarmed at the thought of appearing narcissistic, but very quickly you find that they are unavoidable. Someone has gone to great lengths to position them around the room in such a way that whichever way you look there are always at least three images of yourself peering back at you. Unable to escape them, you rush through your training programme in faster and faster times, tormented by sweaty contorted postures of yourself, chased by vain demons.

I detest training and all the vanity of body sculpting for its own sake. The tedium of endless leg-raising, swinging chrome dumb-bells up and down, squats, thrusts, pounding up rubber-stepped hills and chasing cartoon boats on the computerised rowing machine drives me to distraction. I seem to do it from a distance, as if looking down from above and questioning why I'm strapping myself into some horrifically complicated gizmos designed to isolate one muscle into spasms of agony. Some of the machines seem better suited to torturing cattle than gaining spurious fitness. I dread waking up in the morning feeling as if I've been hanging from the ceiling all night on meat hooks thrust through my nipples. Then there is the agonised stagger down to the bathroom on legs so wire-tight and muscle-bound that I feel sure I can hear the sinews shredding, with calf muscles so hard that it feels as if a rivet gun is about to fire bolts out through them. I confess to a nagging suspicion that it's only making me fitter and stronger so that I can train even harder. When eventually I escape the gyms and find myself in the mountains, I don't seem to be any fitter than my companions and a whole set of arcane unusable muscles, honed to the peak of perfection, soon wither and shrivel from lack of use.

Although I loathe training, I am addicted to it. I don't know what it is – some endorphin-flooded fixation about having three days a week in the gym. I never used to train before I broke my legs, never thought about it until months, if not years, of physiotherapy, dire warnings about never climbing again, and the withered stick of a leg after eight months in plaster prompted me to join a local fitness club. By the time the leg had regained its muscle mass I was hopelessly trapped. Oh, I know the importance of it and how quickly my legs will deteriorate if I don't train, but that doesn't mean I should be addicted to it.

I remember the first gym, a slick room of chrome and mirrors and neatly ranked machines of torture. Three of us had somehow wangled six months free membership and we turned up in tatty shirts and track suit trousers with holes in the knees. A trainer cheerfully put us through a regime that left us near weeping on the floor.

'Do you lads fancy some Quando aerobics?' he asked.

'Quando what?' we chorused from a collapsed heap by the buttock-separating device.

'Fit young lads like you,' he sneered. 'You'll love it. Come on, let's feel the burn.'

He handed each of us a pair of plastic-coated dumb-bells and led us into a small room surrounded by wall to ceiling mirrors and dominated by an enormous pair of stereo speakers.

'Hey, these weigh nothing,' I said, hefting the dumb-bell experimentally. 'Less than a bag of sugar, I reckon.' I grinned confidently. 'This will be a doddle.'

'Yeah, what are we worrying about?' Richard swung the weights nonchalantly over his shoulders. 'Nothing to it.'

'Have you done this before?' Tom asked as he tested

himself with a few stretching exercises. Bending forward from the waist, he was struggling desperately to touch his knees. He had the flexibility of an iron bar.

'Nope, but it can't be bad,' I replied. 'He said we'd only do forty-five minutes.'

Twenty minutes later we were barging drunkenly into each other as we tried to follow the trainer's instructions. Dance music thumped hypnotically from the speakers and I watched our regimented rhythmic choreography descend into uncoordinated rag-doll spasms. The dumb-bells now weighed close on fifty pounds and our bodies were wracked with burning muscles from holding them continuously in front of us, over our heads, and out to the sides. I could barely see for the sweat flooding into my contact lenses and someone appeared to have removed one of my lungs. I was grateful for the odd painful crack of a wayward dumb-bell in the ear to keep me going.

'Lift those legs higher, pump it, pump it, PUMP it.' The man yelled into the microphone curled in front of his mouth. In ragged unison we reeled off to the side, collided with a mirror and bounced roughly back into line, making pathetic little hopping steps. He was virtually chinning himself with his kneecaps, holding the dumb-bells ramrod straight in front of his chest.

'Lift.'

The weights arched above his head. There was a loud thump as Richard dropped his and howled as it crushed his foot.

'And out to the side, one, two, three . . . and lift. Get those knees up. Feel that burn.'

Burn! I was standing in flames. Tom was resting his dumb-bells on his shoulders. In an effort to raise one above my head I twisted to the side and let the left one drop. I lurched out of line like Quasimodo on acid, wondering who the manic, twisted creature in the mirror was. Richard staggered into view clutching one weight in both hands and bending himself almost into the crab position in an effort to get it to stick out in front of him. He sank slowly to his knees.

'And down,' the torturer said, lowering his weights. He kept jumping lightly on his toes. He hadn't broken sweat.

'Okay, slow it down lads.'

Slow it down? We stared at him in horror from our kneeling positions on the floor.

'Okay, warm up over. Let's go!' he yelled, making us shrink back in alarm.

'Warm up?' Richard croaked. 'Warm up? If I get any hotter my blood will start boiling. Bugger this.' He tried throwing his dumb-bell to the floor in disgust only to find he had already let go of it. Tom had got to his feet but didn't have the stretch to lean down and pick up his weights. He bent from the waist and flapped his hands pitifully at his knees.

'Sod it!' I gasped, and leant back to back with Richard on the floor. The music suddenly stopped. The room was filled with the stentorian rasp of our breathing.

'What's up with you guys?' the fitness god inquired.

'Knackered,' I whispered.

'Help . . .' Richard added.

'Have you been listening to Walkmans?' the trainer asked, as he shepherded us from the room.

'No, why?'

'Well, you seemed to be dancing to different music, that's all.'

It took a couple of weeks before we got over the shock.

'Must have been the Quando bit that did us,' Richard speculated optimistically.

'Which bit was that exactly?'

'The dumb-bells, I suppose. Why don't we do the normal aerobics class? I'm sure we can cope with that,' Tom suggested. We looked at him balefully.

'You're kidding,' I hissed.

'May as well give it a try,' Richard said. 'After all, it can't be any worse than carrying loads at twenty thousand feet.'

'And when did you ever carry a load at twenty thousand feet?' Tom and I chorused at his departing back.

'Why's he so keen?' I asked, amazed by Richard's uncharacteristic lust for pain.

'Have you seen the rest of the class?'

We went over and looked into the mirrored room. Ten gorgeously attired young women were limbering up in two lines facing the mirrors. A fearsome-looking body-fascist was adjusting her throat mike. Richard was enthusiastically bending and stretching at the back. The women sported big hairstyles, make-up, jewellery, tight multi-coloured body suits, and bodies that would make a professional model weep. *This isn't a keep fit class,* I thought, *if this lot gets any fitter they'll snap.*

'He's got a point. I mean aerobics might do us some good,' I suggested to Tom, who was already getting into line at the back next to Richard. I shuffled furtively into the room just as the music boomed into life.

'Hey, this isn't bad,' I whispered to Tom after thirty minutes. 'It's nothing like that Quando stuff.'

'Well, there is some distraction from the pain.'

'Yeah, I noticed.' I executed a few nifty high-faluting kicks and spun round on the instructress's command. Tom was still facing the front and Richard seemed to be dancing with the side wall.

'Hell, I've seen more fat on a chip,' I said as Tom and I spun neatly to face one another while the rest of the class jigged in perfect precision, eyes to the mirrored front. Richard danced with the door.

'And down!' Everyone sank to their knees. 'And stretch that pelvis!' I looked sideways across the line. A tangerine-spangled shapely leg whipped back, narrowly missing Tom's face. I lifted my leg up and back copying the contorted kneeling position.

'Oh Jesus! Ouwch!' I yelped as something parted company between my buttocks and my lower back.

'And stretch up!' Miss Lycra Thighbreaker sang cheerfully from the front. My head pressed down on the floor and my left buttock seized up in a tight knot of cramp. I lowered the leg and writhed on the floor, trying to release the cramp. Glancing sideways, I saw Tom and Richard on their hands and knees staring up and forward, necks outstretched, eyes bulging. Richard was craftily resting his leg on the mirrored wall behind me and I noticed the oddly fascinated stare on his face. A whole row of shapely lycra buttocks were arrayed in a row in front of him. There was less than a foot between them and Tom's and Richard's faces.

'Well, that's not such a bad exercise. My pelvis could do with loosening up,' I muttered, abandoning my cramped bum and hastily getting to my knees. I assumed the position and stared expectantly forward. To my horror, I was confronted with a pair of hairy testicles hanging from the loose shorts of some hearty rugger-bugger type who had insinuated himself into the class after we had started.

'Yeargg.' I pulled my face away from the awful sight to see Tom in spasms of laughter. Richard was miles away.

There is a peculiar contradiction of signals in some of these establishments which I have never been able to resolve. On the one hand, everyone is there to train, to work up a sweat, tone those muscles and get fit; on the other hand, sometimes it seems more akin to a fashion parade than a no-pain no-gain routine. I know it's rude to stare. Naturally it's politically incorrect to display the slightest attraction for your fellow devotees of agony, but it is also well nigh impossible. If everyone wore baggy loose-fitting tops and track suit trousers, there wouldn't be much of a problem, but life isn't so easy. The trend of ladies' gym wear makes it hard, so to speak. There seems to be an obsession with leotards, body suits, buttock-splitting Lycra thingies, swim suits worn-over swim suits, countless variations of attire that leave absolutely nothing to the imagination.

From a practical point of view, I can't think of anything sweatier and more uncomfortable to wear during training sessions. Performing squats while wearing a cord-thin g-string that threatens to split your cheeks up level with your shoulders looks unspeakably painful. And if you are wearing, say, a black leotard, why then put a skin-tight swim suit on top of it with the legs cut so high that they seem to go up to your armpits? Or pull on what looks like a scarlet pair of bikini bottoms so lacking in material that they merely create a vivid red triangle which for the average man has the effect of a hypnotist swinging a fob-watch?

Some of the leg machines found in gyms today place the athlete in the most undignified and vulnerable positions imaginable. To wear such luridly revealing clothes and then climb on to a machine that threatens to spread your legs so wide that you're in real danger of having your ankles meet behind your back seems to me absurdly illogical. The more so when some unfortunate male, already plagued by mirrors, happens to look up at the wrong moment and finds himself helplessly transfixed by an overtly sexual vision in red and black who glares back in ferocious condemnation of his lechery.

I'm not sure it is lechery in fact. When the very style of clothing is screaming out 'look at this body', and the design makes the legs look twice their length, the buttocks split and lifted, the breasts outlined perfectly in fluorescent colour, what are you supposed to look at? Nine times out of ten, looking away simply brings another colour-isolated part of a woman's body squeezing and thrusting and spreading in front of you. Short of staring fixedly at the ground and finding the exercise machines by feel, it is impossible not to look.

I was once accosted in the gym by an irate lady who angrily demanded to know what I was staring at. Since I was struggling to release myself at the time from an overweighted pecs machine that was threatening to dislocate both my shoulders, I found it hard to gather my thoughts.

'You,' I said bluntly. 'Your scantily dressed body that leaves absolutely nothing to the imagination, that keeps leaping into view wherever I go. What did you think I was staring at?'

Well, that's what I would have liked to say instead of spluttering a mortified apology, feeling my face blush with shame. To be honest, I don't think I had been staring. In fact I think I was in one of those aerobically bored vacuous states that gyms induce. She stalked indignantly away and I felt too embarrassed to ask whether she could help me retrieve my elbows which were touching behind my head. To me, it seems a bit unfair to confront us with virtual nakedness and then accuse us of disgustingly lewd thoughts. All I was trying to do was torture myself in a gym.

It seems that the prim and proper message is that such garments are worn not to be sexy but because they make the wearer feel good. They simply display the wearer's confidence in herself. Well, that's as maybe, but it strikes me they display a damn sight more than that, and to deny it is plain self-delusion. I'm not easily offended or prudish in any way, far from it, but I do resent being the victim of a dishonest conspiracy. If these clothes are the uniform of the post-feminist woman, as I've heard said, and are about woman's empowerment and not men's desire, then I'm a wildebeest.

To wear outrageously enticing apparel and at the same time profess the sensibilities of a sentimentalised Victorian spinster is shamelessly deceitful. Sure, I'm not allowed to touch. I know that. But faced with spread-eagled semi-nakedness, can't I just leer a little? It might help both sexes if they took all the mirrors away. The men wouldn't be ambushed by horny visions at moments of muscle-ripping effort and the women wouldn't have a constant reminder of how beautifully empowered and confident they are.

However, all things being equal, I'd much rather cope with the women's sense of gym fashion than that of the average male. Wobbling beer bellies straining through unwashed sweat-stained t-shirts are bad enough, but it doesn't stop there. It is odd the way men bare their arms in tank tops, all the better to show off their bulging biceps and allow them conveniently to forget the blubbery sphere of fat quivering above the tight belt of their shorts. Some wear wide leather weight-lifting belts, either to look tough or more probably to restrain the verandah above their toyshops, as the Australians so delightfully describe beer bellies.

The worst gym I've known was attended by four huge bouncers from a now bankrupt Sheffield night club. They were big both in height and musculature but they were not honed into the sort of symmetry, however unnatural, that body builders acquire – broad shoulders, small 'v-shaped' waist and powerful legs. These guys were utter slobs. They went in for bench pressing horrendous stacks of steel, curling dumb-bells so heavy that I doubted I could lift one off the floor with both hands, making animal grunting noises and sweating profusely. When not displaying their awesomely pointless machismo, they glared around the gym, exuding an atmosphere of raw violence.

There was something truly repulsive about their flabby white arms and shoulders, biceps as thick as my thighs, short bull necks with ludicrously small cropped pin-heads balanced on top. They walked with muscle-bound ponderous gaits. I had seen them in action in the club and listened to their monosyllabic conversations in the changing room. These consisted almost entirely of accounts of the unfortunate wretches battered into a pulp the previous night. If they changed the subject at all, it was to discuss the relative merits of various different steroids and body-building drugs. In time I developed a keen sense of disgust whenever I met them and tried to avoid eye contact in case their walnut-size brains suddenly recognised my impudence.

So it was with some horror that I found myself trapped by their hulking presence in a six-foot by six-foot sauna. It was the first and last time I will ever go into one of those hell holes. They barged in just as I came to the decision to leave.

'Can't take the heat?' one of the slobs sneered as he laid his towel on the slatted wooden bench and lowered his vast naked buttocks on to it.

'Are you wimping out, youth?' his mate said as he thrust a leg the size of a tree trunk against the door.

'No, no,' I said quietly. 'I've had my go.'

'Have you heck as like,' pin-head in the corner snarled. 'Tha's been two minutes. What's the problem? Too hot for you, or are you scared?'

'Scared? Scared of what?'

They laughed and I sat down disconsolately.

'I'll show you what's hot lad.' Pin-head leaned forward and began ladling water on to the coals. Steam erupted and the temperature soared. At least it hid the sight of their gross bodies. I was tempted to point and laugh at the sight of their minuscule genitals squashed like chipolatas between the bulge of their thighs and bellies, but I decided that I quite liked my arm in one piece and bit my lip. Instead I bowed my head and breathed slowly, feeling the dry burning pain of the steam in my throat. *What a bunch of wankers!* I thought.

When they grew bored with the heat competition, they took to shaving and squeezing the mass of pimples covering their heavy rounded shoulders and broad backs. I wondered whether it was the steroids that caused the body acne.

'I fancy that bint in red,' pin-head growled as his mate dug his nails into the white-headed pustules on the back of his neck.

'Aye, I'd give her one.'

Give her one? You'd crush her to death, I almost yelped and bit my lip. I edged towards the door.

'Going somewhere kid?'

'Er . . . no, no. Just adding some more water. Not hot enough yet.'

'. . . bet she'd go,' pin-head continued his fantasy. '. . . like the shit house door in a gale.' He roared with laughter.

'Bet you wouldn't find your dick,' I murmured under my breath.

'Yer what?'

'Nothing, nothing. Just talking to myself,' I said hastily.

'Best shave you can have,' pin-head's companion announced with satisfaction as he dragged the disposable razor across his unlathered cheek. A rash of beheaded spots began to bleed copiously. He wiped the stubble from the blade with his thumb and smeared it on the wall.

'Right, I'd better be off,' I said brightly and grabbed the door handle. I had it open and was half-out before the thigh came across the jamb. I hopped over it and slammed the door, cutting short the rant about 'poncey fooking students'.

I changed as fast as possible and was heading outside when I spotted the broom in the corner. I glanced at the sauna door with its tiny window pane and back at the broom. The door had a stout wooden loop handle and opened inwards. It was the work of seconds to slide the broom through the handle and across the door, jamming it firmly in place. I sprinted out, half-expecting to hear insane bellowing and the sound of splintering pine doors. I ran from the gym, never to return and never to set foot in their night club again.

Now, at last, I have found a pleasant, friendly gym in the Y.M.C.A. and train there three times a week. I still dislike the monotony of it but I go all the same. Without building the strength in my legs, particularly around my knee, I know that the doctors' dire warnings would very soon come true.

'How's things?' Clive asked as he handed me my membership card. 'Haven't seen you for a while?'

'No, I've been in Tibet and Nepal, trying Cho Oyo.'

'How did it go?'

'Five topped out, so that was good, but I got a chest infection and had to give up.'

'That's bad luck after giving up smoking.'

'Yeah, tell me about it.'

'Where to next?'

'Peru,' I said. 'Next week.'

'Well, have a good one.' He smiled.

'Yeah, thanks. I will.'

I had been back from Nepal for less than three weeks, barely time enough to shake off whatever had infected my chest and resume my usual twenty-a-day smoking habit. I was due to guide three clients for a Sheffield-based trekking company in the Cordillera Blanca. It was to be my first time in Peru since the dreadful accident on Siula Grande in the Cordillera Huayhuash had crippled me nine years before.

The bell rang time as Richard came back from the bar with two foaming pints of bitter.

'How do you feel about going back?' he asked as he handed me a pint.

'Oh, it'll be great,' I replied airily. 'Why do you ask?'

'Well, you know. Bad memories, that sort of thing.'

'Oh no, I'm looking forward to it, and I'm being paid. Anyway, it wasn't Peru that did me, or even the mountains. It could have happened anywhere. I have been on ten trips since then, you know, and the medics said I'd never go again. No,

I feel okay about it.'

I had accepted Bob Lancaster's offer to lead a party in the Cordillera Blanca for his trekking company High Places. Ric Potter and I would guide on various acclimatisation peaks before attempting Huascaran (6768m), the highest mountain in the Tropics and the fourth highest in South America. After the trip, Ric and I planned to do some climbing for ourselves.

'Just easy routes, okay?' I had warned him. 'Nothing hard, nothing new, all right? I'm not getting into any more epics, ever again.'

'Sure,' he said, 'but good easy ones. Alpamayo, perhaps, or Artesonraju.'

A week later, as Heathrow approached and Sheffield faded down a long ribbon of grey motorway, I was feeling less sure of myself. I felt superstitious, as if I might be tempting fate, as if going back could be the end of a journey. I knew it was irrational, and I tried not to believe that I could be closing the circle of life I had been blessed with since Siula Grande, but the sudden rush of apprehension was hard to dispel.

'Don't be stupid,' I kept telling myself. But the feeling absorbed me and wouldn't go away. I lit a cigarette and watched a Jumbo defy logic as it hung in the empty sky above the terminal.

'Are you okay?' Pat asked as she pulled into the Terminal 1 car park.

'Yes, of course I am,' I snapped defensively. 'Why shouldn't I be?'

'Just checking. You look a bit tense, that's all.'

'Oh, it's nothing. Just the thought of flying,' I lied fluently, and she smiled, knowing it wasn't true.

'It'll be fine. There's nothing to worry about,' I said as I lifted the rucksacks out of the back of the car.

'I wasn't worrying. You're the one who's worrying.' She laughed at the look of surprise on my face.

'Well, just a little, I suppose,' I admitted and felt my heart skip a beat. I swallowed nervously and headed towards the check-in desks.

18

A DIRTY WAR

'Now don't be alarmed. Just remember to be very careful on the streets,' I said to Tony, David and Malcolm as we collected our gear from the carousels in Lima airport. They all looked duly alarmed.

'I know it sounds paranoid but I can assure you that street theft is rife here, okay?' They nodded seriously.

'Don't wear watches. They'll be snatched. Carry money in the front pockets of your trousers. No jewellery; it'll be snatched. If you need to carry a small day sack have it on your chest not on your back.'

'Why's that?' David asked.

'Knives,' I replied bluntly. A flicker of fear crossed his face. 'It's okay, they won't use them on you, unless of course they're cornered. It's all opportunist stuff – pick-pocketing, bag-snatching and so on. But I tell you, they're bloody good at it and they're very fast. As often as not you won't know it's happened. They'll walk discretely behind you, slit your rucksack open with a razor and take what they want. You won't even know anything's gone.'

'What about this?' David pointed to his huge camera case which appeared to be surgically attached to his body. 'I'll be safe with this, won't I?'

He had taped a finger-thick wire to the camera strap and connected it to the D-rings about his body.

'Might be, but remember they can't see the wire so they might grab it anyway. What would you do then? I mean, if they did it from a motorbike they'd be dragging you down the street by your neck.'

'I hadn't thought of that.' He looked apprehensive again.

'So long as you keep it tight against your chest it should be okay,' I reassured him. 'Look, I'm not trying to scare you.'

'You seem to be doing a pretty good job,' Tony Hamza said.

'Well yes, but that's just how it is. I don't want the trip to be ruined for you by something that could easily be avoided. The thing is to be alert, and look alert – that would put them off and make them find easier targets. Basically, just use common sense. Don't make it easy for them. You've got to remember that most of the stuff we have is worth a fortune to them. It's like wandering around a rough part of London with a wad of five thousand pounds in your hand. Okay?' They nodded grimly.

'Oh yes, I nearly forgot,' I added. 'If you do get mugged, don't resist, and certainly don't chase after them.'

'Why not?' Malcolm asked.

'Because it's just not worth it. I mean you're all insured, right?' They nodded. 'So it's just money. It can be replaced, but these guys are pretty desperate not to get caught. Prison here is no joke. If you catch them and they have a knife, they'll use it. Stabbing you won't make it much worse for them and might mean they can escape.' David looked panic-stricken. 'Just be sensible, that's all. Keep an eye on each other and don't flash your wealth around. It's only here in the city that you have to worry. Once we're in Huaraz there will be no problem.' They let out a collective sigh of relief.

By the time we emerged into the sun outside the airport terminal to meet Ric I had succeeded in thoroughly alarming our three clients with tales of banditry and knife-point muggings. I felt quite pleased with myself. It had an excellent impact and I doubted whether the most desperate thief in Lima would be able to prise a red cent out of them after that pep talk.

Ric looked tanned and fit. His trek round the Cordillera Blanca, culminating in an ascent of Nevado Pisco, had gone well. We piled aboard a transit van for the thirty-minute ride into Lima. I peered out of the window, curious to see whether things had changed in nine years. The roads had certainly improved. The last time I was here we had launched across great gaps in the surface in battered Volkswagen Beetle taxis that seemed to be held together by wire and rust. Earthquakes had created countless stepped cracks in the tarmac that were left for years without repair. It had been like powering into ten-inch kerbs at forty miles an hour, and most journeys were spent suspended somewhere between the seats and the roof.

Apart from the roads, Lima itself was unchanged. The old centre of the town, with its magnificent churches and stately colonial hotels, was just as dusty, dirty and cracked as ever. It appeared to be in a perpetual state of sad decline, in contrast with a brash rich area such as Miraflores, with its chrome and mirror-glass fronted banks and smart apartment blocks.

After a quick wash and money change in the majestic Gran Hotel Bolivar, we set out to explore the city. Having given our three clients the direst warnings about theft, razor-artists and watch-snatching, I myself was robbed within a few minutes of leaving the hotel. I had been so concerned to make sure they understood the risks that I had forgotten them myself. I had felt a sudden hard tug at my wrist and, as my hand flew out from my side, I had spun round immediately. I heard a shout – probably an accomplice's warning – which momentarily distracted me. I had even seen the black leather-jacketed back of someone turning rapidly away from me. I yelled and reached for his arm, taking two jumping strides, but he evaded me and just seemed to vanish. Ric and David went on strolling down the street, quite unaware of what had happened. The man must have been following me for quite some time, staying close behind me, waiting for the opportunity to slide his finger swiftly under the back of the watch and, with a hard jerk, snap the retaining pins on the straps. In an instant he would have had the watch in his hand. I had no doubt that the warning shout came from his accomplice and was meant to confuse me. I found the wrist-band lying at my feet.

I was furious with myself, and at the same time I had a

sneaking admiration for the thief's nerve and dexterity. Unfortunately it was no ordinary wrist-watch but an altimeter worth £150. It was galling to have been so dumb as to forget to take it off and irritating now that I would not be able to make use of it in the mountains.

'We'd better get a police statement if you're going to make a claim for it,' Ric had said.

'Yeah, I suppose you're right.' I was still feeling angry at my stupidity. 'We'll do it when we get back. No point putting the wind up the clients by taking them to the police station.'

'No.' Ric conceded. 'It wouldn't be the best start to their holiday.'

When we caught up with Tony, Malcolm and David, and I told them what had happened, David asked why I was wearing an altimeter at sea level. I had to struggle to control my temper, and kept telling myself that it was highly undiplomatic to go around punching clients on the first day of a trek.

I threw away the useless wrist-band and followed the others towards the church and monastery of San Francisco, beneath which lay an extensive system of catacombs. There had been a brief argument about what to see before we narrowed it down to three alternatives: the catacombs, the Museo de Oro, which was packed with thousands of gold artefacts, or the Museo Rafael Larco Herrera. I was especially keen on the latter since I knew that it housed a famous collection of pre-Colombian erotic pottery illustrating the acrobatic and intellectually stimulating sexual practices of past Peruvian cultures. Given a choice between death, wealth and sex, we chose death.

Since I am both claustrophobic and have serious hang-ups about anything to do with churches, I was surprised to find how enjoyable the guided tour of the cloisters, the library, the religious art museum and the labyrinth of catacombs turned out to be. A young lady, speaking Spanish at incomprehensible speed, showed us round the church which had been badly damaged by an earthquake in 1970. The dusty and quiet library had antique texts dating back to the times of the conquistador, Francisco Pizzaro, in the late 1520s.

As we crept down a flight of dusty stone steps towards the catacombs I couldn't help thinking that it was about the worst place in which to find yourself caught in an earthquake. The lady cheerfully announced that there was nothing to fear since the catacombs had been designed to be earthquake proof. Dubiously examining the mouldering brickwork, I came to the conclusion that breaking wind loudly could bring the whole thing crashing on to our heads, let alone the shattering impact of an earthquake.

She led us along a maze of narrow brick-lined tunnels through which we had to stoop to avoid the roof. We whispered among ourselves, making nervous jokes about safety and trying not to touch the walls. Wooden troughs lined the edges of the tunnels, filled to the brim with neatly arrayed patterns of bones. On one side would be a long line of thigh bones laid across each other to form a symmetrical v-shape, snaking off into the darkness, on the other would be arm bones, similarly patterned.

Every now and then the tunnel would widen and there would be deep circular brick shafts sunk into the floor. These were filled with femurs and skulls arranged in geometric ringed shapes. Despite – or due to – the litter of crisp packets and drinks cans lying on the bones, it was disturbing to see the remains of so many thousands of past lives lying there in plain view. Staring at the serried lines of grinning skulls, I tried to imagine what they had been like as individuals; what age they had lived in, and what had finally brought them to this lonely dusty mausoleum. There was a musty smell in the tunnels, and I began to feel edgy. I wondered how many people had been buried here after dying of some awful plague.

'I once read that spores of the bubonic plague can live on buried bones for as long as a thousand years,' I said to Ric, who was closely examining a thigh bone. He hurriedly dropped the bone and wiped his hands on his shorts.

'You're kidding?'

'I'm not,' I replied. 'Apparently, when they accidentally uncover old plague burial pits in London, everyone gets highly excited. I wouldn't bite your finger nails if I were you,' I added cheerfully.

'Yeah, thanks,' Ric said, and thrust his hands in his pockets.

'What's behind that?' I asked pointing to a bricked-up tunnel.

'She says it is closed,' Ric translated. 'Earthquake damage.'

'What? She said this place was earthquake proof.'

'Apparently not. Good God!' He listened to the rapid Spanish. 'She says that some of these tunnels go as far out as the airport.'

'Come off it . . . ! That's nearly twenty kilometres away. Christ, how many people are buried here?'

'Somewhere between seventy and a hundred thousand she thinks. They stopped using the vaults quite some time ago.'

'Seventy thousand . . .?' I looked around the arched chamber which was lit by a single bare electric light bulb. It gave me the creeps.

'How do they sort out the bodies; get all the arms and legs and heads out, and who does all the nifty patterns?'

She went on to tell us how the bodies were dumped into large pits and left for long enough to decompose before some poor fellow had to get in and sort out all the bones. They seemed only to use a few specific bones, although I did see a jumbled heap of what looked like pelvises that had been piled in an unused trough. It looked as if someone had had an idea for a new bone pattern and then forgotten where he had put the pelvic bones that he had painstakingly dug out of the charnel pit.

As we emerged, blinking in the bright sunlight, Tony Hamza asked me the time and laughed when I looked at my bare wrist and swore under my breath. I'd forgotten about the theft.

'Let's get down to the police station,' Ric suggested, when we had returned to the hotel. 'I asked the receptionist about getting a proof of crime form for the insurance and he said that he knew an officer who could validate it immediately instead of waiting the normal twenty-four hours.'

'Do you think it's necessary?' I asked.

'Well, it'll save any bother when you make a claim.'

'How come this policeman is so helpful anyway?'

'We have to bribe him.' Ric said with a grin.

'Oh, great!' I muttered. 'I don't like the idea of going into that place, and I certainly don't fancy getting caught trying to bribe a copper.'

'Everyone does it,' Ric said airily. 'There's nothing to worry about.'

'I've heard that phrase before,' I complained as I reluctantly followed Ric's confident stride. After leaving the clients at the hotel and getting a note from the receptionist, we hailed a taxi to take us to the police station.

It was a grim concrete shell of a building. Just entering it made the hairs on the back of my neck stand on end. Ric, who was fluent in Spanish, did all the talking while a bored overweight policeman laboriously typed out a statement. I sat in the damp cell-like room and looked nervously around me. There was a nasty atmosphere in the place. I glanced at the typist, who looked up in surprise when Ric gave the value of the altimeter. He had close-set cruel eyes in a round sweating face. His uniform was awry and his hair hung slackly in black greasy hanks from his balding scalp. I knew something of Peru's recent history and had no doubts about the number of victims that had 'disappeared' within these cold grey walls. A shiver ran up my spine.

Another man leant against the wall by the door, prodding under his finger nails with a tooth pick. I wondered why they had closed the door. I looked away hurriedly. If anything, he seemed more sinister than the desk-bound typist. There was a thin white scar on his chin, and he had a hungry wolfish face with eyes that were disturbingly blank. They lent him an unsettling appearance, as if he could do anything at any time without reason or emotion. A pistol was holstered on his hip, attached to a belt of bullets. I wondered how many people he had killed with it. Even if there were no records of death squads executing street children in Lima like vermin as they did in the cities of Brazil and Guatemala, the Peruvian army and the police certainly had a reputation for brutality even by the extreme levels of South America.

In 1985, when I last visited the country, 'the people's war' had already been in full swing for five years. Alan Garcia Perez had just been elected President and, despite the troubles, there was immense popular support for him. His plan for undermining the Shining Path – a Maoist terrorist group, which sprang from the Peruvian Communist Party – had come to nothing. Perez had seemed to have the right approach – respect for human rights, social reforms to improve the lot of the peasants, control over the military – but the economy had continued to decline, the poor became poorer, and the army continued its dirty war against Abimael Guzman Reynoso's Shining Path. Since the start of 'the people's war' in 1980 an estimated 27,000 people had been murdered and $15 billion dollars of damage done to the Peruvian economy.

Guzman had joined the Communist Party in 1960 after seeing the terrible plight of the poor in the earthquake which struck Peru that year. He began to move closer to the Maoist faction until, in 1965, he visited China and returned greatly impressed by what he had seen. It was then that he formed The Shining Path and styled himself Chairman Gonzalo. Whatever Guzman saw and learned in Mao's China he put to good use. The Shining Path has been described as the world's deadliest revolutionary force and its victim has been Peru, mired as it is in the international drugs trade, terrible degrading poverty, and a government described by its own Vice President as being in the hands of the murderous drugs mafia.

It would be inaccurate to portray this beautiful country either as the legendary mysterious land of the Incas or as a place riven with violence and crime and corrupt extortion. The Peruvian people pride themselves on their freedom and decency and strive to defend the principles of democracy and the rule of law. It is a richly varied land with three distinct regions – a narrow desert coastal belt, in which half the twenty million population lives, the wide Andean mountains, and the vast Amazonian rainforest which accounts for 60 per cent of the country's land and only 5 per cent of its population. The remainder live in the highlands, mostly as peasants, *campesinos*, existing on subsistence agriculture. Half the population is Indian, a third *mestizo*, 12 per cent are white with a small minority of blacks, Asians and Chinese. The dominant religion is Roman Catholic, although the Indians tend to blend their traditional beliefs with the Catholicism imported by the conquering Spaniards in the sixteenth century.

The web of corruption, drug trafficking, terrorism and widespread abuse of human rights is not immediately obvious to a visitor. When the Shining Path collaborated with the drug cartels in their efforts to disrupt the country's stability and the army joined forces with the police in a vicious war against them, it was the *campesinos* who became the victims caught in the middle.

Plantations in the Huallaga valley in the north-east of the country produce 70 per cent of the entire world's supply of coca, the raw material from which cocaine is produced. The potential income from this trade is staggering. Peru's estimated revenue from coca production in 1992 alone was nearly three hundred million dollars, and this was well down on earlier years. Such a source of illicit wealth breeds crime and corruption on an unparalleled scale, and with it comes a spiralling uncontrollable wave of violence and brutality that feeds endlessly upon itself.

The *campesinos* suffer intimidation by both the terrorists and the military. The army has a grim reputation for the indiscriminate torture, rape and murder of hundreds of people in their efforts to root out the terrorists. The terrorists have been no less ruthlessly trigger happy. This vicious circle of brutality is best illustrated in the Upper Huallaga Valley where, once Shining Path had gained control of the drugs trade, the peasants growing coca found themselves in a desperate position. Assuming that the farmers supported the Shining Path, the army treated them as enemies. At the same time, Shining Path expected nothing short of total loyalty from the peasants in their struggle for control. Torture, deaths and disappearances increased through the 1980s as the bodies of more victims floated down the Huallaga river. Both sides fought to control the profits of the coca paste trade, and both sides accumulated huge profits. Innocent civilians were the losers. The mutilated corpses dragged from the river were testimony to that.

These events taken out of context give the impression of a hopelessly evil land, which is far from true. A tourist could travel with relative safety and never catch the slightest glimpse of what lies darkly in the background. In my travels in Peru I have found it to be a charming and friendly country blessed with breathtaking scenery and a vibrant sense of confidence. This is because it has given me exactly what I went there to find. I saw only what I wanted to see and remained happily ignorant of the dark side and the menace lying uneasily beneath the surface.

The influence of the Sendero ebbs and flows, and the areas of the country where it is most dangerous to travel occupy a relatively small portion of central Peru. Few visitors would believe on the evidence of their eyes that the world's deadliest terrorist organisation and the Peruvian army are engaged in a dirty war of horrifying brutality.

However noble the terrorists saw their cause to be, they nevertheless used savage methods to achieve their aims. Following the principles of Mao's Cultural Revolution, they adopted the rigorous internal disciplines employed by Mao's Red Guards. New members had to submit totally to the Party's authority, writing exhausting self-criticisms and accepting complete relinquishment of all personal ambitions, feelings and ideas. Only total obedience to 'Gonzalo Thought' was tolerated.

The solution to the problem as far as the government and the army were concerned was the capture or death of the Shining Path prophet, Abimael Guzman Reynoso. This proved more difficult to accomplish than anyone foresaw. Guzman became legendary, and even with his removal, there was no guarantee that the movement's effectiveness would be destroyed. Atrocities were committed by both sides in the name of the other until it was hard to distinguish which had become the more depraved. In 1986, a year after I had crawled out of the mountains with a shattered leg, mutinies by jailed terrorists were brutally suppressed by army death squads. In the main prison in Lima, Lurigancho, 124 Shining Path guerillas died, most of them after they had surrendered. Due to poor intelligence, the army could only fight the guerillas by means of terror, and when brutality feeds upon itself, men become inured to it. Only the victims experience its full horror.

At last, in September 1992, Guzman was captured by policemen who could scarcely believe that he actually existed in the flesh.

'I have lost one battle,' he said to General Vidal, the arresting officer. 'You yourself know, General, that the Party is everywhere in Peru. We have now advanced sufficiently to be able to win.'

So far it appears that his prediction has not come true. The situation in the country greatly improved over the next two years and tourism, an important source of income, began to revive. Our presence there was evidence of that. Yet, despite Guzman's capture, there is still a shadowy fear that the Shining Path has not been defeated.

When, in April 1995, the Shining Path unleashed a new campaign of terror in an effort to disrupt the general election, eleven peasant villagers in the remote Andean settlement of Calemar were murdered. Bullet-ridden and decapitated corpses were strewn across the village square, many bearing notices saying: 'We will kill those who vote. Traitors to our cause will die.' Simultaneously army camps were attacked in the north, and bomb and grenade assaults carried out on government buildings. All this took place in areas close to the centre of Peru's cocaine production.

Abimael Guzman, the tubby, bearded prophet of the terrorists, may be behind bars and calling for a peace accord, and thousands of terrorists may have since surrendered their arms, but there is still a frightening undercurrent of terror. Cutting off the head of the movement may have come too late.

Self-interest and greed spawned by massive profits from drugs may have taken a higher priority over the revolutionary zeal of Guzman's Maoist ideology. So far, the police and the army may have won, but their on-going battle with the drugs trade is just as vicious and brutal.

I stared at the scar-faced policeman leaning against the wall and suddenly felt an overwhelming desire to get outside. I knew that this man had the means and the ability to execute me, if he so wished, without a moment's hesitation. It seemed perfectly possible that Ric and I could disappear without trace in that cold, damp concrete room. *Don't be an idiot,* I told myself. *We're just innocent tourists.* The logic didn't help. It was the simple, clear realisation of the power wielded by these men that made me shudder. I was in a place quite beyond my experience, discovering for the first time in my life that the comforting notions of human rights, justice, fair play and the rule of law that were so fundamental to my culture had precious little value in much of the world today.

I had the empty stomach and dry mouth of a guilty man as I looked nervously at my feet, wondering whether he had recognised my fear. I listened to Ric chatting happily in Spanish, quite unaware of my unease. *It's because you can't understand the language,* I comforted myself. *They wouldn't do anything to you. You're British.*

I nudged Ric's shoulder. 'Are we done?'

'We are going to have to pay him now,' he whispered.

'Fine, fine, do it,' I stammered. 'Come on, let's get out of here.'

'What's the rush?'

'It's this place. It gives me the creeps.'

When at last we hurried out into the early evening shadows on the city streets, I felt a huge release of pent up tension. I ran across the six-lane highway outside the police station and was narrowly missed by a truck. I waited for Ric on the other side, holding the flimsy piece of paper that would enable me to recover the value of the altimeter and wishing I hadn't bothered.

The fearful atmosphere of the police station had tainted my attitude to the country. Standing there on the sidewalk, looking at Ric as he waited outside the police station for a gap in the traffic, I tried to convince myself that it was all in my mind, that it wasn't important. I was here to climb mountains, not to try to solve someone else's problems. So long as it didn't affect me directly, why should I care? The truth was uncomfortable to live with.

On the Nangpa La I had walked past columns of poorly equipped people escaping from torture and tyranny and had not lent a helping hand, despite wearing and carrying the very latest expensive clothing and equipment. Perhaps there was nothing I could have done for them, but the vast difference in our fortunes was inescapably obvious. In Lima I stood outside a police station feeling unnerved and menaced by an aura of brutality vicariously experienced while filing a report of stolen property to support an insurance claim for a £150 gadget.

'It makes you wonder whether we should come here,' I said to Ric once we had returned to the splendid luxury of the $90 a night Gran Hotel Bolivar.

'How come?'

'Oh, I don't know, the poverty, and the violence and the human rights abuses.'

'We don't take part in them, so why shouldn't we come here. After all we bring in a lot of money and boost the tourist trade.'

'Yes, I know, but it's almost as if we sanction it by coming here. And anyway most of that tourist money goes straight to the people who are already rich. I mean the really poor bastards just get poorer and more screwed.'

'That's not entirely true. The trade filters all the way down. The guy with a few donkeys benefits from the extra work as much as some fat city slicker, relatively speaking that is.'

'Of course he does. I'm not suggesting it should be some sort of socialist paradise, fair play for all and so on, but we can't get away from the fact that by ignoring the death squads or the drugs trade we are in a way sanctioning them. It's like saying we're not at home so it doesn't matter. If it's not in my back yard, then it doesn't exist.'

'I think that's a bit of an exaggeration, don't you?'

'But there is an element of truth in it. Take Tibet. Would you go climbing there?'

'Given the money and the chance, I'd jump at it.'

'Even knowing what has gone on there, and still is going on, and knowing that the money you bring in goes directly to the Chinese authorities.'

'Yes, well maybe . . .' Ric said uncertainly.

'You see?' I said triumphantly. 'You're not sure, are you, eh? You want to go because you're a climber but deep down you're uncomfortable about it. You're not sure.'

'Tibet is a bit different,' Ric said defensively.

'True, but not entirely different. If you accept that travelling to a place indicates that you're happy with how the country is governed, then it means you sanction what goes on there. Whether it's the Chinese in Tibet or the drugs war and human rights abuses in Peru makes no difference. You can't be there and pretend it has nothing to do with you, can you?'

'No but things are not that simple. People are not that moral, or guilty for that matter. Look, you've just been in Tibet and now you're here so you're not exactly setting a shining example.'

'Oh, I know that,' I said. 'That is precisely what's bugging me. Sometimes I think I feel guilty about it only because the guilt makes me feel better. I still go, but I can thrash myself with all sorts of moral recriminations and think that that goes some way towards solving the dilemma – which, of course, it doesn't.'

'Would you go back to Tibet then?'

'No,' I said firmly. 'Somehow that is different. What happened there was deliberate plunder. You could say the troubles in Peru have all sorts of causes – greed, politics, corruption, drugs – which are all bad, but the country still operates. Most people manage to live perfectly normally. There are elections and there is democracy and so on. Whereas all you have in Tibet is an invading authoritarian regime and a police state, with the people almost crushed deliberately out of existence.'

'So where is the difference?' Ric asked. 'I mean, is torturing and executing a Tibetan any different from killing a Peruvian peasant?'

'No, but the degree to which it is done and the intention behind it has some bearing. It was genocide in Tibet, make no mistake about that. A quite deliberate systematic attempt to eradicate an entire culture. Here people get innocently caught up in it. The violence and brutality is no different, not in the way it is inflicted, but it is random here. It's just a messy dirty corrupt war, whereas in Tibet it was genocide.'

'You knew that before you went to Cho Oyo? Why is it suddenly so different?'

'I thought I knew. Until I saw them actually trying to escape I didn't really believe it.'

'Yeah, I suppose it's hard to believe,' Ric said. 'I mean, we just don't have that sort of corruption, or brutality at home.'

'Well, that's debatable,' I replied.

'What d'you mean?'

'Okay, sure, we don't have genocide and widespread corruption but it isn't perfect at home either. I mean a corrupt society, or a brutal and violent one, is simply a gathering of corrupt or violent individuals. There is enough of both in the west – it's just harder to see . . .'

'That's going a bit far, isn't it?' Ric interrupted. 'Genocide and wars mostly arise out of deliberate government decisions and policies.'

'Yeah, and governments are simply a collection of individuals. In the end it comes down to what those individuals are prepared to do, or think they can get away with. Does some thug robbing and raping a pensioner behave any differently?'

'I don't follow you.' Ric looked puzzled.

'It comes down to human nature. I mean, if as individuals we can't control our behaviour, our aggressive instincts, then surely we'll always be beset by the collective thuggery meted out by governments.'

'Yes, but we're not all like that,' Ric protested. 'Just because a few individuals are bad doesn't mean we are all tarred by the same brush.'

'I'm not so sure. It's a reflection of our nature. However conceited we may be about how civilised we are, that same violence lies not far below the surface in all of us. I mean, how the hell do you think we've managed to send generations of young men off to slaughter in all the wars we've had in Europe? They wouldn't fight if it wasn't an innate part of themselves.'

'Maybe,' Ric conceded. 'And I suppose, even in a democracy you'll get the kind of government that most people want.'

'Even Hitler came to power by winning a couple of elections,' I added.

'Yes, but your argument is still a bit over the top for me. Surely there must be checks and balances in human beings, just as there are in nature. After all, most people want good things, not bad, to happen. What about compassion, self-sacrifice and love? They're strong and good . . . No civilisation would have lasted a week without any of those, surely?'

'You're right. Let's change the subject,' I said hastily, somewhat relieved to find myself outflanked.

'We can forget about the police. We'll be out of Lima tomorrow.'

'What do you think about climbing Huascaran? It looks huge to me.'

'It is,' Ric said. 'I failed the last time I tried, and I didn't have any clients with me.'

'Do you think they're up to it?'

'I haven't got a clue,' Ric replied. 'I was more worried about us,' he added with a laugh.

19

GHOST STORIES

I heard the voices and the laughter more loudly in my ears as if carried by the icy gust of wind cutting across the snow slope. I stopped and pressed a hand to my ear, shaking my head trying to make them go away. Sometimes they sounded like faint background whispers and then they would surge in volume. I looked up and saw the yellow flashes of head-torchlights cutting across the night sky and the sweep of the slope. Tony Hamza was following the Peruvian guides, Ankel and Ubaldo. Ric was leading David slowly a hundred feet above me. Fragments of ice tinkled down on to my sleeves as I drove my axe back into the snow. My shoulders were beginning to ache with the effort of the repetitive arm movements.

'How are you doing, Malcolm?' I shouted down into the darkness beneath my feet.

'Fine,' came the faint reply from the shadows.

'I'm not going too fast for you?'

'No, I'm fine.'

For a moment, in the silence after the shouted conversation, I thought the voices had gone but then I heard them again far back on the edge of my hearing. They had plagued me ever since we had left the high camp at the Garganta col at two in the morning. At first I thought I might have left my Walkman on with the volume turned down. On checking, I found it switched off and carefully wrapped in a scarf in the top pocket of my sack. I pulled back the balaclava exposing my ears to the icy wind, thinking that it might be the rubbing sounds of the fabric. The voices were still there.

When they surged loudly there was something oddly familiar about them. I dredged my memory, trying to think what it was. Although muted and distant, the noise was instantly recognisable as human voices and laughter. It had the same cadences, the rising and falling sounds of murmured conversation, and every now and then the high-pitched shriek of a child's laughter at play. *Child's laughter. That was it!* I could hear children playing in a schoolyard.

As soon as the memory of that familiar sound came rushing back to me I knew what I was hearing. I looked around in confusion. *Where was it coming from?* The full moon cast a silvery sheen across the upper slopes of Huascaran Norte. I was perched on a steep icy snow slope on the rising flanks of Huascaran Sur which rose above the col separating us from the summit pyramid of Norte.

Earlier, in the star-strewn darkness before the moon had risen, there had been nothing to see but the bobbing yellow head torches above and below me. I had put the voices down to a vivid imagination caused by the strange atmosphere of sensory deprivation that comes with climbing at night. There were no surrounding distractions apart from the small pool of light from my torch beam and the repeated blows of my ice axe. It felt as if I were in a separate, suspended world. There was no drop below me, no looming mountain wall above, just a ring of yellow light and a few square feet of snow. I didn't seem to be with anyone. The man to whom I was tied climbed far below me in his own cocoon of light, oblivious to everything.

Sometimes in the dark it is possible to convince yourself that you are not actually there on a steep mountainside; that if you fell nothing would happen. You would remain trapped in your tiny yellow bubble of light, not falling or climbing, simply there because nothing exists around you.

The voices came again, muttering and whispering conspiratorially in my head. I faced into the snow, pressing my forehead against the head of my axe, and listened carefully to the sounds. They were beginning to unnerve me. I couldn't explain them away. It wasn't the wind, nor was it the headphones. It wasn't my imagination either; I could hear them clearly. I had thought perhaps it was the effort of the climb, or pressure related, or some strange manifestation of an ear infection, but as I stood leaning against the slope I realised I could hear the sounds just as precisely as I had heard Malcolm's reply.

I pulled back the cuff on my mitts and checked the time. It would be light in an hour and a half. Already there were the tell-tale bandings of light blue in the eastern sky, just above the horizon. The moon was dropping low towards the jagged black crest of the Cordillera Negra, its silver light gradually softening to a creamy rich saffron glow. Below the crest of the hills the valley lay silent and black. I could see that we were far above the summits of the dry rocky horizon. I thought I could detect the curve of the earth in the crescent of moonlit hills.

The voices surged back again. They seemed to be coming from my right, from the dark shadows of the valley beneath the black jagged hills. I stared down into the darkness, listening intently. *Could sound travel so far?* I dismissed the thought with a shake of my head. Even if it could, what would a schoolyard full of children be doing laughing and playing at this time of night? And anyway, it wasn't only schoolyard sounds. There was also the deeper note of adults talking, a busy everyday sort of sound that was familiar, like a market on market day, haggling voices, children playing, ordinary greetings and shouted prices.

'Why have we stopped?' The clearer sound of Malcolm's voice came up from below. I shook my head and looked down. There was a winking yellow dot set against the blackness of the col below.

'Waiting for David,' I yelled.

I started moving again, irritated now by the incessant murmuring. I am not a believer in ghosts, although I have experienced a number of strange, inexplicable events in the past. Once, beneath the Croz Spur in the Alps, while tramping down the Leschaux glacier in the dark of the night, I was followed by something. I can't say what it was. I saw nothing, yet Ian Whittaker and I were definitely in the presence of something. We both sensed it independently and kept quiet for fear of appearing ridiculous. I remember the hair standing up on the back of my neck and the utter conviction washing over me that something was walking right behind me. I kept turning quickly to see who it was and there was no one there, just the rope trailing over the gritty ice and the distant light of Ian's headtorch.

I became convinced I could actually hear the phantom footfalls and kept stopping abruptly, expecting to catch him out and hear a couple of late footfalls. There was nothing. Only much later, as dawn was breaking, did I ask Ian if he noticed anything odd, and at once he blurted out that he was sure that he was being followed. When I said I had experienced exactly the same thing and added that it felt menacing as well, we both began talking rapidly and nervously about the same eerie sensation of being followed.

From then on, Ian insisted on leading. I had felt uncomfortable enough at the front not to want the added anxiety of knowing there was only empty black space behind me. After that we kept close together, side by side where we could and all the way down the glacier something followed us until we reached the junction with the Mer de Glace.

I know it could have been auto-suggestion, the consequence of sitting in a keyed-up state in the dark for hours beneath the huge threatening sweep of the Grandes Jorasses, anticipating the serious climbing to which we were about to commit ourselves. Maybe it was due partly to the cold and partly to the anti-climax of having to abandon the attempt because of dangerous rockfall. I knew that many climbers had lost their lives on those fearsome cliffs above where we had sat sheltering in a small crevasse, listening in the darkness to the machine-gun rattle of rockfalls on the ice fields high above us. I tried to convince myself that this knowledge predisposed me towards imagining ghostly visitations but it didn't explain why, independently, and at the same time, we both felt that we were being followed by an unfriendly and menacing presence, something quite outside our experience . . .

Almost a decade later, in the Gangotri region of the Garhwal Himalaya, a similar thing took place when Bob Drury and I were camped beneath the Fyffe Barton route on a mountain called Bhagirathi III. On the previous day we had dumped a heavy load of equipment at the base of a huge overhanging boulder that protruded from the glacial moraines beneath the west face of the mountain. It was early evening before we started down with empty rucksacks towards base camp.

We became separated on the way back, and as I had trudged wearily through the darkness I became convinced that someone was walking alongside me. I thought nothing of it at first, assuming it must be Bob, and carried on down in companionable silence with my shadowy partner. The sense that he was there with me was incredibly strong. I felt that, if I reached out, I would touch him. On a couple of occasions I stopped and looked around me to get my bearings but I could see no sign of Bob in the darkness. I hurried on, not wanting to be left behind, and soon sensed that I was once more close to him.

When I reached camp I was surprised to find Bob relaxing with a brew of tea. I couldn't understand how he had made it back so quickly since he had been with me only minutes before. Bob assured me he had been waiting in the camp for almost an hour. I was somewhat shaken by this news and wondered who on earth had been walking with me. I asked if Paul or Johnny had been out on the hill, but Bob told me that they had been in the camp all day. I didn't tell him about the presence for fear of appearing foolish.

The next day, as we camped in a portaledge tent hanging in space from the overhanging boulder beneath the west face, the presence returned. Darkness had just descended as I zipped the tent door closed and lay back in my sleeping bag. I felt my head begin to prickle before I heard the sound. I held my breath as I listened to the footsteps moving at a measured even pace round the tent. It sounded exactly as if a man was walking slowly on a loose gravel driveway. The sound was the same distinctive crunching and slithering of small stones being regularly disturbed. I waited tensely for the sounds to stop, for the overwhelming and stifling sensation of something stalking me to go away. I tried to tell myself that it was my imagination as I listened to the footsteps circling the tent site. When I shifted nervously in my sleeping bag and heard the nylon rustling, I could still hear the footsteps in the background.

There was definitely something outside. It didn't make sense. We were surrounded by a vast jumble of heavy boulders. There was nothing in the area that could possibly have made such a gravelly crunching sound. It must be an animal, I reassured myself, despite knowing that no animal other than a man on a gravel path could have made such a sound.

'Joe?' Bob said in the lightest of whispers.

'What?' I whispered back, straining my ears and tensing up.

'Can you hear that?'

The crunching footsteps continued their measured pacing around the tent. I was suddenly deeply scared.

'Yes.' There was no reply, only an intense watchful silence as we both lay utterly still and listened to the footsteps. They continued pacing for more than twenty minutes during which time Bob and I became increasingly terrified.

'What is it?' Bob hissed after a long pause.

'I don't know,' I hissed back, hearing the frightened vibration in my voice.

'Why don't you stick your head out and have a look?'

'Will I fuck?' I gasped breathlessly. It was the last thing I intended to do.

'What shall we do then?'

'God knows,' I said. 'But I am not sticking my head outside.'

It sounds foolish now, but I've never been so unnerved in all my life. We were two confident, fit men. We were not drunk, nor exhausted, and not dehydrated. We were not suffering due to altitude sickness nor hypoxic from lack of oxygen. We were spending a relaxed and calm night out, bivouacking beneath Bhagirathi III and listening to the eerie sounds of someone walking round and round us on a gravel path that didn't exist, and we were both utterly terrified.

Eventually the sounds faded away. We awoke the next morning and made a minute examination of the area, confirming to ourselves that we couldn't possibly have heard what we heard. Then we sat and chain smoked cigarettes and giggled nervously, trying not to think what it must have been. Later we learned that a few years before a young climber had fallen to his death close by in the glacier where we were camped. It was possible that he had actually fallen into that very cirque. I have never really known what to make of it. All I know is that something strange happened to us that night, and even with the passing of the years I'm no less convinced that we were listening to the lonely phantom footfalls of a man who didn't exist in our time and space.

I listened to the murmuring voices as I continued thrusting my axe into the snow in a slow progress up Huascaran's summit slopes. There was no sense of the menace that I had felt before. I remembered the times on the Leschaux glacier and beneath Gangotri and tried not to think about them. These were no ghosts encircling me with whispering voices. They might be wind sounds, or the product of a feverish imagination, but they could not be ghosts. They were too commonplace, too ordinary to be phantom sounds.

I watched as an immense moon slipped behind the distant ridges of the Cordillera Negra. The rising sun set it alight, so that it seemed to sink as a vast glowing fireball into the belly of the black hills, melting into the land itself. We stood in a silent awestruck group, watching an incandescent moon subside into the hills where dawn had already begun to pick out the shadows of valleys and river gorges. The snowy flanks of Huascaran Norte were burnished with the colours of molten metal, changing from leathery silver, to saffron yellow, to gold, and finally to an icy hard blue sheen as the moon disappeared and dawn threw its tentative cold light across the precipitous landscape. In the gap between the twin summits a sea of spectacular ice mountains was suddenly revealed rising dramatically from dark shadowed valleys. The horizon was coloured with distinct graduated blue layers and a thin sand yellow band formed between the horizon and the sky.

'That must be the desert,' Tony said, shading his eyes as he looked at the horizon.

'What desert?' I asked. 'You mean the coastal strip? That's over a hundred kilometres away.'

'I know, but surely at this height we can see that far. We're well over twenty-two thousand feet now. Yes, I reckon that's the desert.'

And at that moment the voices stopped. They didn't fade slowly; they stopped abruptly, and I remember it distinctly. For the first time since leaving camp nearly five hours before I no longer had the voices whispering to me. The contrasting silence was so sudden that I looked around to see what had happened. The darkness had gone. We sat huddled in the freezing blue light of dawn, waiting for the warmth of the sun to creep down from the summit slopes.

'That's Yungay,' Ric said, pointing down into the valley where the moon had been swallowed.

'Yungay?' I said. 'The place that got wiped out?'

'Yeah, it's there, see?' Ric pointed to a spur descending into the river valley. There was a grey scar plunging down towards the river. 'You can see where the avalanche went. There, see that grey area?'

I peered down at the spot where eighteen thousand people had been engulfed, where a whole village had disappeared, had simply been buried as if it had never existed, and thought about the babbling murmur of the voices in the night. *No. It couldn't be anything to do with that, surely?*

Later, when we got safely down from the summit to the shelter of the tents, I told Ric what I had heard, expecting him to laugh at me.

'You'd better not tell it to Ankel, or Ubaldo,' he said earnestly. 'It will freak them out.'

274

'How do you mean?' I was surprised that he had taken me seriously.

'Well, with the earthquake and all. I don't believe in ghosts but they will. They're pretty superstitious about these things, you know.'

'Well, so am I now.' I stared uncomfortably at Ric. 'I did hear those voices. I swear I did.'

'Probably the wind,' Ric said dismissively.

'It wasn't you know. I tell you, it wasn't the wind.'

20

COLLATERAL DAMAGE

The children laughed and clapped as the clown entered the ring, his face set in a beaming painted red smile, eyebrows arched in high curves of permanent surprise. He took three steps in his oversized shoes, and as the drums rolled he flipped forward, landing flat on his face. The crowd of children shrieked with delight.

Outside in the hot sun of a Sunday afternoon stalls had been set up selling sweets and balloons and all manner of food and drink. Whole pigs turned slowly over glowing charcoal in mobile barbecue stoves. Roasted guinea pigs, spread out and flattened, hung from a post by the stoves, their rodent teeth displaying agonised rictus grins across crushed golden roasted heads. Another chorus of laughter rose from the tent amid the sound of drumrolls. The earth rolled imperceptibly with them.

In the beautiful nearby town of Yungay the market was beginning to close down. People began packing away their goods in stout sacks and cardboard boxes. Donkeys tethered to railings were expertly loaded with recently purchased sacks of rice and flour. Great mounds of guinea pig food lay heaped by a stall like a monstrous green eruption of chickweed. A man sat on a box beside it holding closed the neck of a wriggling sack. A woman haggled with him over the price of the guinea pig that she held casually by her side. She had a firm grip on the scruff of the guinea pig's neck and it hung limply from her hand as if paralysed.

A bus pulled into the main square, the Plaza de Armas, where four tall palm trees provided welcome shade from the hot, high altitude sun. A priest stood under the carved arch doorway of the church. Light clouds drifted high above the summit of Huascaran, which was still shrouded in heavy layers of early season snow.

The busy murmur of voices suddenly fell silent. People turned and looked questioningly at the sky. There was a shuddering vibration. For a brief moment the view of the summit of Huascaran, looming twelve thousand feet above the town, shimmered as if through a heat haze. Small explosions of snow clouds puffed from its shoulders. People shuffled nervously. Voices were raised again, high-pitched questioning voices. The earth had moved; then it began to roll, and their world began to end.

It was 3:21 p.m. on 31st May 1970. The idyllic market town of Yungay had three minutes of existence left. An earthquake of shattering force had just been triggered deep below the coastal town of Chimbote 150 kilometres away. There had been a sudden shuddering slippage, momentarily releasing an immense amount of energy as the Nazca plate ground its way beneath the American plate. The epicentre of this massive earthquake was close to the busy fishing port of Chimbote. It measured 7.8 on the Richter scale.

The quake lasted fifty interminable seconds, and in that time tens of thousands of people died. The tremors destroyed virtually every town in the Callejon de Huaylas, the long agricultural valley of the Rio Santa river running the entire length of the Cordillera Blanca from Huaraz in the south to Huallanca and beyond to the north. To the east of the range the lush vegetated remote valleys of the Rios Mosna, Yurma and Shiulla known collectively as the Callejon de Conchucos, were devastated. Bridges, roads, buildings and whole villages were levelled. Ninety per cent of Huaraz, the largest town in the area, was utterly destroyed and more than 15,000 people – more than half the total population – were crushed under the flattened town. Aftershocks, sixty-four separate tremors, continued to wreak havoc for the next two days. As a result, rescue services were rendered helpless. Even helicopters could not land in some areas, due to the dust clouds.

In all, some 80,000 people lost their lives. If the disaster hadn't struck on a Sunday, when children were not attending school, the death toll would have been even higher. An estimated one million people were made homeless. It was the worst catastrophe in the history of the Americas.

International aid flooded into the region as gradually the extent of the destruction became apparent. Aid came from governments, private organisations, including many mountaineering clubs, and hastily set up charities. Huaraz was rebuilt and now has a population of 100,000 – three times more than before – but it has lost much of its charm. It had to be reconstructed quickly and style was not considered important. The old maze of narrow streets that were to trap so many of the inhabitants in a chaos of collapsing houses have gone, replaced by airy open avenues. It is now in a better state, with stronger modern buildings, to withstand future quakes. The main road to Lima on the coast was completed with the help of foreign aid. This should prevent the long wait for rescue that isolated communities endured in 1970. It has also brought the region into much closer contact with the rest of the country.

People all over Peru helped with the reconstruction, and then, taking advantage of the opportunities to buy land, settled in the new city. Many of the mountain dwellers moved down to Huaraz from their shattered farming settlements, and as a result the Cordillera Blanca is now much less populated than it was.

Yungay, the most beautiful town in the Callejon de Huaylas, was to suffer the most shocking fate. As the first sickening tremor rolled through the earth, silencing the horrified people in the market and cutting off the shrill laughter of the children just outside the town, buildings began to tremble and sway. Twelve thousand feet above where Yungay nestled behind a protective ridge in the valley floor Huascaran's mighty flanks shuddered convulsively. Great pillars of granite were shaken loose from the side of Huascaran Norte and plunged down the mountain, tearing immense cliffs of ice away as they fell. Formerly stable serac bands collapsed in clouds of icy particles and heavily laden snow slopes avalanched in all directions. The mountain came alive. An enormous bombardment of rock, ice and snow thundered thousands of feet down towards the valley.

The west face of Huascaran Norte crumpled like a pack of cards as fifteen million cubic metres of rock peeled away. As it hurtled down the almost vertical face of the mountain it combined with millions of cubic metres of ice, mud and earth picked up in the unstoppable flood. It is estimated that a staggering total mass of some seventy-five million cubic metres of debris eventually formed the bulk of the alluvion triggered by the earthquake.

This immense alluvion – part avalanche, part landslide – gathered speed with ferocious acceleration until its momentum lifted it up and it became airborne on a cushion of air. Freed from the dragging friction of the mountain's flanks, it plunged down 4,000 vertical metres, riding the cushion of air at an estimated speed of 400 kilometres an hour. Everything in its path was obliterated.

A fifteen strong team of Czech mountaineers were camped at 4,000 metres on the slopes of the mountain overlooking Yungay. They included some of Czechoslovakia's most experienced climbers as well as the celebrated mountain photographer Vilem Heckel and the sculptor Valerian Karousek. They were still in a state of shock and grief at the death of one of their members, Ivan Bortel, the previous day. He had slipped during the approach march to the camp and suffered fatal head injuries. Less than twenty-four hours later his companions were also dead, buried under an enormous mound of boulders and conglomerated muddy screes.

A shock wave, like the blast from a bomb, was pushed ahead of the main mass of the alluvion. It blasted the Czech camp into oblivion and no one was ever found. It surged into nearby lakes raising the levels by as much as twenty-five feet, and careered down into the valley of the Rio Santa below.

The alluvion reached the Santa River fourteen kilometres away and four vertical kilometres down in three minutes. It thundered into the river valley, surging past the town of Caraz, where hundreds were at that moment dying in their shattered houses, and entered the precipitous narrow river gorge of the Canon del Pato, a total distance of sixty-five kilometres.

As it swept towards Caraz a small portion of this mass of liquefied rock, ice and mud slopped over the ridge protecting Yungay. The people never had a chance. Most of them probably knew nothing of what was surging towards them. In seconds an enormous wall of sludge and pulverised moraines appeared from nowhere, surging monstrously over the 700-foot ridge, and landed on the town, burying it in a layer of debris thirty feet thick.

Eighteen thousand people ceased to exist. The whole town was eradicated, wiped out as if it had never existed. The houses were smeared from the earth. Those few that were strong simply became sludge-filled tombs. The church, with its high steeple, crashed into the flood and sank from sight. A bus careered across the surging surface of the slowing alluvion like some child's toy in a storm drain. The bus came to a halt half-buried, pointing imploringly upwards at an angle of forty-five degrees at the mountain which had destroyed Yungay. The four stately palm trees in the central plaza miraculously survived the carnage but now gave shade to a devastated landscape littered with boulders and silent rocky mud pools.

Silence flooded over the buried town. There were no agonised screams of the dying, no wails of grief from the survivors. All in the town were dead and buried, never to be recovered. A group of children enjoying the circus outside the path of the alluvion was spared, although in an instant they lost everything else – grandparents, parents, brothers, sisters, uncles, aunts, their homes, their church, their whole world. The only other survivors were 240 people who managed to run up a knoll to the cemetery carved into the summit of a circular dome-shaped hillock. It was ironic that the town's place of death became, for a brief moment, the only place of life.

The alluvion flooded round the base of this mound of earth pulling under those unfortunate enough not to have reached the steps which led to the serried ranks of graves cut into the concentric walls of the ringed summit. The crowd turned from their panic-stricken flight to find that they and the graves were all that was left of Yungay. While the enormity of what

280

had taken place settled upon them in the clearing dust, the rest of the region was being devastated by the main shocks of the quake. They must have expected immediate help, assuming that it was simply a massive avalanche that had burst through moraine dams on the mountain above their town – as had happened in the past. No help came, and no one witnessed the total disappearance of their homes and families and friends. News filtered down to them of the slaughter that had befallen all the other villages and small towns in the valley, though none of them suffered the pitiful fate of Yungay.

Twenty-four years later, I boarded a bus in Huaraz with Matt and Helen Ward, two climbing friends that Ric and I had bumped into in town. The journey to Yungay took less than an hour along the smooth tarmac highway through the Callejon de Huaylas. Matt told me that his uncle, a doctor, had helped in the immediate aftermath of the disaster. He had flown over the buried town and seen at once that there was nothing to be done. They simply flew on to other areas where help was needed.

I looked at Huascaran looming into the clear blue skies above the Rio Santa. It was hard to believe that I had been standing on the summit only two weeks before. It seemed so distant, and so impregnably solid. There was an oddly benign, almost benevolent atmosphere in the way its huge bulk dominated the valley. It seemed as if it would always be there, unchanging and constant.

The bus drew up at the white concrete arches marking the entrance to the old town of Yungay. A new town had been constructed out of the danger area about a kilometre further north, sheltered by the ridge that had offered no shelter in the past. It still looks like a temporary city struggling bravely to achieve its own new identity, yet there is an air of bright optimism about the place.

Alluvions, earthquakes and destructive spillages from glacial lakes have always menaced the region and the people have always returned and struggled to rebuild their shattered settlements. In 1941 an alluvion caused by avalanches plunged into the glacial lake, Laguna Palcacocha, breaching the weak moraine dam of rocks, gravel and boulders. The surge of mud and boulders burst through the lower lake, which no longer exists, before sweeping twenty kilometres down the Cojup valley and pouring through the centre of the town of Huaraz, killing some 5,000 people. In 1950 Laguna Jancarurish was similarly breached and much of the Quebrada (valley) de Los Cedros destroyed. Another one in 1965 from Laguna Tumarina crashed through the Quebrada Carhuascancha. The 1941 disaster prompted a programme to be set up to stabilise the lakes in the area. Water levels were lowered by cutting through the moraine dams, or kept from rising by digging tunnels through the dykes.

However, not all alluvions can be stopped. In 1962, only eight years before Yungay was buried, a huge serac collapse caused by movement 'of the ice cap on the summit of Huascaran Norte spilled down into the valley, completely destroying the towns of Ranrihirca and Shacsha and several smaller settlements, killing four thousand people in the process. On that occasion the ridge protecting old Yungay managed to hold the alluvion back from the town, and this gave rise to a false sense of security among the inhabitants. These recurring disasters are testament to the enduring strength and optimism of the people struggling to survive in the harsh environment of the Cordillerra Blanca, and nowhere more so than in the bustle of new Yungay.

As we stepped from the bus and it drew away in a choking cloud of dust and exhaust fumes I wondered why I had wanted to visit the buried city. It seemed a macabre and voyeuristic thing to do. As we wandered through the archway I saw a group of people selling snacks and bottles of beer and fizzy drinks that were kept cool in a nearby stream. The ground was strewn with litter and there was an air of opportunist commerce that seemed out of keeping with the site of a mass grave. I was tempted to return to the road and walk up to the new town.

A dry hot wind was blowing down the valley rolling small dust storms across a barren plain of rubble. A few large boulders protruded from the earth. There was nothing to see – just as I had expected. We refused the offer of drinks and wound our way up a conical hill on top of which a huge white statue of Christ stood facing Huascaran with arms outstretched. He seemed to be trying to hold back the mountain as he stood upon the square plinth with the creamy folds of his robe hanging down in pleats of concrete. The statue was nearly thirty feet high, and it dominated the area.

I noticed that the steps had been excavated through walls of conglomerated mud and rock until they reached above the tidemark of the alluvion; above that the pebble-dash surface changed to dressed stone. I tried to imagine the hundreds of people racing in panic towards the steps.

Looking across the site of the town, I saw a flat desolate plain extended over an area of several square kilometres. There was no indication that it had ever been a town. Dry stunted bushes waved in the wind, blackened scorched areas showing where fires had been used to keep the ground from becoming overgrown. Dust and balls of tangled grasses tumbled across the plain, blown by a strong wind.

Above me, the expression on the face of the Christ figure seemed to be one of helpless, pitying compassion, as if to say: 'What could I do?' The plinth on which the statue stood had a blue painted band on the side facing Huascaran with a prayer apparently written by one of the survivors on an ochre yellow stylised scroll.

Padre Mío. Diós Mío. Porqué?
. *(My Father? My God . . . Why?)*

Even with my sketchy Spanish, it was clear to me that this was no ordinary prayer. It was a bitter lament verging on disbelief in God – a pathetic cry for comprehension, for reasons. Reading it aloud without attempting to translate, I could hear the agony and confusion in the cadences of the words; the repeated pitiful question marks. Why? Why this, why us? *You made me witness of such pain. Why? My heart bleeds with the memory of the dying . . . screams of children, of young and old, rich and poor united in a single pain. And they were looking towards me!*

Mi Yungay, dejo de existir. My Yungay taken from existence.

I turned my back on the statue, feeling angry and sensing

the pain of betrayal in the words. Clouds had massed over the twin summits of Huascaran, shielding them from view. I could see the rocky cliffs of Huascaran Norte where millions of tons of rock had cascaded down. There was an old grey scar gouged from the lower flanks of the mountain. A wooded ridge came down steeply to a low point directly in line with the scar. I wondered what that roaring wall of debris had looked like when it first appeared, spewing out high over the security of the ridge.

I stood on a terrace that circled the steps leading up to the statue. A wall of white stone some twenty feet high ringed the terrace. Dug into the white stone were ranks of graves seven deep from top to bottom and extending in even lines around the whole circumference of the walls. Looking down, I could see the levels of stepped terraces of two more concentric burial walls. The graves looked like dome-shaped oven doors set into the rock. There was a strange dry rustling sound above the wind. Dust lashed against my face. The ovens reminded me of a dreadful image from the past.

Walking slowly around the burial walls I read the hundreds of names and inscriptions on the faces of the grave doors. In some places there were small glass framed photographs of the deceased staring blankly out across the shattered town in fading sepia browns. Bunches of desiccated flowers were tied to some of the doors. They rustled and crackled across the stone as the wind harried them. It produced an eerie unnerving sound, as if someone were scratching to get out.

As I read the years and ages of the dead behind their doors I realised that there was not one single burial in the year of the alluvion. There had been no one to bury. I hurried down the steps to the next level and searched the tombs. None in 1970, and very few for many years afterwards. The walls were kept meticulously clean, and in places on the terraces there were iron fenced graves similar to others I had seen in England. White crosses stood silhouetted starkly against the cloud-covered summits. It was as if they were ashamed to be seen, hiding their brutal legacy behind grey depressing cloud caps.

I saw Matt and Helen moving slowly away from the foot of the hill towards the centre of the plain. They walked slowly, slightly apart from one another. It was then that I noticed the small shrines and crosses dotted among the debris. We had all been silent since reaching the cemetery. The melancholy atmosphere and the daunting realisation of what had happened in this place had made us mute, almost frightened.

I crossed the dusty plain, following a barely distinguishable path through scrubby bushes and rough rocky gravels. Slowly I began to get a sense of the scale of the destruction. Matt and Helen were two distant dots. Here and there family groups wandered quietly as if looking for something in the ground. I searched around me for any sign that might suggest where a road had once been, the foundations of a house, scattered brickwork. There was nothing to betray the presence of the buried town. Everywhere I turned there was a metal cross or a white stone shroud. The inscriptions were pitiful. In this area lay the house of such and such; beneath this ground lies the father, mother, sons, daughters, uncles, aunts of this family. Even the shrines were placed only in rough approximation of where people thought the houses might have been.

I was overwhelmed with the impermanence of things. It wasn't simply the huge number of lives lost in an instant, or the fact that a whole town had disappeared, but a sense of dismay that things so solid, so vitally alive, a whole community could cease to exist so abruptly. It challenged my own notions of security and mortality, belittled any sense of worth I felt about the significance of life.

The Christ figure stood high and clear and white against the brown hills of the Cordillera Negra. Whatever omnipotence people invested in that idol seemed pathetically misplaced by comparison with the earth's all-consuming dominance of our lives. I had spent years on the high mountains of the world, teetering gingerly across their ice fields and rock buttresses, convincing myself that they were solid and safe. I knew the dangers of avalanche slopes, unstable ice cliffs, and loose exfoliating rock faces and I could use my experience to avoid them. For most of the time I climbed over great walls of rock and ice knowing that they were absolutely solid and immobile. Looking around me, I doubted I would feel that way again. Seventy-five million cubic metres? It was unimaginable.

The enormity of it stunned me, and when I reached the centre of the buried town and saw the four palm trees and a few shattered brick arches of the collapsed church, it finally sank in. I felt suddenly uneasy. I had been walking over the unmarked buried bodies of countless people. The sight of the church walls, two mounds of brick no more than fifteen feet high, made their deaths seem suddenly real.

It reminded me of a time, nearly twenty years before, when I had been overwhelmed by the same numbing emotions. My parents were living in Germany at that time and one day they took me to visit Bergen Belsen, the former Nazi death camp which was situated close to a golf club where my parents played. I can't remember now whether I pestered my father to take me there or whether, as a serving army officer, he felt it was something important for me to witness. At any rate, it did not seem strange to me, a fourteen-year-old schoolboy, to be visiting such a place, which was close to a training ground for British and NATO regiments stationed in Germany. Before that it had been a training ground for the German army.

I walked around the remains of the Belsen camp in a distant slightly dislocated mood. I understood what I was seeing but I felt nothing. The great burial barrows, the plaques with apologies from the German people in the languages of the victims, and the small macabre museum were all taken in as if I were in some sort of artificial, recreated place, as if nothing had actually happened there. For me, it was just a strange history park.

Perhaps it was the presence of my parents that inhibited me. It felt like one of those uncomfortable moments I knew from watching television as a child in the company of adults. Something rude and adult would appear on the screen, and I'm old enough to understand what is going on, even to be aroused by the scene, and yet my parents are sitting there in the same room watching it, and suddenly it seems all wrong and I begin to squirm with embarrassment, looking away from the screen, feigning disinterest. My parents don't even notice my discomfort because they are adults and this is a normal part of their knowledge, but to me it seems strange to witness such things with them sitting there, and I want to run away and hide.

It was just like that walking round the mass graves in the spring sunlight, wanting to run away and be alone. It was like being confronted by strange unanswerable questions, or the teenager discovering sex for the first time and being ambushed by the idea that his parents must do it, and being quite unable to believe it. You know they must, otherwise you wouldn't have been born, but it seems so unlikely. Surely this new, weird, intensely private and secret discovery could only be experienced by people of one's own age? Parents couldn't possibly get up to that sort of thing. Still less grandparents! It is altogether incredible that such things could be part of their world, despite knowing that it must be. You feel uncomfortable and edgy when such thoughts catch you by surprise.

In a similar way, I felt that Belsen had nothing to do with me. It wasn't my world; it wasn't important. I remember looking covertly at my parents, knowing that this atrocity happened in their time, to their generation. It was their world, their war, their responsibility. Oh, I knew it wasn't their fault. I knew who it was had committed the crimes, but it seemed to me that they bore the guilt of it, simply by having been alive at the time. I felt uncomfortable with them there. And at the same time I was filled with remorse that I should even dare to think such things of them, knowing in my heart they were false.

A week later, while my parents were playing golf, I walked back alone down the long straight road lined with trees to Belsen. I remember that a column of tanks crashed down the road past me, making the toughened layers of concrete tremble beneath my feet. I watched the long line of steel behemoths belching great black clouds of smoky exhaust fumes as they thundered past and felt dizzy with the intense bass roar of the engines.

As I entered the concentration camp I noticed an old grey-haired couple standing silently, heads bowed, before one of the great grass-covered barrows. I walked slowly down the avenues between the barrows reading the inscriptions again. It was strangely silent in the camp. There was no sound of trees rustling in the wind, no traffic noises from the nearby road, not even birdsong. It was as if the place was holding its breath. A notice revealed how many bodies were buried under each of the mounds that stretched in orderly lines across the former grounds of the camp. Nearly a hundred feet long, I guessed, by forty wide. The numbers were in tens of thousands.

I stared at one barrow and tried to picture 20,000 people lying twisted and interlocked under the thirty-foot-high mound of earth. It was quite unimaginable. It hurt trying to think about it. I remembered the photographs I had seen in the small museum room' – the huge piles of emaciated naked corpses with sunken hollow faces, dark pitifully weary eye sockets, and the obscene racks of ribs showing through, the jutting hip and elbow joints and the withered limbs like sticks. There was a picture of a British soldier driving a bulldozer that was pushing a rolling tangle of bodies towards the edge of a pit. He had a fixed emotionless expression on his face. God knows how many frightful scenes he had already witnessed during the war: the deaths of comrades, the carnage of high explosives and machine gun fire. He must have been used to death, seen enough of it not to flinch away, but this must have been beyond his comprehension.

The British army unexpectedly stumbled upon the camp in April 1945 during their advance across Germany. They found forty thousand survivors barely alive, wracked with malnutrition and starvation, suffering from the effects of an epidemic of typhus, typhoid and tuberculosis. Great heaps of naked rotting corpses lay scattered all around. One pile of naked women measured 250 feet in length, 100 feet wide and 5 feet in height. Children played nearby. In the preceding month before liberation 30,000 prisoners had died. In total an estimated 100,000 people died in Belsen.

When they opened up the huts where the prisoners had been incarcerated they found scenes of dreadful horror. Sometimes the occupants of an entire hut were dead, locked in, starved to death, killed by disease and overwork. In some huts there was evidence of cannibalism where inmates had struggled desperately to stay alive. A burial programme was immediately instigated, survivors were deloused and quarantined in an effort to contain the ravages of contagion.

Even as British troops entered the camp the Nazi guards were shooting prisoners no longer capable of work, oblivious of the fact that the camp had been liberated. When they realised that the British had arrived they tried to escape. Some were shot, others committed suicide. Many of the guards were captured before they had a chance to flee, including the commandant, the notorious Beast of Belsen and his sadistic female assistant. She had been responsible for appalling atrocities in the camp, including setting her alsatian guard dogs on defenceless prisoners.

The museum room was a grisly testament to the barbarity and inhumanity of these people. A lamp shade made from the tattooed skin of a man's back was on display behind glass. A few crumbling, mouldering white blocks lay nearby – soap produced from human fat in other concentration camps. In haunting black and white photographs survivors stare back from history, eyes unnaturally wide in cadaverous faces, the skin stretched so tightly over their skulls that they are almost unrecognisable as human beings. There are photographs of plump, well-fed female guards swinging naked corpses into the pits by ankles and wrists that looked as if they would snap. Soldiers stand guard beside them with levelled rifles. Well dressed healthy civilians pass at gun point along the sides of the graves. I stared at pictures of the sadistic S.S. woman guard and her commandant, the Beast of Belsen, both later hung after being found guilty in the war crime trials that followed the end of the war.

The British Military Command had rounded up the inhabitants of the nearby town of Bergen and forced them to witness what had taken place. No one believed that these civilians hadn't known all along what was happening in the camp. I stared at a faded picture of the mayor and his wife and various other worthy local dignitaries, standing there with blank faces as the gruesome burials took place.

Belsen was just one of many concentration camps scattered

across the country at the time. It was essentially a labour camp, not one of the extermination camps, such as Buchenwald and Auschwitz, where Hitler's 'Final Solution' for liquidating the Jews was carried out with awesome efficiency in gas chambers. Belsen was simply a slave labour camp, where prisoners were worked to death – yet further evidence of the cold blooded and systematic attempt to erase an entire section of the human race.

As I stood in front of the barrow, remembering the scenes in the museum and all the television films I had seen and the books I had read about the camps, it all suddenly became real. It was no longer some grotesque and macabre voyeurism from a distance but stark reality. I recalled a description of the scene at Auschwitz II, Birkenau – the piles of shoes, spectacles, suitcases, artificial limbs, children's sandals, and 7,000 kilos of human hair. Suddenly I too could sense that rank smell of an evil place and a lingering taint of despair.

With my parents present it had been like watching a film or reading a book, but alone it was devastating. I can remember the sense of helplessness and vulnerability that swamped over me. A cold dark shadow seemed to pass over me and I felt an irrational fear that it might happen to me. I looked around hastily. There was only the old couple wandering towards me along the length of the barrow. I had the feeling that in an instant I could be transported back to 1944 and find myself a prisoner in such a camp.

I decided to leave. I no longer felt bravely adult. I was a child in a nightmare place and I needed to wake up. I turned and walked quickly towards the entrance, swallowing and feeling my throat tighten. As I passed the elderly couple I noticed something on the man's bare forearm. I slowed down and looked closer. It was a tattoo, a blue line of numbers etched into the pale skin. I looked up and saw the man staring straight at me. I wanted to look away, feeling ashamed at having stared so incredulously at them. He didn't seem to be angry and he didn't smile. There was an empty blank expression in his eyes as if he were staring far beyond me to another place, another set of memories.

I wanted to speak to him but had lost my voice. I wanted

to be sorry, not for staring, but for being there when I hadn't been through such horrors, for being young and happy and alive. I wanted to ask him if this was his camp, wanted him to tell me that it was real. He walked past, holding his wife's elbow gently in his hand, guiding her. I stopped at the entrance and looked back at the two small figures. He was pointing to something on one of the plaques. I wondered whether he knew someone under that barrow – his father or his mother, a brother or sister?

I walked back to the golf course feeling cold and numb despite the hot sun. I never lost that memory of the two old survivors and the atmosphere in Belsen. It was the pity of the place that I remembered, and the eerie silence. I thought of all the evil that had been perpetrated there, the agony and the sadism, the individual acts of barbarism and the cold indifference of the local townspeople. Yet all I ever felt was the overwhelming pity, the inconceivable sense of loss.

It was the first time in my young life that I had ever acknowledged the inevitability of dying. I was struck by the impermanence of everything at a time when my whole world seemed solid and unchangeable. It left me vulnerable in a way I never expected to feel again. I could conceive of nothing so emotionally draining as Belsen until I stood in the wreckage of Yungay, watching dust clouds whipping across acres of barren rubble, absorbing the silence.

A ball of dried grass blew against my bare legs as I walked to where Matt and Helen sat in the distance. Desiccated stalks clacked mournfully against each other in the wind. The scattered shrines became more numerous as I approached a broken stump of vaulted brickwork – the remains of the church ceiling, poking like a broken tooth from the earth. A strange skeletal mass of twisted steel protruded from the boulder field where four huge palm trees thrust defiantly straight into the air near the site of the old Plaza de Armas. Their dark trunks had been painted with a ten-foot band of whitewash. Three of the palms were dead. The fourth, nearest the church wall had a triumphant spray of green foliage at its head.

I noticed small groups of people wandering aimlessly

among the shrines, as if lost. Massive glacial boulders dotted the plain, almost a mockery of the flimsy houses that had once stood there. I stared at the rusted carcass of the bus sticking incongruously out of the earth. It had been plugged solid with the muddy conglomerate. Spars of metal had been peeled from its chassis like the rind of fruit. The windows ran down into the ground like gun ports on a stricken warship. Nearby a wrought iron cross with a white placard on it listed yet another dead family. Apart from the palm trees and the stump of a church wall, it was all that was left of Yungay.

I walked past the vaulted brick wall and saw an Indian woman, head bowed against the wind, squatting in the shadows. A tin pail full of water cooled a handful of coca cola bottles. She held on to her straw hat with her hand and turned her face to the wall. The bright blue of her bolstered dress and the vivid pink of her jacket stood out against the grim shadow of the wall. I took a photograph without her noticing, feeling guilty. I turned quickly away and framed the bus in the viewfinder. A stinging blast of dust hit my face and I flinched away as my eyes burnt with the pain of grit under my contact lenses. As I walked past the woman I wondered whether she thought I was crying for the dead. As in Belsen, I had no tears, only a numb feeling of worthlessness and fragility.

I came to a wide circular mound of cobbles with steps leading up to a heavy granite slab of an altar. A pattern of black cobbles formed a cross in the circle of stones. An empty coke tin rattled back and forth on them. Matt and Helen were walking slowly away towards the new Yungay. Matt stopped abruptly and pointed up at Huascaran. A huge serac avalanche was pouring down the buttresses and spraying out in a soft harmless powder puff of white ice fragments. It looked small on that massive mountain yet I knew it was the equivalent of a five storey building falling down.

Hurrying to catch up, I saw a man carrying a bundle of firewood laid horizontally across his shoulder. He stopped at a boulder and crouched to sit in its shadow. As I drew near I could see that he was about the same age as me, but his face in the shadows looked old and lined. He seemed rooted to the earth, whether by fatigue or grief I could not tell. When the alluvion fell he would have been about fifteen. I wondered whether he was one of the children who had been watching the circus. Was this the site of his lost home, the loss of his entire family? I walked past, remembering that it was Sunday, and glanced at my watch. It was three thirty – almost exactly the time of the disaster. Suddenly I realised why the man in the shadows had sat down. His wood pile on top of the boulder chattered in the wind.

I joined Matt and Helen as we crossed a fresh clear bubbling stream. The debris and boulders had ended and we walked past rows of neat houses, watched by the silent occupants. I expected that they would resent our gawping presence and was surprised when a woman waved cheerfully to us from her porch. I waved back and a man raised his hand in grave salute. Perhaps they were glad that people have not forgotten; that they still come to bear witness and acknowledge the pain.

> My Father ... My God ...
> Why?
> You have made me be
> a witness of such pain,
> Why?
> My heart bleeds
> with the memory
> Of having seen the dying,
> Of having heard the screams and cries
> of children young and old,
> Of the rich and the poor.
> United in a single pain,
> they cried out for salvation.
> And they looked to me.
>
> It was 3.25 p.m. on 31st May 1970,
> My Yungay ceased to exist.

Andy Cave's translation of the inscription
on the Yungay memorial statue.

21

FIRST ASCENT

In three weeks of near perfect weather we had climbed the South-east Face of Urús Este (5420m), the South Ridge of Ishinca (5530m), the East Ridge of Point (5520m), and finally the long and (in my opinion) dangerous slopes of the Garganta route on Huascaran Sur in four tiring days. As the bus taking the clients – Tony, David and Malcolm – pulled out of sight I turned to Ric.

'What do you reckon?'

'Oh, I think they'll be happy with the trip. Hundred per cent successful and all that. They had a good time.'

'No, I mean that,' I said, pointing to the white sail of Ranrapalca piercing the sky above Huaraz.

'I thought you didn't want to do a new route?'

'Well, I didn't before, but I do now. The man who likes to say yes, that sort of thing.'

'Okay then, you're on. Let's get sorted.'

As we headed for the centre of town I couldn't help wondering if I had just made a very big mistake. I had promised myself that I wouldn't try any difficult routes on this trip, and certainly not attempt to make a first ascent. At the shuttered tin door of Pyramid Adventures I wanted to grab Ric's arm and tell him it was a bad idea, but he ducked through the door before I could speak and greeted Eudes.

With the help of Eudes Morales we organised transport, burros, an *arriero* (or donkey driver), food, fuel and a camp guardian for Ric and myself. Having earlier bumped into two of Ric's friends, Matt and Helen Ward, who were on the

294

South American leg of their worldwide travelling and climbing tour, we invited them to join us. The total cost for an eight day excursion up the Ishinca valley came to £40 each, although that was a special deal from Pyramid Adventures because of our work for High Places.

Peru, and Huaraz in particular, is a climbing wonderland – no peak fees, no liaison officers, no permit applications in triplicate, no baksheesh or hassle. Step off the plane in Lima, get on a night coach to Huaraz, book into a cheap clean hotel like Edwards Inn ($10 for a double room) and acclimatise with some frantic Pisco slammers and sangría induced chicken-dancing until five in the morning in Tambo's nightclub. Huascaran, Copa and Ranrapalca loom over the small town only one day's walk from the road, and behind them lie the true beauties. Alpamayo, Artesonraju, Piramide, Santa Cruz, Taulliraju and the fearsome Chacraraju. It is a climber's paradise.

Two days out from the town Ric and I left base camp carrying huge rucksacks and trudged towards the Ishinca glacier where we planned to bivouac beneath the face. It was not long before I collapsed in a heap beside Ric, with Jimi Hendrix's voice shrieking in my head-phones. Seventy pound rucksacks and dodgy legs were not a good combination.

'This is counter-productive,' I snapped. 'Far too much gear, too much food, hardware – too much bloody everything . . .' Ric sat there with a calm smile, gazing appreciatively at the north face of Ranrapalca soaring above us and ignoring my whining complaints.

'Looks good, doesn't it?' he said when I had spluttered to an indignant silence. 'Should be fun.'

'Could be,' I muttered as I lurched to my feet again and staggered drunkenly in circles trying to get my legs into some meaningful dialogue with each other. There was a piercing shriek in my ears as the tape changed over, making me throw my arms in the air as if I had been shot in the chest.

'Pump it up, pump it, pump it, pump it . . .' The dance music thumped through my head with an hypnotic mega bass beat loud enough to make your ears bleed. I tottered unsteadily towards the mountain, legs lurching forward in staccato rhythm to the song.

By four o'clock the next morning we had climbed a snow ramp that led to a loose rock step beneath the ice fields of the north face. A fireball hurtled across the night sky, ending a journey of unimaginable time from the depths of space as it dipped towards the gloom of a nearby valley.

'Did you see that?' Ric yelled excitedly from the shadows above.

'What?'

'My God, you should have seen it!'

'Seen what?' I shouted as I teetered up a chimney of loose granite blocks.

'It was a meteorite. Really close, a huge fireball, like a crashing plane, but silent . . .' he told me in a rush as I struggled up to his stance, cursing the rock, the cold and the fact that I clearly had just missed one of the most wondrous spectacles in the world. I couldn't imagine the odds against being so close to such an event. I wondered for how many light years it had hurtled through space before it crashed into our tiny piece of the world? How typical that I had had my back to it when it landed.

We sat on a dusty block and peered around, trying to distinguish features on the ice field above us. The yellow beams from our torches criss-crossed crazily in the night until we fixed on the shadow of a serac and pinned it against the darkness. In the east the faint glimmer of dawn showed as a thin light blue band rising above a jagged black horizon of peaks. For an instant flame flashed gold and white above them and the clouds on the horizon flickered.

'Lightning,' I said.

'Are you sure?' Ric asked anxiously. The sky flashed again. There was no sound.

I watched the silent bursts of lightning flare on the horizon with a mixture of foreboding and depression. Until then I hadn't realised how much I had wanted to climb the North Spur. It was an unclimbed-line, an eye-catching new route up the centre of the face, and perhaps – most compelling for me

– a chance to cap a great trip, the most successful I had ever had, with a fitting memory. I wanted something with which to exorcise the superstitious anxieties that remained nine years after the disastrous outcome of climbing Siula Grande. That first ascent had almost destroyed me, and it seemed suddenly vital to restore my brittle self-confidence by climbing this new route. I wanted to close the door on the past. It was perhaps not a very good reason for climbing, but important to me.

'Shall we go down?' Ric asked in a voice that screamed 'Let's go up'.

'I don't know. Once we're through the seracs we might not be able to retreat safely and if that stuff hits us . . .'

'It seems to be holding back. There's no thunder. It must be miles away, over the Amazon somewhere.'

I looked at huge banks of cloud building up against the eastern walls of Palcaraju. Streamers of silver-grey moon-lit cloud poured slowly over the crest of the walls and then slowly dissipated. I remembered how we had noticed from Huaraz that Ranrapalca, for some odd reason, had seemed to remain clear of bad weather. These clouds welling up over the mountains looked strangely lethargic, as if unable to summon the strength to push forward and envelope us. A flash of lightning silvered the approaching storm.

'I suppose we could go on a bit further, at least until the seracs.'

'It should be light by then,' Ric said, 'might look a bit more promising.'

We pitched on up a diagonal ramp line leading into the seracs of the lower ice field, always looking east and counting the sporadic bursts of lightning.

The Americans Slaymaker, Rourke and Johns had been this way eighteen years before, fixing ropes for 700 feet up to the top of the seracs before climbing the 2,000-foot north face ice fields above in a single push. In the intervening years the face had changed enormously. The serac barrier had been a huge cliff of ice blocking all access to the North Spur far out to the left. Much of it had since disappeared, plunging off the overhanging cliff above the glacier. What remained was an area of fractured and unstable ice pinnacles and small shattered seracs. Once we had climbed past them, we intended breaking out to the left and heading for the start of the North Spur by crossing the lower edge of the ice field towards a narrow rock chute that led to the spur. To our left the ice field plunged off a 350-foot overhanging wall of rock to the Ishinca glacier. As we approached the seracs it felt intimidating to be edging across this precarious ice slope above the long airy fall.

Just as the Americans had found in 1975, our progress was slowed by the most extraordinary ice and snow conditions I had ever encountered. The whole face seemed to be corrugated. The surface was a serrated band of sharks' fins, six inches apart and eighteen inches high. It was as if someone had poked millions of slate tiles into the ice at an angle of about sixty degrees to the slope – a common feature of north faces in the Andes.

These fins, known as *'penitentes'* because they are said to resemble lines of monks at prayer, often form late in the climbing season in the Southern Hemisphere where north faces receive plenty of sunshine. The late afternoon sun melts the *penitentes* and the whole face becomes unstable and slushy. Higher up the good névé conditions of early dawn steadily deteriorate, forming what is called cheese ice – a fractured honeycomb structure on which it is unnerving to climb. I had already experienced some of the horrors of Andean snow conditions on Siula Grande where steep flutings of fluffy powder snow had made climbing with no protection on the summit slopes both exhausting and frightening. In choosing our line on Ranrapalca I had made the basic error of forgetting that in the Southern Hemisphere north faces are sun traps and not the cold and shadowed places I was accustomed to in the Alps.

In the early morning cold we could teeter up on the *penitentes* with minimal fracturing but it made for awkard off-balance high-stepping manoeuvres. I hammered in an ice screw and waited for Ric to arrive. Above me blue obelisks of ice hung out over the ice field. A large fractured wall draped in icicles and eaten away into honeycombs caught the first rays of dawn. There was a popping sound that made me jump and an odd tinkling like breaking glass, or like crystal chandeliers rattling in the wind.

'The lightning has stopped,' Ric said, taking the screws from me.

'I noticed.'

'How do you feel?'

'Nervous,' I said, nodding towards the decaying ice cliffs.

'Yeah, let's get out of here.' Ric set off diagonally leftwards through the heart of the seracs and was soon out of sight. The ice suddenly began to creak and pop all around me, making me jerk from side to side with fright. A slab of candy-floss ice tinkled past me. There was another sharp report and then the ice settled ominously, as if the slope to which I was belayed had dropped abruptly a few inches.

I looked nervously at the ice-screw; it was both a belay and a trap. I couldn't move away from it. The rising sun gleamed through the blue ice walls around me, flashing white off the lattice of ice bubbles. I thought of René Daumal's story of *The Hollow Men* who 'in ice appear as bubbles in the shape of men', and who at night 'wander through the ice and dance during the full moon. But they never see the sun, or else they would burst. They eat only the void, in the form of corpses and get drunk on empty words and all the meaningless expressions we utter.'

I was just concluding that Daumal was a nutter, although pleasingly imaginative, when one of his hollow men saw the sun and burst. There was a crack, a slow ominous creak and then a whooshing sound as part of the serac above keeled over and tumbled towards me. I lurched to my left with a squeal of fright and came up hard against the sling on my ice screw. Within a second or two the serac had gone crashing past me, a chunk of blue ice the size of a supermarket freezer, cart-wheeling down the ice field before vaulting out into space above the over-hanging rock wall. It hovered there for a moment and then plunged out of sight with shocking suddenness.

Cursing furiously, I began unscrewing my belay.

'Are you okay?' Ric's faint call came from above.

'Get a belay, quickly,' I yelled, flinching as the seracs popped and cracked with a burst of enthusiasm. I was surprised to see my hands shaking as I tried to clip the screw to my harness. I set off after Ric without waiting to see if he was safe.

'Were you hit?' Ric asked when I reached him.

'If I had been we would both have been taking flying lessons by now. It missed me by a few feet. God, that was scary!'

'Well, I might add that this isn't much better.'

'Why?'

'I was digging for a belay and came to the conclusion that the ice isn't attached to a rock underneath.'

He pointed at a hole he had excavated in the ice where I could see dark shadows and the gleam of smooth wet rock. I leaned forward and thrust my head into the hole. Sunlight streamed in past my shoulders as I peered with mounting horror at the slab of rock extending away into the darkness beneath the ice field. There was a gap of nearly a foot between the ice and the rock. I remembered how the slope had moved ominously just before the serac collapsed. I hadn't been imagining things after all. I pulled my head from the hole and looked warily down to where the ice field plunged into the abyss of the over hanging rock wall 300-feet below.

'This whole ice field could go, couldn't it?' Ric asked, with a nervous tremor in his voice.

'That's what I'm thinking. If we can get to the rock gully and up on to the spur we should be safer.'

'Get moving then.'

'Right, I'm out of here.'

By mid-day we were clear of the lower ice field having exited through a narrow rock chute at its left-hand end to reach the base of the North Spur proper. The north face basked in sunshine and heat waves seemed to shimmer across the vast expanse of ice. Far to our right we could make out the Americans' 1975 North Face route, the shark's fin surface sweeping up towards thin rock spurs that reached down from the summit headwall two thousand feet above us. I was glad to be on the relative solidity of the spur and wondered whether the Americans had thought the slope would go. They were either brave or foolish.

As we climbed up the crest of the spur the heat intensified and the sharks' fins began collapsing under our weight. The snow took on the consistency of wet sugar. It was no use placing screws or even ice stakes. We edged closer to the shattered rocks that hung from the crest of the spur. To our left the rocky central couloir plunged down to the glacier and was hemmed in by vertical walls of broken rock and fringed by curtains of icicles near the summit. Massive bombardments thundered into the couloir, making us jump until we realised we were safe. The glacier below was blackened in a wide fan by the dust and debris.

The treacherous snow conditions forced us to climb the shattered rock ridge that protruded out from the spur and hung over the awesome drop of the central couloir. Our position was unnervingly airy, and the loose rock and snow was beginning to fray our nerves. At first I found the climbing enjoyable, perched above the drop, tip-toeing up snowed-up cracks and leaning blocks of rough rock. As the sun melted the ice and snow that glued the unstable rock ridge together doubts began to crowd in upon me. I was putting slings round rocks to protect my progress, but as more and more debris collapsed beneath my feet I saw that they were of little value. After one long pitch Ric was forced to dismantle his belay and move together with me until I could find a solid anchor. As I edged around a wing of rock hanging out over the drop there was a sudden grinding noise and I felt my feet slide away. My axe, hooked over the top edge of the wing of rock, held firm as the ledge on which I had been standing fell away with a roar into the couloir below.

For a moment I swung out into space on my outstretched arm, hoping the rock wing would not take to the air as well. There was nothing between Ric and myself if I fell and I didn't trust the rope to hold as it sawed across the jagged crest of the ridge. With a yelp of alarm I swung back towards the rock, hooked it with my ice hammer and scrambled fearfully out on to the cheese ice of the face.

As night closed in we had slowed almost to a standstill, unnerved by the precariousness of our position and the instability of the snow and rock. We were forced to treat everything with gentle, probing touches. When Ric was three pitches from the top of the face he came to a halt. The crest of the spur curled out in cornices to his left, and I watched as he made increasingly tentative digs with the shafts of his axes into the corrugated open snow slope.

'This is lethal,' he yelled over his shoulder.

'Why?'

'It's all falling down.'

I watched him stamp his crampons into the slope and slide down a few feet.

'See if you can reach that rock above you,' I yelled, feeling my throat tighten in anticipation. I looked around to see if I could improve my belay, which consisted of two axes buried in wet sugar.

'If you're going to fall, for God sake's fall into the couloir!' I called out. A muffled curse came back in reply.

It was dark when I reached the tiny stance on which he was balancing.

'We're going to have to stop. That was terrible.'

'I know,' I said, face down in the snow, trying to recover my breath after all the exhausting wallowing. 'Let's dig a cave.'

'Where? It's not deep enough. We're on another hollow ice field – or hadn't you noticed?'

'Well, let's try and dig into that cornice.'

'A cornice?'

'Got any better ideas?'

Three hours later we had excavated a hollow under the curling lick of a cornice. There was enough space for us to lie on top of one another and perch the petrol stove on a balanced slab of rock by the open doorway. Darkness hid the abyss of the central couloir just a few feet away. It was the only safe option to wait for the night to freeze the shark's fins into climbable condition and glue the rocks back together. A fall was not worth thinking about. The cave was a chance to regain control over a situation that had been getting out of hand. Fear, cold, and tiredness had been making their play for our souls.

Having spent a cramped night, we quickly climbed the last four hundred feet to the summit headwall. There we found an old piton at the point where it narrowed. It was the first piece of gear we had come across, and this was clearly where the 1975 route exited on to the summit slopes.

After thirty hours on the face, and with wind-whipped clouds and driving snow, we decided not to go on to the summit. Instead we tried to find the start of the north-east ridge by which we hoped to find our way down. After many anxious probing searches we began to descend in the hope of coming across a rock anchor from which to abseil. I kept peering down at murky shapes in the shifting clouds, looking for the dark shadows of rock buttresses.

The ice fell away abruptly at sixty-five degrees as I crossed a few small crevasses. I hammered a screw into the brittle water ice and continued down towards a small outcrop of dark rock that refused to get any nearer. Coils of rope began curling around my arms. Ric was coming down, we were moving together on steep ice with inadequate anchors. A mounting tension built up inside me. I had been here before. *This is where things go wrong,* I kept telling myself, *this is how it always happens*. At last my crampons skittered on to the jumble of granite blocks and I gratefully fixed a belay.

After four abseils we began trudging through a chaotic icefall as clouds formed dramatic shapes, backlit by the setting sun. Snow flurries eddied around us as Ric picked his way confidently through a maze of gaping holes. I tottered after him, whining that I didn't like crevasses much and was he sure this was the right way. Just as exhaustion overtook me and I decided it was time to dig a snow cave we came out on to a col above the Ishinca glacier which led down to our first bivi site.

We were enveloped in soft purple cloud as the last of the sun glimmered through from above. A chocolate bar revived me, but Ric had slumped after his magnificent effort in the icefall. I knew something was wrong when I watched him trying to burn his toilet paper in a snowstorm. Even the most fanatical environmentalists wouldn't do that.

All at once the tension evaporated, and we were laughing and hugging and apologising for all the angry exchanges, and looking in delight at our manic purple faces, knowing we were safe. We had done it. The new route was ours forever, never to be taken away.

As we staggered down to base camp we kept looking back at the line of the route and grinning at one another, our heads full of magic and that temporary sense of invincibility that comes after good days on the hills. When at last the tents came into sight the feeling was replaced by the dull aches of tired bodies. The following day Ric said he wanted to climb Toclaraju (6032m), a beautiful ice pyramid at the head of the valley. I said no, I was too tired. Matt and Helen, who had just climbed Urus, wavered, but by three in the afternoon we were all struggling up steep scree slopes to a high bivi beneath the north-west face of Toclaraju.

The next day we climbed gingerly up towards the base of the heavily corniced summit not daring to go any further. I sat and watched the shadows of small cumulus cloud drifting across the north face of Ranrapalca. The line of the spur was etched clearly by the low morning sun. It had been worth breaking my promises. In less than a month, Ric and I had climbed six mountains, one by a new route. I chuckled to myself, thinking how nervous I had been about returning to Peru. It had been the most successful summer's climbing I had ever had.

22

STRANGE CONNECTIONS

I stood at the small wooden bar of El Encuentro Cebiche, waiting for someone to appear. The room had white plaster walls and plants hung in earthenware pots from the low wooden ceiling beams. It was refreshingly cool. Behind the bar a television was showing an odd version of *The Water Margin*, which seemed to be about two young girls making wishes while holding a weirdly obscene horn and magically appearing in swimming costumes. They then began a rather vicious kung-fu fight with a monkey and an implausible rubber dragon.

Tearing myself away from this bizarre soap opera, I looked around the room. At one of the tables, which were neatly covered with red cloths, a balding middle-aged man in a sheepskin-lined denim jacket sat in a creaking wicker chair, chatting up a young woman who could have been his daughter. She wore knee-length leather boots and a tight black pencil skirt. Her silk blouse in patterned pink and gold set off the long, sleek, plaited black hair that reached to her waist. She had a bewitchingly beautiful smile. A man stepped through a beaded curtain that hung in the kitchen doorway and carried two cups of coffee over to the couple. I walked out on to the patio which was roofed with red clay tiles and took a seat in the sun. I ordered a beer from the waiter who had followed me outside.

The bar was situated behind the shell of a half-built church in the centre of Huaraz. Across the grassy lawn from where I sat I saw an elderly couple knitting hats and baby clothes. Two

305

boys in school uniform approached the table and tried to sell me embroidered table cloths. A four-wheel drive pick-up truck drew up and two men got out. They settled themselves at a table and shouted for beer, then they stared at me in a curiously disgusted sort of way. I stared back until their beers arrived.

The barman began talking to me in excellent English about rock music before bustling back inside. The calm was shattered by 'Credence Clearwater Revival' blasting out at full volume. The old men stared at me with renewed ferocity as if the twangy bluesy guitar sounds were my fault.

I reached into my pocket for the packet of pills the doctor had given me, popped two into my mouth and washed them down with beer. I had been diagnosed as suffering from pneumonia when I visited a local clinic with a severe chest pain. It felt as if I had been shot in the side. When I returned home I was pleased to discover that it wasn't pneumonia but a cracked rib, sustained through falling over outside Tsambo's night-club at five in the morning.

A woman sat down at an adjacent table and waved to a young woman on the other side of the lawn. I looked across at the seated woman and guessed from her appearance that she was European.

'Are you on holiday?' I asked.

'Yes, we were,' she said with a sad, wistful smile.

'You're Dutch, aren't you?'

'No, Belgian,' the woman said and smiled tenderly as the second woman approached and sat down. 'This is my daughter.' They talked intently in what I took to be Flemish for a while. The mother's face looked strained and tired.

'Ah well,' she said, turning to me. 'And you, are you on holiday?'

'Yes, in a way,' I replied. 'I've been climbing.' I saw her face light up with interest. 'I guided a party on Huascaran and after that I went climbing with my friend.'

'It has been good?' she inquired politely.

'Wonderful,' I said. 'Seven weeks of unbroken sunshine, six mountains climbed, and a new route. I've never had such a successful trip.'

'I'm pleased for you.' She said it quietly and bit her lip with a sad expression on her face. 'My husband is a mountain climber. He loves the mountains very much, I think.'

'Do you climb?'

'Oh, no,' she said hurriedly. 'No, I just came to walk, see the beautiful lakes, to enjoy the mountains while my husband was climbing.'

'When do you go home?'

'That is difficult,' she replied, looking distracted. 'I have been here now for too long. My daughter arrived last week to help me.'

'To help you? Is something wrong?'

'Yes.' The woman glanced at her daughter, as if for confirmation. 'You see, my husband is missing.'

'Missing? On a mountain do you mean?'

'On Pisco. He went to climb alone. No one has seen him since he set out for the summit.'

Pisco? I remembered the missing Belgian Ric had told me about after he had returned from guiding Pisco with some clients. They had found the man's abandoned tent. At first no one knew what had happened, and then fragments of the story were pieced together.

Huaraz is like any popular climbing centre, with its grapevine of gossip and rumours passing around. With an increasing number of climbers visiting the Blanca, now that the threat of terrorism had receded, there was also a spiralling rash of fatal accidents. We met a Scottish climber who had returned from Artesonraju with a smashed rucksack he had found on the descent. It had belonged to a Spanish climber who had slipped descending from the summit and fallen to his death. He wondered what to do with it. A man had broken both his legs and knocked himself into a coma in a paragliding accident. I remembered the tall, red-faced, over-weight climber Ric and I had seen preparing to climb Copa. He had looked like a heart attack waiting to happen. Ric and I had both laughed.

Three days later we heard the news that the big man had been standing at the edge of a crevasse during the descent from the summit when suddenly, for no apparent reason, he toppled into the gaping hole, dragging a woman and a guide with him. The guide was uninjured, the woman had badly broken an arm, and the man was found to be dead. The Peruvian guide, who had managed to hold the weight of the three people, broke his left leg. We heard from Eudes Morales of Pyramid Adventures, our agency in Peru, that an autopsy indicated the man had indeed died of a massive heart attack. In all probability he was dead even before he came on to the rope. I felt guilty remembering my light-hearted laughter.

Eudes had also told us about the tent on Pisco. The Belgian man had set off alone in good weather to climb the normal route up the mountain and had failed to return. It was thought that he had probably fallen into a crevasse at night during the ascent. Ric remembered one large crevasse with a substantial well-trodden snow bridge.

'Do you know what happened?' I asked the woman cautiously.

'We have not found him,' she said, and shrugged. 'The guides have been searching three times now and have found no sign of him. Only his tent.'

'Was he trying a difficult route or . . .'

'No, no, he was going only the easy way. He was an experienced climber,' she explained, 'but he did not go on the very hard climbs, you understand.'

'Yes, I see,' I said. 'My friend was climbing Pisco just before your husband disappeared and he told me that there was a very large crevasse . . .'

'It is all right. I know all this. The guides believe he has fallen in this crevasse but they cannot find him. I do not understand it. They have been down digging in the crevasse but he is not there. This is why we are still searching.'

'Why? Where else do you think he could be?'

'I don't know.' She shrugged helplessly. 'Sometimes he was not good with directions. Maybe he went the wrong way; maybe he is on a different face.'

'How long ago did this happen?'

'More than three weeks ago.'

'Oh, I see . . .' I felt momentarily at a loss for words.

'Do not be concerned.' She smiled sadly at me. 'I know that he is dead now. I have accepted this; there is no hope after so long.'

'No, I'm afraid there isn't. I'm very sorry.'

'They are dangerous, the mountains. You know this.'

'Yes, they can be.'

'The guides are on the mountain now,' she continued. 'They make one last search in the crevasse again.'

'Are they sure they have the right crevasse?'

'Yes, they are certain, but I don't understand. The bridge over the crevasse was not there when they found his tent but they know from other climbers who had descended the day before his climb that it was intact on that day. They believe it collapsed. But they cannot find him. With digging they should find him, no?'

'Ah well, not necessarily.'

'Why is this? Do you know about crevasses?'

'Yes, a little.' I replied hesitantly. 'I'll try to explain.' I arched my fingers to represent a snow bridge. 'You see when a very big bridge collapses, or even just the edge, it doesn't always mean that the person falls on top or with the snow. Often he breaks through, falling into the crevasse with a great mass of snow following on top of him.'

'Yes, I can see that, but if you dig, then you will find him, no?'

'Well, no,' I said. 'Big bridges are not just made of snow. They may be very thick hard ice, and therefore also very heavy. When this falls into the confines of a crevasse it comes under tremendous pressure. Where the gap between the walls of the crevasse become narrow, squeezing the falling ice and snow, it is often compressed so tightly by its weight and momentum that it can form a solid block of ice too hard to dig through.'

'So you think he is under this and they have hit the ice?'

'It is possible.' I hesitated, feeling uncomfortable at presenting her with the stark truth. She spoke earnestly to her daughter, who nodded seriously.

'Are you sure?'

'I'm sorry, I cannot be sure,' I said, wishing I had never started the conversation. 'I know of one man who fell into a crevasse when the edge gave way. His two companions, standing nearby saw the fall and noted exactly where it had taken place but the rescue services could not find any trace of the victim – only solid blue ice.'

'It was quick then?'

'Er, yes, I should imagine so,' I said, taken aback by the question.

'He did not suffer?'

'Sorry, who . . .?'

'My husband.'

'If that is what happened, then I think it would have been very fast. Instant.' I knew that this probably was not entirely true. I remembered the dreadful night I had experienced in the crevasse on Siula Grande wondering how long it would take to die. I had been lucky to escape. I was determined not to let her know what had happened to me in case it raised false hopes for her.

After a long pause, she looked at me with a forced smile and said, 'Good. Thank you.'

'I'm very sorry.'

'No, no, it has been good to talk. I think the guides are tired of me asking so many questions and making them do this work. If what you say happens, could someone live a long time?'

'Maybe.' I shrugged, feeling more and more uncomfortable at the direction the conversation was taking. 'But in this case I think it would have been very quick,' I assured her hurriedly.

'I hope so.' She smiled at me. 'I had to know, you see. It is hard to think of him alone for a long time, injured, with no help. It would be bad to be left like that.'

'Can I ask you something?'

'Yes, what is it?'

'You say that you know he is dead?'

'Yes.'

'Then why are you still looking? I don't mean to be rude,

but your husband obviously loved the mountains and I was thinking that perhaps it is better to leave him among them. Isn't it harder for you to keep searching like this . . .?'

'You are not rude,' she interrupted me gently. 'I know he is dead. You are right. I just want to be sure; I need to know what happened. It is easier then, you understand.'

'Yes, of course.'

She paid for her drinks and then stood to leave.

'Thank you for your help,' she said and shook my hand. 'I am happy that you have had such good climbing.'

'I'm sorry,' I said again, thinking how inadequate a word it was. I could have cried for her. There was something about her that triggered off a whole weight of memories from the past. On the one hand there was a sense of resignation, almost tranquillity, in the way that she expressed herself and she seemed controlled, almost serene in the acceptance of her loss. Yet I could see behind her mask a painful lost state of loneliness and bewilderment. Nine years before, I had experienced the deepest, most traumatic loneliness, so traumatic in fact that it made me live – made me keep fighting. I had always seen that time in terms of myself and never in what it would do to the ones who loved me if I had not survived. I had recognised immediately the awful possibilities in the manner of the Belgian's death but now, looking at her sad, weary face, I could see what it really meant to those left behind. It was such a selfish thing that we chose to do.

'No. Don't be sorry. He knew, like you, what could happen, and he did love the mountains so much. It is over now.' With a slight wave she turned and walked across the lawn with her daughter. I watched them go towards the mountain guides' office. I secretly hoped they wouldn't find him. It seemed better that way.

When the sun dipped behind the skeletal walls of the half-built church I finished my beer and walked down towards Edwards where I had been staying for a week. I had to pack for the journey to Lima and the flight home the next day. I passed a signpost outside the Casa de Guias, with an arrow on it pointing east. It said 'Suiza Peruvanos Huaraz – SUIZA

10,426 Km.' I burst out laughing. It was typical of the highly efficient Swiss, who had helped so much in the reconstruction after the earthquake, that not only should they have a sign showing in which direction home lay but also the exact distance, as if travelling Swiss always needed to know how far from home they were.

As I turned from the sign a young lad came careering towards me on a bright yellow ice cream bicycle. A large refrigerating box was attached to the front wheel. Steering with one hand and sounding off on a hunting horn with the other, the lad rattled past me at breakneck speed. There wasn't much hope of buying an ice cream, and I didn't rate his chances of negotiating the steep right-hander at the bottom of the hill.

In the narrow subway leading through to the main street I stopped to watch a chess game being played on a long trestle table. Five chess boards were painted on the surface of the table and the young man who tended the nearby stall that displayed all manner of merchandise was playing four opponents at the same time as trying to make his sales. I had played him a few days earlier. He had swiftly annihilated my carefully prepared strategy, but I had been happy to part with the 500 intis it cost me. I watched, fascinated, as the young man negotiated the price for an item from his stall with an old woman and then quickly made four abrupt moves, one on each board while he rummaged for change in a wooden cash box. Only one of his opponents looked as if he had the slightest chance of beating him.

While walking across the market place it struck me that Huaraz seemed to be awash with oranges. There were great mounds of them everywhere. The hustling vendors competed aggressively with each other. A man pushed a barrow past, heaped high with oranges, while he spoke rapidly into a little battery-powered microphone so that his sales chatter boomed out from a speaker balanced on top of the fruit. Another vendor immediately started yelling into his microphone, and then another. When I had first heard this I kept looking around to find the car with the political candidate calling for votes through his tannoy and instead found an enthusiastic orange war in progress. The vociferous enthusiasm of the vendors made me wonder how often they broke into all out violence. Like the canvassing politicians, I imagined that their claims became further and further from the truth, more wildly optimistic as the competition increased. At that point the lad on the ice cream bicycle came barrelling through the market, hunting horn drowning out the exhortations from the orange sellers. He clipped the side of a trolley and oranges cascaded on to the road. At once the vendors united in outrage and a cacophony of tinnily amplified abuse chased after the lad as he pedalled furiously away.

The next day a Boeing 747 lifted me out of a smoggy overcast Lima. I gritted my teeth and prepared for the long fifteen-hour flight home. I opened my pouch of tobacco and rolled a cigarette, reading the informative little messages that were written on the inner side of the pouch flap. 'Travel is the art of feeling at home' it read, and I laughed. What, then, was the point of leaving in the first place?

In Bogota, Colombia, we had to change planes. I stood in a long queue looking out through the huge glass terminal windows at the baggage carts busily swarming around our plane. It was hot and muggy even with the air conditioning of the terminal building going full blast. Three boisterous young men were joshing and fooling in the line of bored passengers, rudely barging into people, and knocking their luggage over. No one complained despite their obvious irritation.

My bad ankle felt stiff and sore after six hours cooped up in a cramped seat in the plane from Lima. One of the men suddenly shoved me roughly forward. Momentarily off balance, I twisted my ankle and a shooting flame of pain ran up my leg. I turned around and, placing my palms against the chest of the young man, I shoved him violently away. He stumbled backwards and then fell down. His friends crowded round me aggressively shouting at me in French. One of them held his hand up in a placatory manner and said 'Tranquilo, tranquilo.'

'Fuck you,' I said diplomatically. He shrugged and

313

muttered something about the English. His companion stood up and dusted himself down and the three of them glared at me. I glowered back.

Glancing out of the window, I noticed one of the baggage trolleys being loaded from the belly of our plane. When it was full the driver set off at high speed, hand-brake turned and then screeched away in a cloud of blue exhaust fumes. A large rucksack tumbled from the pile and was left sitting in a stain of fuel oil on the tarmac.

The French lads noticed it as well. It wasn't my bag, which cheered me up, and it was still there half an hour later when I reached the head of the queue and was issued with a transit pass. The three lads looked anxious and kept glancing at the abandoned rucksack and muttering darkly among themselves. As they reached the desk an animated argument erupted with much pointing to the abandoned rucksack. I strode off to find a bar, giggling happily.

I found a seat in the corner and ordered a beer. After a while the French lads turned up. They looked grimly furious. Since I had nothing else to do I tried cold staring them for a bit. They shared a papaya juice and stared back. I heard them mention Huaraz and saw them nodding in my direction and then realised why I had thought them vaguely familiar. I had seen them in Tsambo's night-club on the night I had been chicken dancing in Lucio's place. I stopped glaring at them.

I thought of the bereaved Belgian woman and the lost expression in her eyes. She had appeared composed but I could imagine the turmoil she must have been in. However many times she told herself that he was dead there must still have been that irrational flicker of hope as she waited for news from the guides. If they did find his body it would come as a crushing blow, but in the long run I reckon it would free her from years of wondering.

I remembered her when the plane had lifted out from Lima and headed – as I had thought – towards Caracas in Venezuela. The air hostess had come along the aisle, closing the window shutters as an inane film about a man with a mask had flickered on to the video screen at the end of the cabin. I put out my arm when she leant across me and slid the shutter down. I said that I wanted to see the Cordillera Blanca and Ranrapalca, and maybe identify Pisco, and would close the shutter in a few moments. The stewardess looked irritated and I waited until she had moved further down the cabin before lifting up the shutter again and peering out.

Directly in front of me, probably no more than a mile away, Siula Grande was framed against a clear blue sky. I felt a shock run through me and sat back suddenly. *How could that be there? Where was the Blanca?* I knew that we couldn't see the Huayhuash on the flight path to Caracas. *Was I on the wrong flight?* In a state of confused shock I stared at the mountain from my past unable to believe what I was seeing. There was no doubt that I was looking directly at the West Face of Siula Grande. I could see the line of our ascent in 1985, the steep ice fields and the distinctive yellow rock buttress. It was like looking at a slide projected on to my window frame. The ramp line and the bivouac sites and the flutings were all there, exactly the same. I could see the point on the north ridge where I had fallen and broken my leg, the line down which Simon had lowered me again and again on 300-feet of rope. There was the chaotic crevassed glacier, the two copper green lakes, the jumble of moraines and the dry river bed where we had our base camp. It looked such a long, long way. I felt suddenly cold and frightened.

I never thought I would ever see it again, and had made sure I would go nowhere near it on this trip. The sight of it, framed like a photo in perspex, made me cold and sick with a long-remembered dread, a feeling that I was trapped, that there was no escape. Writing the book about the accident had been painful enough, reviving untold fears of being left for dead, dying a slow, bitterly lonely death. Since then I had spent so many hours staring at photos of this mountain, giving slide lectures about what had happened there, that the whole ghastly event had become unreal. Repeatedly talking about it had become a sort of therapy until the whole traumatic episode had been reduced to just another story, a fantasy in which I had no part. Now I never think about those days, even when I'm giving a lecture. I just seem to be telling someone else's story; it means nothing. I thought with shame of what I had said to the Belgian woman. It came too close, revived too many fears.

As the image in my window grew smaller and more distant I found myself staring fixedly at it as if hypnotised. I sat rigid, with a chill, tight stomach, and for a few moments everything came rushing back so hard and real that I almost cried out. After the success we'd just had in the Blanca I thought I had exorcised all my ghosts, detached myself from the past until it was no longer real. Then, through a window, there it was hurtling back from my past as if it had only just happened, obliterating everything else with a memory so bright and lucid, hitting me with flashes of emotion and dazzling little snapshot recollections. Suddenly, in a plane full of people, I felt desperately alone.

I lit a cigarette and inhaled with a shudder as I watched Siula Grande recede into the distance, into my past, and began to feel easier. Once over the shock, I watched it go with a surprisingly contented feeling, as if I knew it was gone for good now. It had been strange to see the line of our route snaking up the west face, knowing we had been there, and feeling proud of it. It was our route, Simon's and mine, always would be, and that was what it had always been about. The accident and the struggle to survive were incidental. Though these had taken over the story, had taken over reality and changed my life, they were not what we had set out to do. It was the route that counted, the mountain, our mountain, and it would always be there. For a moment I had remembered the bad times in a totally unexpected and overwhelming way, and then it had faded. I was happy with it now, glad to have experienced it, in a way, honoured by what it had given me.

I stared out at the brown foothills of the Andes as the Cordillera Blanca began to loom into sight. It was little more than fifty kilometres north of the Huayhuash. I saw the massive white bulk of Huascaran come into view. The beautiful pyramids of Alpamayo and Artesonraju poked jauntily into the sky with a great shadow thrown across their lower flanks by the mass of Santa Cruz. I knew that I was staring almost straight down at Pisco but I couldn't pinpoint it. I thought of the man lying buried in the crevasse and his wife's lonely vigil in Huaraz. I imagined the guides digging in the crevasse as we flew by, and it made me shiver to think of it. I didn't tell the woman what had happened to me. It seemed so unfair to have had so many chances. I hadn't wanted to arouse in her false hopes of miraculous survival, and I didn't want to confront the cruelty of chance that had killed him and spared me.

'Señor?' I turned at the touch of the stewardess's hand. 'Please?' she said, pointing to the shutter.

'Yes, of course,' I said and shut out the view of the mountains.

'Que quieran beber?' she asked.

'What?' I said, having to drag my eyes away from the closed shutter. 'A drink. Oh, yes please, I'll have a gin and tonic. Could you make it a double?'

'Certainly, sir.' She scooped ice cubes into a glass and passed me two miniature gin bottles.

'We are going to Caracas, aren't we?' I asked.

'No señor. We always go via Bogota on the return flight except when there are storms in the mountains.'

'Oh, I see. I didn't know. Thank you.' I said as she turned to serve the passenger across the aisle.

I lit another cigarette and reached for the in-flight magazine in the pocket on the seat back in front of me. It was printed in both English and Spanish and I decided to make comparative readings to test my command of the language. After ten minutes, when I was tiring of the exercise, my eye was caught by the word Buchenwald.

There was a small piece about a surrealist poet called Robert Desnos who had died of typhus and malnutrition two days after being liberated from the Buchenwald Nazi concentration camp. They found on his body the last poem he had written to his wife Yaki. I thought of Yungay and the bleak memories I had experienced of Belsen when I had wandered past the huge burial mounds. I read the poem slowly, ignoring the Spanish. It reminded me of the poignant prayer etched on the plinth of the statue of Christ at Yungay. As I was about to close the magazine I noticed the date of Desnos's death on release from Buchenwald – 8th June 1945.

June the eighth! Exactly forty years later to the day I had broken my leg on Siula Grande. I glanced suspiciously out of the window. The mountains had long since disappeared. Green jungle and brown rivers stretched as far as the eye could see. It was just a coincidence that the dates should have been the same, but like so many things in life there always seemed to be strange connections. Perhaps if I hadn't visited Belsen, and Yungay, or unexpectedly seen Siula Grande, I would have paid it no attention. But I had and all of them fitted neatly together.

'Excuse me?' I said as the stewardess returned.

'Señor?'

'Could I have another drink, please?'

'So soon?' she smiled. 'Of course, one moment please.' I watched her walk down the aisle and then turned to look out at the jungle.

'Your drink, señor,' she said when she returned.

'Oh, thanks. That was quick.'

'The mountains,' she said nodding towards the window, 'you like them, yes?'

'They are gone now, but yes, I like them, just a bit.'

'They are very beautiful, yes?' she said with a smile. 'And very powerful.'

'Yes, sometimes they are.'

'Always, I think,' she said with a laugh. 'You like them?' she asked again, as if I might have changed my mind.

'Yes, I do.' I sipped the drink and smiled at her. 'Sometimes.'

23

TAKEN ON TRUST

The post box rattled as mail and a newspaper dropped on to the doormat. I put down my coffee cup and picked the paper from the floor, shaking flakes of melting snow from the front page. A small headline caught my eye. 'Tibetan monk, tells of Chinese torture – page 12.' I opened the paper at the overseas news section and glanced through the headlines. 'Amnesty discloses Kurdish atrocities', 'Car Bomb Kills 70', 'Church blamed for Rwanda genocide'. It was a bad day for the world.

I saw the photograph of Palden Gyatso framed by these grim headlines. He held his hands in front of him; both thumbs were clamped into medieval thumbscrews. Lord Wetherall sat beside him holding up a pair of ratcheted handcuffs. An assortment of serrated knives, electric batons and other implements of torture lay incongruously on the polished veneer of an expensive table in the House of Commons. Below the main picture was a smaller one of the monk holding a tissue to his eyes, weeping. His face, with its gaunt high cheek bones, had a startled expression. His eyes stared fixedly from the broadsheet, hiding a lifetime of agony. There was something sanitised about the photograph of the torture instruments. They appeared unreal, unused, out of place.

Palden Gyatso recounted his thirty-three years of ritual humiliation, brutal beatings and sadistic torture in Chinese prison and labour camps. It could not, he claimed, break his spirit. 'I have seen the destruction of Tibetan civilisation and culture. The only drive to stay alive was that I was determined to tell the outside world what was happening in Tibet.'

Thirty-three years! I was two years old when he was first imprisoned. I stared at his picture, trying to imagine the utter misery of his life. It was impossible to grasp. He described the tortures that had been inflicted on him, the permanent bends left in his arms from the excruciating air-plane torture whereby the victim has his hands tied behind his back and is then hoisted into the air and chained to the ceiling. It was a matter of routine for him to be kicked unconscious, to be beaten with nailed sticks, forced to witness the execution of his friends, and all the time urged to accept the rule of China as some sort of liberation.

He was arrested in 1959 for defiantly leading a protest against the Chinese invasion of his country. As is common in Tibet, the first seven-year sentence was delivered before his trial. His continued defiance in prison brought further sentences and more beatings. He told of the time in 1966 when he and his fellow prisoners were forced to sign confessions which justified their executions. Then, so as to deprive them of the last shreds of dignity before they died, many were forced to enact a grotesque series of songs and dances before being shot. Families were sent invoices for the bullets and equipment used during prisoners' executions and imprisonment. Palden Gyatso was released from Drapchi prison in 1992, but he remained a marked man. Instead of returning to his monastery, he saved the money to buy the torture instruments from corrupt prison guards and then escaped to India by way of a two-week walk through the Himalayas.

He described the routine use of electric batons through which a high voltage discharge is specifically designed to create maximum pain without death. At one time a baton was thrust into his mouth and triggered. He awoke in a pool of blood and urine, having lost twenty teeth; the rest fell out shortly afterwards. The batons are a favourite instrument of torture for the Chinese, often being applied to the most sensitive areas of the body, such as the soles of the feet, the nipples, mouth, eyes, and the genitals. There are accounts of them being inserted into the anus and into female prisoners' genitals. The shock produces convulsions and excruciating pain, and the heat often causes strips of flesh to be torn away as the baton is removed.

Palden has been left toothless, almost deaf, physically disabled and psychologically scarred by the incessant tortures he has endured. Chinese claims that they respect human rights are preposterous. The fact that we seem to believe it, or at the very least sanction the lie, is shameful.

It is exactly one year since I returned from Cho Oyo. In that time I have worked, climbed, trekked and had a lot of fun in Peru, Ecuador, Nepal, Australia, Canada, and Ireland, not to mention my home country. It has been a whirlwind year of travel and adventure, and I have enjoyed almost every minute of it. My one regret is Cho Oyo. I wish now that I had never gone. It has left a stain on my conscience.

I know in my heart that we did nothing wrong by going there. By approaching through Nepal we avoided paying the Chinese authorities the huge fees due for renting Himalayan summits. We did not provide them with funds to fuel their propaganda, the tourist land that they have cobbled together out of the debris of Tibet for the consumption of rich western travellers. Yet we gave nothing back. We played our games and left. But for the uncomfortable appraisal from the small boy with adult eyes, a stream of escaping refugees and a woman's lonely grave, I might have been happy with that in my ignorance.

In truth, the expedition proved to be, if nothing else, an opportunity to learn more about myself; about ego and ambition and weakness and self-deception. Most of all, it made me think about what I was doing; what I took for granted; what I chose to see and chose to ignore. Accepting my own hypocrisy has not been easy, but through learning of the tragedy in Tibet I have discovered what I have always known but have not really wanted to face.

The world is a cruel place. Life is inherently unfair. It could be argued that what has happened in Tibet is not so different from what has happened in almost every country throughout the world at some time in history. There will always be aggression and violence, war and genocide. These are nothing new. They simmer just below the surface of our civilised lives.

Whether we like it or not, we are violent, uncaring and destructive in a way that no other form of life is on this planet. Whether it is in the slaughter of a culture, the thoughtless destruction of a rainforest, the extinction of countless species of wildlife, the unbalancing pollution of the world's atmosphere, the perpetrators are the same. Human beings are the guilty ones. In a BBC radio interview early in 1995 President Kennedy's Defence Secretary, Robert McNamara, said that more than 180 million people have been killed in wars around the world in the twentieth century, and that it was time for the United States to apologise for the mistake of Vietnam. Our most urgent task, he said, is to find a way to stop the killing in the next century if the human race is to survive.

Should we worry too much about Tibet when in our past history we have all been just as guilty as the Chinese? What right do we have to claim the moral high ground? The native Indians of North and South America suffered terrible depredations at the hands of European settlers. The Aborigines, hunted to extinction in Tasmania and classed as non-human by Act of Parliament in Australia in 1908, have fared no better. The Irish peasants, dying gaunt hollow-eyed deaths in the famine of 1846, could lay some claim to being slaughtered by the indifference of the British. The Irish potato famine left a million dead and three million driven into exile. Was the potato blight and the consequent failure of the harvest just a freak of nature or did we British allow it to happen? Was it a natural culling of the population or part of our historical development? We persuade ourselves it could never happen again in our countries, and so presumably do the Chinese.

It is ironic that many centuries ago China was one of the most advanced cultures in the world. In many ways the Chinese were the world's teachers. Their artefacts, their writing, architecture, science and governance, the essence of their civilisation were an example to the world. Now they have deliberately and systematically destroyed all that inheritance and obliterated Tibet's culture as well. Bernard Levin called the destruction of Tibet's monasteries 'perhaps one of the greatest crimes in history'. The mercilessness of the crime lies in the intention to wipe out completely a harmless, peaceful, enclosed, old and venerated nation for no apparent purpose. As Tibet now goes down for the last time, drowning under the Chinese flood, we are left to wonder whether China understands what it has done.

There is a sense in which Tibet is just another secret in China's past that the Communist Party could never admit to, even under the sternest international pressure. It is another awkward fact that has been conveniently dropped down George Orwell's imagined 'memory hole' – a useful device for embarrassed totalitarians. China has a lot of secrets. Only now, when there is an increasing demand in the country for the basic human right of an accurate memory of the past, is there the hint that things might change. How much the Chinese people want to know or can face knowing is another question altogether.

Owning up to complicity in the murder of millions of people is not something a nation's population likes to face. It would be like waking from peaceful sleep to find oneself in a burning house from which there is no escape. Not that the recent past in China itself has been so very peaceful. Mao's Great Leap Forward led to the worst famine in human history, in which an estimated forty million people died, but it is not possible to lay the blame on him alone. The whole population took an active, even enthusiastic part in his Cultural Revolution. Jung Chang's book, *Wild Swans*, draws a vivid picture of how little it took to persuade people to participate willingly in the reign of terror. They may not wish to be reminded of how pupils turned on teachers, children on parents, how they took part in the insane killing, maiming and persecutions of their fellow citizens.

What strikes me so forcibly about all that I have learned since returning from Cho Oyo is the ease with which people can become brutalised; the speed with which we can be seduced into barbarism. Beyond the enigma, the secrets and the politics in China lies the simple fact that individuals were capable of the most unspeakable acts of sadistic violence. In the end it doesn't matter who gave the orders, somebody was willing to carry them out. What makes a whole population turn upon itself like that? Is the root of it any different from that which brings ritualised violence to our football terraces, or prompts a racist skinhead to kick some poor Asian schoolboy to death?

At the time of the savage killings in Beijing's Tiananmen Square in June 1989 the world was outraged by what it saw on its television screens. It was as if, for a brief moment, the real China was exposed. Journalists talked of the tanks and armoured personnel carriers, the piles of bodies, the screams as the bullets lashed in vollies across the square. There were images of police clubbing students to the ground and shooting them where they lay, of hospital mortuaries stacked high with corpses, and the unforgettable sight of Wang Weilin standing alone in front of the tanks, a plastic shopping bag in each hand. China has worked hard on its image since then and we have soon forgotten.

When I flicked on the television one day and saw the Chinese figure skater, Lu Chen, winning the world championship, I was filled with fury. Why is she even allowed to take part in international competitions while her country is inflicting such horror upon Tibet?

I watched as the pretty, petite woman in her bright blood-red dress scythed around the ice, jumping and spinning as the music swelled and the crowd applauded. Advertisements for luxury goods swept past as the cameras tracked her performance – Elizabeth Arden, Baileys, Evian – and then it was finished, flowers cascaded on to the ice and the diminutive red figure collapsed weeping into the embrace of her trainer. For a moment I loathed that figure skater. It was nothing personal. The poor girl was simply doing what she loved to the best of her ability. And this was exactly how China wanted to be perceived – the clean, healthy image of the dedicated athlete. No wonder they had applied to host the Olympic Games. It was all a lie. She had no right to be there. I thought of the nuns being tortured with electric batons because they called for independence and I watched Lu Chen's smiles with a sick heart.

I placed the paper on the table with Palden Gyatso's anguished eyes staring up at me. It made no sense any more. While I filled the kettle I listened to the final harrowing news reports on the radio about a man who had just been executed in the electric chair in Atlanta, Georgia. His twelve-year wait on Death Row and countless appeals for mercy had finally been cut off. There followed an impassioned debate about the morality of capital punishment, with gruesome details of how the electric chair killed its victims. It could take up to thirty minutes for the condemned man to die, an expert said, during which time he would be fully conscious as he was in effect fried to death. Why exercise justice in such a barbarous manner? Some 25,000 people were murdered in the United States last year, a staggering figure when compared with 370 or so in Britain. If so many people were still being murdered, I thought, then perhaps the death penalty was not a deterrent. I learned later that in an average year American doctors dealt with more than 100,000 gun-shot wounds.

As it happens, 25,000 is also the number killed in the dirty war between the Shining Path and the army in Peru in a decade! Dividing quickly by 365 days, I came to the figure of sixty-eight and a half murders a day in the States. Why on earth were American tourists scared of coming to Britain when a few dud I.R.A. mortar bombs landed on Heathrow's runways? If the world's most powerful nation, the proud defender of peace and justice and human rights, has that level of anarchy raging on its streets, then what hope is there for the rest of us?

I sat down at the table and stared at Palden's face and the thumbscrews attached to his hands. The world community poured three billion dollars into Cambodia in an attempt to rescue it from the misery of Pol Pot's year zero. Billions were spent rescuing Kuwait, hardly a model respecter of human rights, from Saddam Hussein's clutches. Aid poured into Rwanda as the world recoiled in horror at the butchery last year. Nothing but empty words has ever been offered to Tibet. We stood by and allowed a fabulous non-violent Buddhist culture that has survived for thousands of years to be swept away.

Meanwhile the Chinese medicine market has created an illegal trade in tiger bones, rhinoceros horn, bears' fat and bile, derivatives of antelope, musk deer and cobra. Tigers and rhinos are now on the verge of extinction. The idea that tigers, one of the world's most magnificent creatures, should be wiped out to provide questionable Chinese medical practices with supplies is difficult to grasp. Are we really to believe that the tiger's whiskers will help cure toothache, that its penis will make a man virile, its skin prevent mental illness? How does a tiger's testes cure tuberculosis of the lymph nodes? Could its teeth cure me of asthma, rabies and penis sores, and if I eat a tiger's brain would it help against pimples and laziness? Even if all these things were possible should the tiger be made extinct because of its miraculous properties? Tibet was no less magnificent than the tigers.

Recently my travels have made me feel ill at ease, but that in itself is no bad thing. It has forced me to see what I don't want to see, and to learn more about how other people have to live. It helps me to be more tolerant of other lives, other religions, other cultures and provides a more balanced view of the world – a world in which the poor and the deprived have to fight for continued existence, where the powerful fend off threats to their privileges, and everyone has to defend a living space from the depredations of the greedy. In today's climate it all comes down to pride, lust, avarice powered by modern technology which we do not know how to handle.

That night in the Broadfield, as I bent down to pot a ball on the snooker table, I caught sight of a menacingly familiar figure. The shaven head, the tattoos, and the macho swagger sent a chill down my spine. I missed the pot and straightened up.

'Haven't seen that idiot in here for a while,' I remarked.

'Who?'

'The guy who called me outside,' I said, as I cold-stared the man at the bar. 'You know. The one who believed in his hairstyle.'

'Oh him!' John said, scrutinising the man too closely for my liking. 'No, that's not him.'

'Isn't it?'

'No. The one you're talking about is long gone. He grew his hair back and wore suits for a while and acted all meek and mild. Then one day some lad who he had terrorized in his skinhead days came in and kicked the crap out of him.'

'You're kidding?' I said, instantly delighted by the news, but at the same time feeling guilty at taking pleasure in the man's discomfort – however much he deserved it.

When I got home I found a envelope on the doormat with a hurriedly scrawled note inside from Andy Cave explaining why he had been so long translating the prayer on the Christ statue at Yungay. It took me back to that windy desolate place and the words made me think I could hear the victims screaming. I thought of the Tibetans and the Chinese, Mao and the Dalai Lama, the tortured eyes of Palden Gyatso and the skinhead's dumb violence. I remembered thinking of Belsen in the rubble of Yungay, and felt confused.

I went to bed with the uncomfortable feeling that there were more bad dreams to come.

ACKNOWLEDGEMENTS

In writing this book I owe a great debt to the knowledge, experience and writings of many others, and not least to my friends who have listened to my questions with kindess and offered so much useful criticism and advice. To them all I give my heartfelt thanks.

In particular I must acknowledge two books for opening my eyes to the tragic fate of the Tibetan culture and people. Mary Craig's shockingly bleak account in *Tears of Blood: A Cry for Tibet* was an unpleasant lesson that prompted me to examine my conscience. Read it and weep. David Patt's book, *A Strange Liberation: Tibetan Lives in Chinese Hands*, is also a powerful indictment. Other authors whose books on this subject have been important to me include John Avedon, Catriona Bass, Elaine Brook, Victor Chan, Jung Chang and Heinrich Harrer.

Among individuals who have been hugely supportive are David Breashear and Jeff Long – both were an inspiration. Audrey Salkeld brought her encyclopaedic knowledge of mountaineering history and a sharp editorial eye to bear at a crucial time. Robbie Barnett of the Tibetan Information Network was unfailingly helpful. Mike Shrimpton, Mal Duff, Ric Potter, Richard Haszko, John Simpson and Ian Smith provided photographs, and Magnum Press and *The Times* newspaper kindly gave me permission to reproduce theirs. Pat Lewis gave me tireless support, as well as advice on scanning the photographs. My brother David and his wife Sukie were kind enough to read the proofs, while Geoff Birtles, Jim Curran, Tom Richardson, Pete Cranwell (the Landlord's landlord), Ray Delaney, Ian Tattersall and John Stevenson were, as always, generous with their patience.

Tony Colwell, my editor at Cape, has worked with me on all my books since the first which, without him, would never have been written. He has been a great friend and has taught me so much. I am immensely grateful to him. In short, he has changed my life.

BIBLIOGRAPHY

Avedon, John, *In Exile from the Land of Snows*; London, Michael Joseph 1984

Bartle, Jim, *Trails of the Cordilleras Blanca & Huayhuash of Peru*; Peru, Jim Bartle 1981

Bass, Catriona, *Inside the Treasure House: A Time in Tibet*; London, Abacus Books 1990

Bezruchka, Stephen, *A Guide to Trekking in Nepal*; Katmandu, Sahayogi Press 1974

Brook, Elaine, *Land of the Snow Lion: An Adventure in Tibet*; London, Jonathan Cape 1989

—— *The Windhorse*; London, Jonathan Cape 1986

Chan, Victor, *Tibet Handbook: A Pilgrimage Guide*; California, Moon Publications 1994

Chang, Jung, *Wild Swans: Three daughters of China*; London, HarperCollins 1993

Craig, Mary, *Tears of Blood: A Cry for Tibet*; London, HarperCollins 1992

Danziger, Nick, *Danziger's Travels: Beyond Forbidden Frontiers*; London, Grafton 1987, Paladin paperback 1988

Jefferies, Margaret, *Sagarmatha Mother of the Universe. The Story of Mt Everest National Park*; Auckland N.Z., Cobb/Horwood Publications 1985

Harrer, Heinrich, *Seven Years in Tibet*; London, Rupert Hart-Davis 1953

—— *Return to Tibet: Tibet after the Chinese Occupation*; London, Weidenfeld and Nicolson 1984, Penguin Books 1985

Hopkirk, Peter, *The Great Game: On Secret Service in High Asia*; London, John Murray 1990; OUP paperback 1991

Levin, Bernard, 'China's Final assault on Tibet'; *The Times* 1994; and earlier columns concerning Tibet.

Long, Jeff, *The Ascent*; London, Headline 1992

—— 'Climbing in the killing fields'; *Climbing Magazine USA*, No.145, June/Aug 1994

Parris, Matthew, *Inca Cola: A Traveller's Tale of Peru*; London, Phoenix 1993

Patt, David, *A Strange Liberation: Tibetan Lives in Chinese Hands*; New York, Snow Lion Publications 1992

Prakash A Raj, *Kathmandu & the Kingdom of Nepal*; Australia, Lonely Planet 1985

Salkeld, Audrey, *People in High Places: Approaches to Tibet*; London, Jonathan Cape 1991

Seth, Vikram, *From Heaven Lake: Travels Through Sinkiang and Tibet*; London, Abacus 1984

Simpson, Joe, *Touching the Void*; London, Jonathan Cape 1988

Simpson, John, *Despatches from the Barricades: Eye Witness Accounts of the Revolutions that Shook the World 1989-90*; London, Hutchinson 1990

—— *In the Forests of the Night: Encounters in Peru with Terrorism, Drug-Running, and Military Oppression*; London, Hutchinson 1993

Tibet Information Network. *An independent research and information service collects and publishes accurate information and analysis of current events and conditions in Tibet.* Robbie Barnett. T.I.N. 7 Beck Road London E8 4RE.

Film

Breashears, David, *Red Flag Over Tibet*; US TV, Frontline 1994